The Private Life of an
ELIZABETHAN
LADY

An unknown Elizabethan lady, 1595.

The Private Life of an
ELIZABETHAN
LADY

The Diary of LADY MARGARET HOBY

1599–1605

Edited by
JOANNA MOODY

SUTTON PUBLISHING

First published in 1998 by
Sutton Publishing Limited · Phoenix Mill
Thrupp · Stroud · Gloucestershire · GL5 2BU

British Library Cataloguing in Publication Data
A catalogue record for this book is available from the British Library

ISBN 0 7509 1349 5

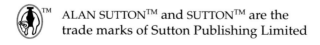 ALAN SUTTON™ and SUTTON™ are the
trade marks of Sutton Publishing Limited

Typeset in 10/12pt Palatino.
Typesetting and origination by
Sutton Publishing Limited.
Printed in Great Britain by
WBC Limited, Bridgend.

For Richard

they are vnworthye of godes benefittes and
especiall fauours that can finde no time to
make a thankfull recorde of them

Margaritt Hoby:

Lady Margaret Hoby
April 1605

Contents

Lady Hoby's Yorkshire, showing places mentioned in her diary.

List of Illustrations

List of Illustrations

Foreword

Information about the private lives of women in Tudor and Stuart times is scarce and valuable. Diaries and letters are the main sources, but they are not very numerous, and few deal with the routines of domestic life. The best known of these documents show their writers interacting with the public world of their time: Lady Anne Clifford's diaries record her life in great houses and on her huge northern estates; Lady Anne Conway's letters display her intellectual engagement with developments in philosophy and religious thought in the mid-seventeenth century. Lady Anne Fanshawe's memoirs deal with affairs of state as she experienced them in company with her husband. In contrast, Lady Margaret Hoby's diary takes us into a more circum-scribed world, but one that is truly representative of her age and class. Here we have a rare access to the household of a pious member of the Yorkshire gentry. There can be no doubt that Lady Margaret's diary was intended primarily as a record of her religious observances, kept as an assurance of her constant attentiveness to the life of the spirit. The frequency of her devotions is remarkable, and her diary is indeed a revelation of the procedures of Protestant piety at a domestic level. But through this record of prayer, reading and discussion runs the everyday business of the manor house at Hackness. Lady Hoby appears to us as the provident Elizabethan housewife, supervising her house and its gardens, engaged with her tenants, caring for the sick and injured in her little community, and offering hospitality to her neighbours. Only the Eures of Malton disturb the noiseless tenor of her life, but even while the litigation between the two families goes forward, she manages to maintain good relations with Lady Eure in a spirit of friendship and charity.

In this present edition of the diary, Joanna Moody has skilfully filled out the background to Lady Hoby's activities. Particularly interesting is her account of the books Margaret Hoby was reading and the religious issues she was exploring, often with the help of the local minister Mr Rhodes, who seems to have acted as her personal chaplain. Although Hackness was situated in a remote part of north-east Yorkshire, the life of the mind and spirit burnt brightly in Lady Margaret's household. Remote as Hackness was, family ties linked the Hobys to the larger world of court and culture: Lady Margaret's first two marriages had been to Walter Devereux, brother to the Earl of Essex, whose execution for treason is warily alluded to in the diary in February 1601, and to Thomas Sidney, the younger brother of Sir Philip Sidney. Her third marriage to Sir Thomas Hoby was characterized more by loyalty than love, but the picture of the marriage we have in the diary provides a valuable glimpse of a marital relationship in late Elizabethan England.

Finally, as we read this edition of Lady Hoby's diary, we are enabled to imagine its setting with great clarity, thanks to the illustrations selected by Joanna Moody, and to her exceptional responsiveness to the character of those Yorkshire places where Lady Margaret led her conscientious and God-fearing life. Those who read this book will surely want to visit these scenes in person, to see for themselves the unfamiliar scenery of these unfrequented moors and dales.

Graham Parry,
University of York

Acknowledgements

Many people have helped with this edition. With regard to the original diary I wish to thank the British Library Manuscripts Department, London. Other librarians and archivists – at the Morrell Library, University of York, the York Minster Library, the North Yorkshire County Record Office, the National Monuments Record, the Public Record Office, the Humanities Research Centre, Austin, Texas – have helped me to locate and gain access to rare books and prints, and facilitated the research at every stage. Dorothy M. Meads transcribed and prepared the diary for publication by George Routledge and Sons in 1930 and my thanks are due to Routledge for allowing me to include some of the original illustrations. I am deeply grateful to the Right Honourable Lord Derwent of Hackness Hall for his invaluable help and kind permission to reproduce the Hackness pictures and maps. Special thanks are due to the following: The Squire de Lisle, Sir Roy Strong, Graham Parry, Robin Hood, James Winterbotham, Pippa Brockington, Annie Cooper, Julie Raby, David Whiteley, Gordon Smith, and to Jane Crompton, Alison Flowers and Roger Thorp of Sutton Publishing. My greatest debt is to David Moody who has been deeply involved in every aspect of this edition since its inception.

The publishers have made every effort to contact the copyright holder of the map reproduced on p. 122, but have been unable to do so. We will gladly rectify this omission if contacted.

Introduction

Elizabethan diaries are rare manuscripts, especially those written by private individuals. This diary is unique as it was written by an Elizabethan Yorkshirewoman who lived and worked on her own estate in that part of Yorkshire where the barren moors fall to the bleak North Sea. Lady Margaret Hoby[1] owned much of the land surrounding Hackness, a pretty hamlet sheltering in a wooded valley not far from Scarborough. She brought three husbands there, but the diary is concerned simply with the period 1599–1605; it begins three years after the writer's third marriage to Sir Thomas Posthumous Hoby with whom she lived at Hackness until her death in 1633. The diary is a collection of private meditations and secret recollections, a record of pious endeavour and religious self-examination. Lady Hoby gave a daily account of her spiritual life, but at the same time she could not help but record many of the household tasks which she and her maids performed.

Lady Hoby's conscience was her private audience as she looked for evidence of the hand of God in her daily life and sought confirmation of her worthiness of His love. The quality of her existence was dependent upon His grace. She did not waste time detailing the anxieties and concerns that troubled her; events are simply recorded. We do, however, find suggestive hints of certain preoccupations and a dramatic narrative begins to emerge. The repetitive effect becomes cumulatively engaging and we are drawn in to her mind and world; we discover both her personal communion with God and the ordinary routine of her daily life, enhanced by the particulars of Hackness itself and by actual events. As a result, the diary constitutes not only an invaluable document of the religious and domestic life of a devout woman living through the final years of Tudor England. It also succeeds in taking us on an imaginative journey into the heart and soul of an industrious Yorkshire lady.

---

[1]   There are several forms of spelling in the correspondence and other sources, including Hoby/Hobie/Hobbye/Hobby/ Hobbei. I have chosen the form used by Lady Hoby herself.

Introduction

There is no known portrait of Lady Hoby other than that offered in the diary.[2] The picture to be found here is paradoxically self-assured and vulnerable. She was godly and confident, a woman with great force of will, but frequently in discomfort or poor health and seeking reassurance of salvation from the 'buffetting of satan'. Lady Hoby seems to have been resilient and determined, capable and talented, yet frail in her being and sometimes unhappy. The prevailing texture of her writing is overtly private, that of a lady absorbed by the needs of body and soul, yet making way in her private inclinations for public responsibility. She began and ended her day in prayer and devotion, and in between these times she exercised her skill in household and medical care. She was an avid reader and a prodigious correspondent, maintaining contact with many outside the immediate circle of Hackness. She concerned herself with affairs beyond the domestic domain and the record of her religious reading shows that she was intellectually engaged in some of the most controversial theological issues of the day. During the six years of the diary she made three long trips to London, which enabled her to be up to date with all manner of fashions, and she was frequently on the move to visit her mother, relations and friends. She saw it as her duty to support her husband, particularly when he was away, and her loyalty to Sir Thomas was never in question. The household of Hackness was in fact a microcosm of the godly Protestant commonwealth, wherein the service of God was carried out with a zeal that dominated the lives of all. Regular prayer and meditation determined the organization of its daily existence.

Lady Hoby's success in managing her large manor house with its estates, and in pursuing her firm religious habits, resulted from skills inculcated at an early age. Her mother features significantly in the diary, but much of her education and training lay in the hands of aristocratic guardians. She was born Margaret Dakins sometime in early 1570/1[3] to Arthur Dakins and his wife Thomasin, of Linton in Yorkshire, the largest

---

[2] The only recorded picture of Lady Hoby, mentioned in her husband's will, is nowhere at Hackness. The fine oil on panel portrait [see frontispiece] of an unknown Elizabethan woman (1595) can however give us an indication as to the appearance, elegance and gentle charm of such as this diary's author. I am grateful to its owner for permission to reproduce it.

[3] There were two systems of dating during this period. Generally New Year was reckoned to begin at the Feast of the Annunciation on 25 March, but New Year's gifts to the sovereign, and some other ceremonies, were associated with 1 January. Accordingly, for diary entries and events occurring between 1 January and 25 March, the 'old' year is used.

shire county in England.[4] She was baptized on 10 February in Wintringham Church, and as the only child became heiress to a substantial fortune mainly in land which her father inherited and then augmented. Land was of course the basis of wealth and power and political changes favoured the advancement of a family such as this. Unlike some of his neighbours Mr Dakins was not a recusant holding to the old Catholic faith,[5] and his position was important enough to maintain worthwhile connections throughout England. Among his acquaintance he could count Henry Hastings, Earl of Huntingdon,[6] whose wife Catherine kept a kind of finishing school for the children of the nobility. It was decided that the young Margaret should be educated and trained in their household with a view to making a match worthy of her fortune.

To be a gentlewoman in a big household such as the Huntingdons'[7] was an accepted course for the children of the gentry, for it provided a form of practical education as well as a useful step towards marriage. It was here that Margaret met with two future suitors, Walter Devereux and Thomas Sidney, the younger brothers of famous courtiers, and she spent her formative years being taught how best to

---

[4] Margaret Dakins was Yorkshire born and bred, and spent most of her adult life there in both the North and East Ridings. Yorkshire covers almost 4,000,000 acres, divided into three Ridings (North, East, West), and the self-contained Ainsty of York. The word 'Riding' is derived from the 'thirdings' into which the Danes divided the land. Christopher Saxton published the first real map of the county in 1577, proclaiming in Latin on the title-page: 'The County of York. . . . in length, breadth and population more distinguished than all the rest'. Yorkshire people are said always to have had strong convictions and are unselfconscious about it, but they have much to be proud of: 'Our county, as the curious observe, is the epitome of England; whatsoever is excellent in the whole land being found in proportion thereto . . . Beside God hath been pleased to make it the birthplace and nursery of many great men' (George Hickes, Sermon, London, 1682). Margaret clearly loved the county, especially her own part around Hackness.

[5] In parts of Yorkshire islands of Catholicism survived, focused on noble families which clung doggedly and dangerously to the old faith.

[6] Henry Hastings, 3rd Earl of Huntingdon (1535–95), married Catherine Dudley, daughter of the Duke of Northumberland. He became Lord-President of the Council of the North (1572–95) and subsequently spent much of his time in York, being particularly active in pursuing those not conforming to the reformed faith. Henry VIII had reorganized the Council of the North after the failure of a rebellion in Yorkshire, known as the Pilgrimage of Grace (1536). This had been provoked by economic unrest and was mainly about such matters as rents and tenures, combined with hostility to religious changes. The Council met four times a year, its main powers being judicial, and its primary concern keeping the peace. The first active Lord-President took office in 1538, but the Council's authority and efficiency reached their highest point during the presidency of Margaret's guardian.

[7] At Ashby-de-la-Zouche in Leicestershire, some hundred miles from London.

prepare herself to be a good Christian wife and mother. The Earl and Countess of Huntingdon were an influential and deeply religious couple, members of the staunchly Anglican alliance which feared for the state of the Reformed Church in England. They had close links with the Protestant interventionist party that lobbied against the queen's connections with France, members of which included such as the Earls of Leicester and Essex, and Francis Walsingham, Chief Secretary to Queen Elizabeth I. The Countess of Huntingdon was a formidable woman, strong-willed and renowned for her sternness and Puritan bearing. With no children of her own she devoted her energies to the welfare of others, being a model of obedience and commitment second to none. She instilled discipline into the young women who lodged under her tutelage and her influence upon the young Yorkshire girl from Linton must have been great. From 1581 the Countess maintained regular contact with the royal court where one of her sisters, Mary Sidney, was lady-in-waiting to the queen, and thus Margaret, once old enough, had the opportunity to mix with the noblest and most aristocratic in the land.

As we can discover from the diary, the religious context of her life cannot be overestimated. From childhood she was intimately bound up with her Christian faith and she grew up feeling deeply the moral and religious obligation of persistence and perseverance. With the Huntingdons she not only learnt to read and write, to keep accounts, to sew and to play a musical instrument, but she also found a distinctively Anglican piety that appealed to her own quiet nature. Her guardians encouraged her to work and study with industry, and taught that her soul's salvation depended upon the avoidance of idleness. Above all, she absorbed their religious practices, following a rigorous pattern of instruction and observance. Deeply influenced by Calvin[8] and theological conceptions about the dependence of sinful and fallen nature upon God's grace, these fervent Protestants believed in inward piety and the more intimate forms of religious devotion. Calvinist doctrine, with its concern for election and sanctification, insisted on the examination of conscience; a close study of the Scriptures offered a precious knowledge that would lead the fallen nature out of the darkness of human weakness to further God's cause in the world. Religious convictions were therefore

---

[8]   Jean Calvin (1509–64), theologian reformer in the cause of Protestantism, wrote *Christianae Religionis Institutio* (1536). He systemized Protestant doctrine and organized its ecclesiastical discipline.

applied to daily life with zeal, for it was believed that the surest method of pleasing God and succeeding to earthly happiness and heavenly bliss was to work honestly in the vocation in which you found yourself. Even in such an aristocratic household as the Huntingdons' work was sanctified, in the firm conviction that God was served through honest labour, and Margaret therefore learnt all her skills as her way of serving God. Apart from sewing, reading and counting, she was taught housewifery and husbandry. She attended church daily, she memorized and copied out sermons, she sang psalms, she studied the Scriptures, she read devotional texts, and she learnt to examine herself for wrong-doings – what she herself termed her omissions and commissions. Moral self-examination, with the help of the Scriptures, was seen as the way to improve the inner self and receive salvation in the execution of one's calling, and diligence in such a matter was therefore the means to avoid sin. As we later discover, Lady Hoby used the diary to record the interior questioning to which she had become accustomed since childhood.

In 1588 negotiations began for a union between the seventeen-year-old Margaret and young Walter Devereux, for whom the Earl of Huntingdon had acted as guardian since his father's death.[9] The couple knew each other from childhood and their marriage in 1589 was very much to the advantage of both parties. Walter's famous brother, Robert, Earl of Essex,[10] was the favourite of Queen Elizabeth, and his sister, Penelope, Lady Rich, was well established at court. Margaret therefore married into one of the most prominent, though not wealthy, families of the land, and her husband could make her substantial fortune his own. Educated at Christ Church, Oxford, where he had been placed at the age of fifteen, Walter possessed the independence, high-spirits and strength of character for which his family was well known.[11] It would not be inappropriate,

---

9   Walter Devereux (1541–76), 1st Earl of Essex, 2nd Viscount Herford, married to Lettice Knollys, second cousin to Queen Elizabeth I. As the queen's champion in Ireland he had dealt severely with the rebels but much of his fortune was spent in the process. After his death his widow had married Robert, Earl of Leicester (*c*. 1532–88), brother to the Countess of Huntingdon.
10   Robert Devereux, 2nd Earl of Essex (1566–1601), m. Frances Walsingham, widow of Sir Philip Sidney. Much has been written about him. Lady Hoby mentions him twice in the diary and is clearly concerned for him at the time of his arraignment. See diary, n. 172 and 244.
11   'Mr. Ewre said he would go to the top of the hill and fling down mill-stones and would play young Devereux at the same time throwing stones at the windows': evidence given in the Hoby v. Eure lawsuit, see Appendix 2 (I), *Cecil Papers, Vol. IX*, 88.17, and below.

Hackness Hall in the seventeenth century (oil on panel).

therefore, to consider how suitably the couple was matched, for the quiet Margaret with her serious turn of mind found herself united with a lively, young devil-may-care, devoted to his older brother. He had no home nor estate of his own, and it was decided that lands should be purchased in trust for the young couple. In 1588 plans were put in hand to acquire the Hackness estate in Yorkshire in order to expand Margaret's family holdings in that part of the country. Her father forwarded £3,000, the Earl of Essex, for his brother, £3,000, and the Earl of Huntingdon, as guardian, £500. The sale was completed, but the joint trusteeship led to complications later. Mr Dakins had not fully paid up his share of the transaction, having left it to his son-in-law to meet the outstanding debt out of his daughter's dowry; Walter's failure to do this was to have grave consequences for Margaret some years later.[12] The gift to the young couple, however, was exceptionally generous. Margaret, now Mistress Devereux, became the head of a large household with extensive holdings across a productive and valuable part of the North Riding of Yorkshire.

There is no information about the life of the Devereux couple at Hackness, but their marriage was not long-lived. In 1591 Walter accompanied his brother on a foray across the Channel into France, where the Earl of Essex was sent by the queen to assist the Protestant Henry IV against the Holy League of French Catholics. Walter went as leader of the horse. They left Dover for Dieppe with 4,000 men, but Essex, although in command of the army, was under a tight rein held by royally appointed counsellors. He forced a march through Normandy and in the first skirmish before Rouen on 8 September his brother was hit in the cheek by gunfire and killed.[13] Everyone thought the siege would not last long, so Essex kept Walter's body in France, rather than sending it directly home for burial. The earl and his friends planned to carry it triumphantly into the city at the head of Elizabeth's forces.

Although tucked away in Yorkshire, as a childless and wealthy widow Margaret was only too eligible to the bounty-hunters flocking to the court in London. To protect her interests, her parents and guardians decided

[12]   In 1595, the heir to one of the trustees, the Earl of Huntingdon, lay claim to the estate on the grounds that the purchase money was yet outstanding. See below. It was not until 1601, after a prolonged lawsuit in Chancery, that the property finally became the unchallenged possession of Margaret, its rightful owner.

[13]   'This unfortunate skirmish has robbed me of him who was dearer to me than ever I was to myself' – 'I have lost . . . him who next her Majesty was dearest to me of all the world', in *Lives and Letters of the Devereux, Earls of Essex*, ed. Bouchier (1853), I, 233, and 240.

that a second marriage should take place sooner rather than later, again negotiated by those who had care of her. Quite how Margaret herself felt about this is impossible to discover, especially as no wedding could take place until her late husband's body was finally interred, yet the outcome of the next two months gives as strong a hint as any that she did not regard remarriage unfavourably. She may even have realized that the opportunity had arrived to make the love-match she most desired, for the Huntingdons' favoured choice was their dearest nephew, Thomas Sidney.

Margaret and Thomas had known each other a long time, for they had met as children in the Huntingdons' home. Like Walter Devereux, Thomas had been placed under the guardianship of the earl at his father's death in 1586.[14] He was the youngest in a close and loving family. His father had spent much of his time in Ireland until his death, and his mother was the lady-in-waiting who had successfully nursed Elizabeth through a bout of smallpox, only to suffer badly herself. His older brother's poetic achievements were soon to be celebrated by their literary sister,[15] and the large family of his other brother tumbled happily around the old home at Penshurst. Margaret, young Mistress Devereux, seems not to have been at all averse to the idea of becoming attached to the Sidney family. By her first marriage she had become a member of the glittering Essex entourage at the heart of the privileged world of Elizabeth's court. By this second union, however, she could become linked with a family of altogether greater riches, literary and intellectual.[16]

Within a fortnight of the death of her first husband, the Earl and Countess of Huntingdon were writing letters to Margaret's father in Yorkshire, in which they pressed forcefully for her marriage to Thomas

[14]   Thomas was the son of Sir Henry Sidney (1529–86) and Mary Dudley, sister to the Countess of Huntingdon. His elder brother, Sir Philip Sidney (1554–86), was the famous courtier and poet; his other brother Robert owned Penshurst Place, Kent. Mary, his sister, was married to Henry Herbert, 2nd Earl of Pembroke (*c*. 1534–1601).

[15]   In the 1590s the Countess of Pembroke was still in the process of coming to terms with the death of her eldest brother and starting to build a myth to glorify his name. She published under her own name her translations of works by the Frenchmen Robert Garnier and Philippe du Plessis Mornay (1592) and she then edited Sidney's great work, *The Countesse of Pembrokes Arcadia* (1593). See Hannay, *Philip's Phoenix* (1990).

[16]   The Countess of Pembroke was an important patroness, and her home at Wilton in Wiltshire became an intellectual centre for writers, poets and churchmen. She was very fond of her youngest brother, so we can imagine that Margaret must have visited and shared literary activities there, maybe even taking part in some way in the editing of *Arcadia*. Hannay notes that there is no record of visits by the Countess to Margaret after her brother's death, although they moved in the same circle of friends. See Hannay, *Philip's Phoenix* (1990), 149.

Sidney. His daughter was in mourning at Hackness, but she was encouraged by her parents to leave home at once and to place herself under the protection of her former guardians. Nothing of course could be done until Walter's body was brought back from France and buried. On 2 November 1591, just two months after becoming a widow, Margaret left for London with the prospect of a second marriage ahead of her. Her husband's body was at last brought home when it became apparent that the siege of Rouen would not come to an end before the winter was out. On 22 December 1591 – the Devereux family may well have thought with undue haste – Margaret, 'in affection',[17] was united with Thomas Sidney. He owned property in Kingston upon Hull, and, on the death of her father a year later, other land as well as Hackness became their own. They travelled to Yorkshire to begin their life together, but the marriage was not to last for long. In July 1595 Margaret yet again found herself a widow.

The Dakins' inheritance had of course attracted many potential suitors, one of whom was Thomas Posthumous Hoby, second son of the late Sir Thomas Hoby of Bisham, Berkshire.[18] His mother, Elizabeth Lady Russell, an intelligent and formidable woman, had pushed hard for her younger son to be considered as a serious suitor for Margaret's hand.[19]

---

[17] 'Yf in affection she be gon to Sidney, it is one thing ; if by reason she be willing to be ledd to her owne good, yow will be fownd the better mache of bothe': Lady Russell to her son, in one of several letters relating to the courtship of Margaret by Thomas Posthumous Hoby. See below and Appendix 1, Letter v.

[18] Sir Thomas Hoby (1530–66), diplomat and ambassador to France, died before the birth of his son in 1566. He is best known for his translation of Castiglione's *Book of the Courtier* (1561).

[19] Elizabeth Cooke, Lady Hoby, later Lady Russell (1528–1609). Much has been written about her. She was the third of five celebrated daughters of Edward VI's tutor, Sir Anthony Cooke, of Gidea Hall, Essex. Receiving an education that was unparalleled for girls of their period, all the sisters were known for their intellectual attainments. Elizabeth married Sir Thomas Hoby on 27 June 1558. Her sister Mildred became second wife to William Cecil, 1st Baron Burghley, and another sister, Ann, married Sir Nicholas Bacon, their son being the philosopher and writer, Sir Francis Bacon. In 1574, the widowed Lady Elizabeth Hoby married John, Lord Russell, the son of Francis, Earl of Bedford, and by him she had two daughters, Elizabeth and Ann. Intelligent and energetic, with great force of character, Lady Russell was renowned for her determination and her litigious ways. Widowed for the second time in 1584, she remained a dominating personality on the London scene, with great ambition for her unmarried children. The tone of her letter to her son is typical, showing that she has already planned the wedding, even to putting down a deposit of 5 shillings for musicians. See *Dictionary of National Biography*; Schleiner, *Tudor and Stuart Women*, (1994), 30–51; Mary Ellen Lamb, 'The Cooke Sisters: Attitudes towards Learned Women in the Renaissance', in *Silent But For The Word*, ed. Hannay (1985), 107–25. The Holbein drawing (see p. xxv) has long been thought her portrait, but dates suggest it must be Lady Elizabeth Hoby, the wife of Sir Philip Hoby (1505–58), aunt to Thomas Posthumous.

She is mentioned often in the diary, during Margaret's visits to London, and must have been a significant presence in the Hobys' life. Certainly she was ambitious in her attempt to secure the young widow for her son. Urged on by her in September 1591, Thomas Posthumous Hoby had put himself forward through the particular auspices of his powerful uncle, William Cecil, Lord Burghley.[20] Lady Russell requested that Burghley write to the Earl of Huntingdon stating that his nephew sought the hand of the young Devereux widow. Burghley duly praised his nephew, writing that he was like to prove 'a good and corteous husbande, and a keeper and noe spender'. Other letters followed, including one to Mr. Dakins, in which Burghley regretted pressing his nephew's suit so soon after Devereux's death, but he had discovered that others had done the same and he feared that delay on his part would disadvantage a 'yonge gentlemane of good byrth, honesty and understandynge'. Margaret's father had to write back regretfully informing Burghley that his daughter had already left for London, to place herself in the care of the Huntingdons, and he thereby had no further consideration in the matter. In fact, Lady Russell later acknowledged that he had already given his consent for Margaret 'to match where she list', and in spite of all her efforts to secure the Dakins's inheritance for her younger son, it went instead to Thomas Sidney until his death in 1595.[21]

It is not difficult to understand why Margaret had rejected the Hoby suit first time round, especially if she was fond of Thomas Sidney. The picture we have of his rival is not a particularly attractive one by all accounts. Thomas Posthumous had been trouble since his early years. He ran away from home, rejected his mother's plans for him to train in the Inns of Court, was difficult over the financial matters of his allowance and expenses, and, according to Lady Russell, altogether lacked application. He was of small stature, known as a 'scurvy urchen', a 'spindle shanked ape', and was ridiculed 'as the little knight that useth to draw up his Breeches with a Shooing-horn'. We can see why she despaired of him, regretting a lack of the talent shown in his older

---

[20]   William Cecil, 1st Baron Burghley (1520–98), Lord Treasurer to Queen Elizabeth I, married as his second wife Mildred Cooke, aunt to Sir Thomas Hoby. See Appendix 1, Letters i, ii, iii. His elder son, Thomas, later 2nd Lord Burghley (1542–1623) features in the diary. His younger son, Robert Cecil, 1st Earl of Salisbury (*c.* 1563–*c.* 1612), received letters from Sir Thomas and Lady Hoby. See *Cecil Papers*, Hist. MSS Com., 1883–1923.

[21]   Even Lady Dorothy Perrot, sister to Walter Devereux, wrote to her sister-in-law on Hoby's behalf. See Appendix 1, Letter iv. She was prepared to act as matchmaker, offering Sir Thomas the opportunity to meet Margaret for the first time at her house.

The Lady Hobbei.

Lady Elizabeth Hoby by Hans Holbein the Younger (1497–1543). For a long time this portrait has been thought to be of Sir Thomas Posthumous Hoby's mother. However, dates suggest it is of his aunt, the wife of Sir Philip Hoby (1505–58).

brother, Edward.[22] Thomas Posthumous was, however, strong enough in character not to be rebuffed when the opportunity arose a second time. The prize was too valuable to lose again.

Margaret's responsibilities in Yorkshire's North Riding had substantially increased when her father died and her riches were considerable.[23] Twice she had gone through the solemnization of matrimony, in which the introductory exhortation states that marriage is ordained for three major reasons, the first of which is the procreation of children to be brought up in the fear and nurture of the Lord. There is no question that Margaret would have regarded her barren state as some kind of punishment. Despite the obvious risks of childbirth, in recognition of her 'fallen' nature she would have accepted that the legacy of Adam and Eve – the first married couple – meant that marriage and childbearing must have their difficulty and pain. But it was her duty and responsibility to further God's cause through having children of her own, and this she had manifestly failed to do. The lack of children would seem like a lack of blessing from the Lord, and so she must marry again. This time, however, she was not as ready to give up her widowhood as she had been to marry Thomas Sidney.

When Sir Thomas Posthumous Hoby[24] discovered that Margaret was again free he hastened to press his suit once more. Not only was her wealth an obvious attraction, but he wanted to improve relations with his mother who had been disappointed by his earlier failure to secure Margaret's hand. He presumably also wished to benefit from her intention to leave him a substantial fortune if he married the woman she preferred. He would receive £500 a year, whereof £300 of it would be joynter to Margaret after Lady Russell's death, as well as a fully furnished house to which he could bring his new wife. Within a short time, therefore, the Earl of Huntingdon again received letters promoting the match, from both Lord Burghley and Lady Russell, and the earl even spoke directly with

[22]   Sir Edward Hoby (1560–1617), of Bisham, Berkshire, diplomat and controversialist. Lady Hoby mentions him several times as she and her husband stay with him in London. He rose in high favour at court and his position was strengthened by his marriage to the daughter of Henry Carey, Lord Hunsdon. Sir Edward represented Rochester in the Parliaments of 1601, and Feb. 1603–4. He was instrumental in the negotiations for the accession of James, who made him a gentleman of the Privy Chamber. He entertained both sovereigns at Bisham.

[23]   The 'residue of goods and chattels to wife Thomasine and daughter Margaret who are appointed executricces, 1 May 1589', Arthur Dakins' will, NYCRO ZF 2/1–3.

[24]   Sir Thomas was knighted in 1594.

Sir Thomas about the matter, encouraging him to visit Margaret. The result was that in mid-September 1595 the suitor hopefully rode north to meet his intended for the first time. He was joined by an old friend, Sir Edward Stanhope, who had been asked by the Earl of Huntingdon to take him under his wing. The two went quickly to Hull, only to find themselves barred from Margaret's presence. Utterly distraught, overcome with grief and in deepest mourning for her dead husband, she very reluctantly agreed to see Stanhope, refusing Sir Thomas when she discovered the purpose of the visit. Stanhope informed her that he carried letters from the Earl of Huntingdon approving the match, and she was finally pressured into seeing Sir Thomas, though only briefly.[25]

Throughout that autumn and winter letters sped back and forth encouraging the match, but Margaret remained aloof.[26] Sir Thomas wrote to Huntingdon thanking him for his support, informing him that his position was still very weak but he would persist in his efforts to gain the lady's hand. She, however, successfully resisted all advances, until mid-December when her kindly guardian the Earl of Huntingdon died.[27] His heir, discovering that the Hackness estate had not been fully paid-up by Margaret's first husband, laid claim to the property believing it to be rightly his own. Margaret, lacking allies, was therefore faced with an intimidating lawsuit in Chancery and no one to help with her defence. She felt isolated and vulnerable, with both her father and guardian gone and no husband to whom she might turn for support. Stanhope advised that it would be to her advantage to have Sir Thomas and his influential relatives on her side,[28] and even the dowager Countess of Huntingdon could see that she would be best protected if she allied herself with Hoby and his powerful connections.[29] The extent of Margaret's despair at this time is to be found in a letter sent to Sir Robert Cecil, which although more concerned with her brother-in-law, Sir Robert Sidney, does give an insight into her own sorry condition:

---

[25] See Appendix 1, Letters vi, vii.
[26] See Appendix 1, Letter viii.
[27] A week before he died he wrote to Margaret saying that Sir Thomas clearly would not take no for an answer, and warning her to be careful about all their reputations in her dealings with him. See Appendix 1, Letter ix.
[28] See Appendix 1, Letter x.
[29] Hoby wrote to the Countess of Huntingdon thanking her for her support and informing her of his anticipated success in gaining Margaret's hand. See Appendix 1, Letter xi.

Introduction

1596, July. Though my present state and misery be fittest only to continue in prayer to God for His grace that I may with patience endure this rod of my afflictions, yet doth the 'feeling' knowledge of my brother Robert's estate and despairs when he shall hear of this desolate news, added to her Majesty's former undeserved displeasure, so fright me that I am forced to be a mediator to you that he may not be forgotten. Alas! Sir, his desires were such at his going down as both his wife and I had much ado to make him stay in his own country. Judge then what this new assault of sorrow will work in him; for besides his natural grief, his office of the wardenry which he had under my lord is gone, his office of Norham is to no avail to him, his brother having (by her Majesty's commandment) the commodity of it, so as in that country both countenance and commodity is lost now, and if her Majesty with some remorse do not 'begene' comfort in him that was first overthrown by her, I fear we shall have cause to bewail the untimely misfortune of my brother with the unfortunate loss of my father. 'She that is nothing but grefe and misery, Margarete Hoby.'[30]

This letter was written just a month before she finally surrendered. On 9 August, in a simple ceremony in Lady Russell's home in Blackfriars, London, she became Lady Hoby, wife to Sir Thomas Posthumous. It was a quiet affair, consisting of the solemnity itself, with a sermon and a dinner. There was no music nor dancing and only a few friends attended, these including her brother-in-law, Sir Robert Sidney. Undoubtedly, Lady Russell would have been delighted to have her younger son richly settled at last.

The Hobys returned to Hackness and Sir Thomas quickly developed powerful contacts with members of the Council of the North, where his cousin, Thomas Cecil, 2nd Lord Burghley, would become President in 1599. The death of the Earl of Huntingdon had led to a slackening of persecutions of recusancy until Lord Burghley eventually resumed the pressure[31] with the help of Sir Thomas, who was appointed to many of the Council's commissions to assist in the process. He took it upon himself to crush recusancy in the area, through the zealous searching

---

[30] *Cecil Papers Vol. IV*, 42.34, 301. There is obvious self-dramatizing in the quote marks.
[31] Fines paid by recusants were an important source of revenue for the Council. The more prominent recusants suffered not only fines but harassment and occasional imprisonment, although the severest persecution was not usually maintained for long.

out of those who failed to attend the regular church services. His Puritan leanings, combining his godliness with political aspirations, were therefore enough to make him very much disliked in the north of Yorkshire which still harboured many old and established Catholic or pro-Catholic families. There were other reasons for his growing unpopularity; like his mother, he became an experienced and determined litigant, constantly engaged in quarrels or lawsuits of one kind or another with tenants and neighbours. There were disputes about tenures and leases, and battles over boundaries, pasturing, turve-digging, wall repairs and payment of tithes. Altogether this put him at odds with several of his most important neighbours, including the powerful Eure[32] and Cholmley[33] families, and these unfriendly relations were to have later repercussions. At the same time he was a Justice of the Peace, held a court at Hackness, attended Quarter Sessions, and became a representative of Parliament. We discover from Lady Hoby's diary that he was increasingly absent from home as he became engaged in public affairs; she often mentioned writing to him, presumably about business matters which she was supervising at home.

Lady Hoby comes across in her diary as utterly loyal to her husband. We cannot help but ask, however, whether she really liked him. This union was partly forced upon her by circumstances that, for all she might have wished to, she failed to resist. It is perhaps symptomatic of a lack of resilience revealed through her frequent reference to ill-health. She evidently married Sir Thomas for the security and support offered

---

[32] We shall hear more of the Eures later, for Mary, Lady Eure, is mentioned in the diary as a friend of Lady Hoby, and it is her son who gets the two families involved in the lengthy lawsuit that tears them apart. The Eures had possession of the whole lordship of Old Malton and were later to suffer the results of litigation among themselves. Lord Eure left two granddaughters co-heiresses, who could not agree as to the division of property and the possession of a large castellated mansion. After an expensive lawsuit it was determined to pull down the house and divide the stones between them (1674). Some compromise was effected before the entire demolition, as the lodge and three gateways were left. See Bulmer, *History of North Yorkshire* (1890), 747.

[33] The Cholmleys were neighbouring landowners and supporters of the Roman Catholic cause, supposedly harbouring recusants. As owners of the lands comprising the liberty of Whitby Strand, including Whitby Abbey and its holdings, with the exception of Hackness, they were confirmed in their right to hold courts and pocket the proceeds of justice. Against their wishes, Sir Thomas was granted the right to hold Court Leet and Baron of his independent manor of Hackness. There was no love lost between the heads of these families, and young Richard Cholmley joins his friend William Eure for the Hackness visit in August 1600. See below.

St Peter's Church, Hackness, seen from the south-west.

not only by a husband but by Lord Burghley and others in the forthcoming Chancery suit. At the same time, her marriage was one means whereby she might finally prove that she was indeed worthy of God's blessing in enabling her to start the family she desired. Perhaps the diary was intended as a record of the process. We can never really know what it was that prompted her enthusiasm for the daily reckoning which begins in August 1599, nor can we know if this was the only diary Lady Hoby kept. However, the fact that the emphasis shifts over time to a simple record of routine existence hints at a private inner life conflicting with, and finally giving in to, the demands of household and of a wider world.

Hackness is a small village, situated in the North Riding, inland and not far from Scarborough. It lies in a pretty valley through which the River Derwent runs, fed by streams of spring water that tumble gently from the higher levels. Surrounded by hills and dales, it is in fact well sheltered from the winter cold blowing in from the North Sea and the Yorkshire moors. A peaceful spot, it consists even now of little more than the manor, a few houses, a parish church and a tiny post office. Both village and hall are built of the local stone which varies in colour from buff to yellow ochre. Pastures enclose the hall, its gardens and orchard, and there are abundant woods, planted mainly with oak and ash in Lady Hoby's time. The lands of Hackness had been donated to Hilda, abbess and foundress of Whitby Abbey,[34] and monks were later to live in a dwelling more or less on the site where the Tudor hall was situated. It was an extremely profitable estate in medieval times, yielding high taxes, and with extensive pasturing, timber, fishing, hawking, and hunting.[35] After the dissolution of the monasteries, the

---

[34] The first abbey at Whitby was founded in 657 by King Oswy of Northumbria. Its abbess was Hilda, great granddaughter of a Northumbrian king. She established a 'double' monastery – a community of women supported by a separate community of monks and priests. Hilda's abbey was destroyed by the Vikings in the ninth century and lay in ruins for 200 years. The existing buildings were begun in about 1200, and closed in 1539 when the monks were dispersed by order of Henry VIII. The site was bought by Richard Cholmley. A memorial in the record of Whitby Abbey in the time of William II states that the monks of Whitby made representations to William de Percy regarding the 'theives [sic] and robbers coming out of the forests and dens where they lurked' and desolating the monastery. They were given the church of St Mary at Hackness that they might build a monastery there. After about 1100 Hackness became a cell to Whitby Abbey.
[35] Winterbotham, *Hackness in the Middle Ages* (1985), offers a useful survey of village history before modern times.

estate passed into secular hands, and was finally purchased in 1589 by Arthur Dakins with the help of the other two trustees. It included the manor house and mills, the rectory and advowson, and extensive property in the surrounding districts of Silpho, Suffield, Everley, Hackness Dale, Broxay, Burneston, Hutton Bushell, and Ayton.[36] The Hobys themselves added to it, and Lady Hoby particularly mentions in the diary the acquisition of a farm in Harwood Dale.

The existing Hackness Hall is not the one purchased for the young Margaret and her first husband, for the old dark house was pulled down when it obscured the view of a gracious, airy hall begun as a replacement.[37] However, although the original buildings have disappeared, we have a good idea of what they were like from a wood panel oil painting (undated) at Hackness. Almost certainly Lady Hoby's home was built from the stone and slate of the former monastic settlement, and the gardens and orchard may well have existed for

[36]   The parish of Hackness has altogether an area of about 15,280 acres (6,188 hectares). The church, formerly St Mary's, was later dedicated to St Peter and restored in 1870. In Lady Hoby's time it was possibly still known as St Mary's, for it is referred to as such in the catalogue to Hackness church library. It consists of a clerestoried nave with side aisles, chancel, and tower with octagonal spire (see p. xxx). In the east end of the south aisle is an ancient cross, believed to have been erected to the memory of the abbess Hilda. There are several monuments to the Dakins and Hoby family, and their successors, the Johnstones. The Hackness church library (now lodged in York Minster Library), comprising 116 volumes as listed in a catalogue of 1701, with an additional list of 1862, was put together by the Hon. Sir Philip Sydenham, Lord of the Manor, not long before the whole estate was sold. The collection is a mixture, primarily religious, and the publications dating from the early seventeenth century include books purchased by the Hobys for their own reading. There are two books inscribed with Lady Hoby's own name, both by Philip of Mornai: *Doctrine of Sacraments* (1600) and *A Treatise of the Church* (1606) (see pp. xliii, xlvii). Both are in translation from the French and her interest may well have been inspired by her sister-in-law, the Countess of Pembroke. See n. 15.

[37]   Demolished finally in 1798, nothing remains of Lady Hoby's house except a few bumps in the ground and its position marked by a hawthorn tree. Old estate maps indicate that the house was constructed on the supposed site of the monastic cell. The present house, begun in 1792, is a fine mansion with beautiful pleasure grounds, located north-east of the original. It is very different from that known to the Hobys, being an elegant two-storey, seven-bay-long, classical building, from designs by Carr of York who was much influenced by Robert Adam at Harewood. It is privately owned, the seat of the Right Honourable Lord Derwent, whose forbear John van den Bempde bought the estate in 1707 for £31,000 from the heavily indebted owners. It is partially visible from the road which runs through the park, but the grounds are rarely open to the public. See 'Country Homes. Gardens Old and New: Hackness Hall, Scarborough, the seat of Lord Derwent', in *Country Life*, 19 March 1921, 339–44.

The interior of St Peter's Church, Hackness.

sometime. The monks' fishponds were retained and the village extended beyond the parish church, within easy walking distance of the manor house.[38] In the painting we discover an Early English Renaissance house, typical of its period, with a central hall and subsidiary buildings used as service rooms at right angles at each end. There is a fully enclosed forecourt with an arched gateway, possibly with some classical detail, through which visitors approached an impressive main entrance. The house in which the Hobys lived was therefore large, and we know from estate surveys that it included not only the hall, parlour, and great chamber, but also a chapel, bed chambers, two kitchens, a buttery, pantry, brewhouse, bakehouse, and various outbuildings. The central hall was a single large apartment for general use by everyone resident in the house, and the dwelling and reception rooms were on the upper floors, their mullioned windows fully glazed. The great chamber or gallery over the hall would have had a wide staircase leading up. Bearing in mind her wealth and status, Lady Hoby may well have had her staircase decorated with the rich carvings characteristic of Elizabethan woodwork; stone, plaster, oak and local marble would have been materials used throughout.

The manor houses of this period were generally the headquarters of a considerable estate. The main income came from the profits of rents and farming, and the service buildings were necessarily hives of activity. Lady Hoby's diary informs us that she was herself very much involved with all aspects of housewifery and husbandry, so she must have been familiar with every nook and cranny of her property. Apart from reading and writing letters in her private chamber and office, she visited the granary, she worked in the kitchens, she gardened, enjoyed fishing and went out into the fields and woods. She cooked gingerbread and sweetmeats, distilled aqua vitae, preserved damsons and quinces, weighed and spun wool, pulled hemp, made wax and oil lights, saw to her bees and honey, and checked her linen. Much of her time was spent sewing and embroidering. Such phrases as 'sat and wrought with my maids', 'went down and wrought' and 'I wrought tell dinner time' occur again and again. The diary hints at a lady and her household fully occupied in well-organized activity and recreation.

---

[38] The ponds were to be transformed into a lake in the eighteenth century and the village buildings were moved a few hundred yards further westward to accommodate a later garden scheme.

It is not difficult, therefore, to imagine Lady Hoby moving around her house and gardens, fulfilling those duties so faithfully, but simply, recorded in her diary. Her household consisted of many people: clerics, servants, widows charitably housed, maids in attendance for their education and training, and the children of other families.[39] Although Lady Hoby had no children of her own, she referred to them all as her 'family' and clearly spent much time with them, as she did with visiting friends and relations. There is a sense of constant coming and going, of a generally public life interrupted by moments of quiet study. It was a godly household, dominated by prayer, meditation and honest labour. Whether she was seated with her guests at the high table, or busying herself in the farmery or service rooms, Lady Hoby was generally in the company of other women, helpers and maids. There is evidence in the diary of her ensuring good relations and seeking to end disputes. She counselled one woman who was to be divorced for having lived incestuously with her husband and another who seemed troubled but could not say why. She also gave advice to a servant suffering from some unspecified abuse and admonished one of the men for getting a maid pregnant. She supervised the estate when her husband was away and the diary records her dealing with business affairs and going to judges' chambers in York. She kept accounts, paid the servants, sorted and weighed corn, saw to matters out in the fields and woods, and was altogether busy ensuring adequate provision was made for all the household. One of her major tasks was the nursing and medical care of her workmen and servants, and she tended their ailments, bound their wounds, performed simple operations and gave out medicines and cure-alls to both humans and animals. Her role as a midwife was cherished, and she visited the sick and needy. Altogether, she was an outstanding administrator as well as being a gentle and intelligent wife.

The diary often refers to the partaking of meals at which the household would have sat down together in the great hall. Lady Hoby regularly mentioned breaking her fast, probably around eight o'clock, and going to dinner, the main meal of the day, between eleven and

---

[39] On 24 May 1599 Lady Hoby wrote to Sir Robert Cecil: 'It was my evil fortune to desire and obtain of her Majesty the wardship of Sir Ro. Salsberey's son or heir, who then by the report of his brother captains was supposed to be dead, though since fallen out contrary, yet it is certainly thought that his disease though lingering is not recoverable. I entreat you that I may receive some benefit of my first obtained suit in court; if not, a pardon for thus troubling you'. *Cecil Papers, Vol. IX*, 10.52, 180.

twelve o'clock. A supper was generally provided around five-thirty in the early evening, followed by public prayers. The food eaten was harvested from her own land, the animals – fowl, geese, pork, rabbits – slaughtered in her fields, cheeses pressed from her own cows, cakes baked from flour ground in her mills, honey from her bees, and preserves home-made to last the year. Apples from her orchard, game birds and venison from the woods, herbs from the garden, all were washed down with home-brewed beer and cider, or the clear water springing from the surrounding hills. Vegetables, thought to engender wind and melancholy, were used mainly to flavour meat broths and boiled beef, but Lady Hoby wrote of planting seeds each spring and her garden certainly would have been plentifully stocked with such as carrots and cucumbers, parsnips and leeks. There were also damask roses which she spoke of tending throughout a warm autumn. The godly order of her household emanated from its Puritan zeal and pious routine, and it is hard to tell how much was simply accepted labour or pleasurable activity. There is mention of relaxation when she walked by the river and in the meadows, when she went fishing, or played bowls – a vigorous exercise on roughly cut grass. She also sang and played the orpharion, a pretty lute-like instrument. She went for rides in her coach, and the diary even records her boating at the seaside. There were regular visits to her mother, to friends, and to churches in other parishes, and Lady Hoby made longer trips to York and to London. The 'Road-Roll' illustrations, typical of the time, indicate the journeys and how long they took. In London she had a hectic round of court attendance and social visits, interspersed with church services and shopping at the Royal Exchange. Events are recorded briefly and dispassionately, but enable us to establish a very real sense of the pressures of Lady Hoby's existence. Altogether it was a sociable life, one that was bound up with the affairs of others leaving her little time for herself.

In spite of the very public nature of Lady Hoby's life at Hackness she did nevertheless manage to assert independence of a kind, through her reading and lengthy discussions with the young chaplain who guided her private meditations and prayer. Master[40] Rhodes is often mentioned, conversing and reading with her, supervising her Bible study and directing her religious exercises. Although there is no direct evidence that he lived in the manor house he undoubtedly had a major role in the devotional life of Hackness. It was not unusual at this time for young

---

[40] In Elizabethan times 'Mr' was the abbreviation for Master, and 'Mrs' for Mistress.

men to be attached in such a manner to private households that could afford their keep, and he was in attendance at public prayers and catechism as well as seeing to Lady Hoby's own spiritual needs. Bearing in mind that the diary was intended as a record of pious endeavour it is not surprising that Master Rhodes should feature so often. Perhaps he was even shown the daily record. After all, he was probably more intimately involved with her thoughts and prayers than her husband, with whom she seems mainly to have discussed business and estate affairs, though there is one entry when she mentioned talking with him about their consciences (25 August 1599). There are hints of shared moments between Lady Hoby and Master Rhodes in which they discussed not only religious topics but themselves and such matters as the match he would make with Rebecca, his first wife. One of the longest entries (20 December 1599) concerns the encouragement she received from him to pray for virtue against temptation, and with him she sought confirmation of her own faith even through a reading of Catholic doctrine.[41] Certainly Master Rhodes was in the best position to bring her spiritual comfort, and it appears, at least in the earlier part of the diary, that Lady Hoby did not wish to be long separated from him. He regularly accompanied her on visits to the homes of friends and to her mother's at Linton, although he did not travel with her to London, staying home presumably to minister to the household with which he was so closely bound. His first wife died when Lady Hoby was away in 1600/1, but Master Rhodes married a second time, his wife being young Mercy Hunter who had been resident in the Hackness household for a mere six months as one of Lady Hoby's maids. In 1605 he became parish priest, and his mistress happily noted that the Book of Common Prayer was used correctly for the first time. Lady Hoby was obviously fond of him, and she enjoyed their talk of 'principles of religion' and such 'good things'. He was not, however, the only divine at Hackness, for we also hear of Master Ardington and Master Maude, with whom Lady Hoby talked of 'good maters', and there were other religious visitors who came to converse about their own writings and sermons.

According to the diary, more than half of Lady Hoby's time seems to have been spent in some kind of religious act, with the common pattern being at least one daily visit to church – two on Sundays. The parish church we enter now is still the very same in which Lady Hoby

---

[41]   Not infrequently in this period material was pillaged from Catholics for the benefit of Protestant readers.

worshipped and where she buried her father and mother. This was where she listened to sermons that were painstakingly noted in her commonplace-book, and where she heard the Bible and homilies read aloud for the benefit of the congregation of servants and tenants. To these she gave further instruction at home, while ensuring that the maids within her care also learnt to read and write the Scriptures, the Bible being seen as the foundation of all religious reading. The diary records how she read to her women and in return heard them read. Repetition of the lessons was a regular feature, as was the catechism. Prayer was seen as an expression of obedience to God and took place both in private and in public. Lady Hoby copied out devotional texts, she sang psalms, she wrote in her testament, she meditated and she fasted. At one point she noted a discussion with a young papist maid, probably with a view to conversion, and she often spent a whole afternoon talking about religious matters with her women friends. In fact Lady Hoby possessed an inordinate appetite for pious activity and reading: 'I haue Continewed my duties of praier and readinge, both findinge my corruption and receiuinge stringth' (23 April 1602). Books teaching good morality were seen as a path to piety, second only to the keys of salvation, and leading, alongside the Scriptures, to a knowledge of both the self and of God's providence. The buying and reading of such books was of course a symbol of faith to fulfil that commitment. Much influenced by moderate preachers and writers who were shaping the mainstream of Puritan thought, Lady Hoby read, or had read to her, a wide range of devotional and religious texts. However, as well as published sermons, instructive treatises, books of psalms and rhetoric, she also read herbals for culinary and medicinal purpose, and biographies of martyrs.[42]

Lady Hoby was concerned with the application of theology to everyday life, and her active and enquiring mind was prepared to tackle some of the major controversies of the day. She was naturally exercised by the differences in doctrine between Catholic and Protestant, and a diary entry refers to a sermon she heard in York Minster which did 'defend the truth against the papest' (10 April 1600). Later the same day she listened to another talk on the question of justification by faith or works, and this matter was still under discussion when a preacher came to speak with her at her lodging on 16 April. This led her to find renewed

---

[42]   The Hackness church library contains several of the Hobys' books, marked with their own inscriptions, including Foxe's *Book of Martyrs*. See diary, n. 59.

comfort in God's promise of salvation through faith alone, that is, in the knowledge of justification by faith in Christ, and the profitable text she may have heard was in the New Testament – Paul's Epistle to the Romans, Chapter 8 – which contains some of Paul's most forthright statements on election and predestination and justification by faith. It was a text that was inevitably popular with the Puritans of the time. In the same vein, she also mentioned Master Rhodes reading to her from a book, probably written by Hugh Broughton,[43] which took issue with Bishop Thomas Bilson's theories about Christ's descent into hell (18 January 1599).[44] It is an interesting example of Lady Hoby's concern, for there was a question of doctrine here. The reformed view rejected that of St Augustine, still held however by many Anglican divines, that Christ actually descended in triumph into the place of the damned. Lady Hoby mentioned William Perkins[45] several times, so it is probable she had read the discussion in his 'exposition' wherein he parted company with the usual interpretation, by querying the meaning of the line 'He descended into hell' in the Apostles' Creed. Perkins rejected the absolute view that Christ actually went to hell and opted instead for a more symbolic interpretation, in which the descent represents Christ's lower degree of humilation, answering to the highest degree of his exaltation in sitting at the right hand of God. He suggested that it was symbolic of the necessity 'to become nothing in our selues, that we may be in all forth of our selves in Christ'. Christ's descent 'teacheth eueryone of vs that professe the name of Christ, that, if it shall please God to afflict vs, either in bodie, or in minde, or in both, though it be in most greuous and tedious manner, yet must we not thinke it straunge . . . nor quite despaire of his mercie'.[46] It is not hard for us to believe that, in her own humility, Lady Hoby found strength in this interpretation, discerning hope and comfort for herself in the humiliation and exaltation of her Saviour.

---

[43]   Hugh Broughton (1549–1612), divine and rabbinical scholar; published *Explication* (1599) respecting Christ's descent into hell, maintaining that Hades was a place not of torment but of departed souls.

[44]   Thomas Bilson (1547–1616), Bishop of Winchester, wrote *The effect of certain sermons, touching the full Redemption of Mankind* (1599). He argued against much Puritan thought.

[45]   William Perkins (1558–1602) was a highly esteemed theological writer and probably the most popular Puritan preacher of the late sixteenth century. He had a great reputation as a teacher. Distinguished for his strong Calvinism he was also concerned with the application of theology to daily life. His writings were gathered together in *A Golden chaine: or the description of theology* (1600), which went into many editions.

[46]   William Perkins, 'An exposition of the creede', in *The Foundation of Christian religion; gathered into six principles* (1597), 248, but see 243–9.

Introduction

Apart from her reading, Lady Hoby was also an avid note taker and letter writer. Like many others of her time she kept a commonplace-book in which she wrote down passages that interested her for future reference, such as extracts from pious books and the Bible, psalms, sermons, and so on.[47] She had both a household and table-book for domestic matters, and, of course, she wrote in her diary. Although we have only these 118 folio pages it is possible she had been recording her daily activity for some time. She mentioned her letter writing frequently, maintaining a regular correspondence with friends and with her husband when he was away.[48] Curiously, she even noted writing to him when he was in the house, expressing anxiety and unhappiness concerning a matter about which we can only guess the cause (19 July 1600). She wrote letters on behalf of her servants, and kept in touch with them when she was away. She ensured regular contact with her mother and her physician when she could not see them, and clearly she had business matters to which she had to attend. Writing and the keeping of accounts in her private closet, or office, took up much of her time, and the diary records her regret that she was sometimes too busy to devote herself properly and with as much attention as she would like to the religious exercise she had set herself: 'many sundrie distractions withdrwe my mind from so profitable hearing as I ought, which I humble pray the Lord to pardon, and grant me here after strength, by

---

[47]   Margin annotations in Lady Hoby's handwriting are to be found in her inscribed copy of Philip of Mornai, *Doctrine of Sacraments* (1600), Hackness church library.

[48]   One of Lady Hoby's few letters extant is addressed:
'To my dear and loving husband Sir Tho. Posth. Hoby, Knight, at York, give these'
'Deare harte, I am not sure that I have sent you all right, because I could not find both the bookes so writen of as you tould me, but I have sent you all that is likely to be that you spake of; I pray you if you come hither by York, let John Broune bye me or send it me by this boy 2 pound of starch, for I have none left. W. Rhode had but little speach with Burch because he did think you might then call for him, but willed him to bethink himselfe wherein he had offended which he promised to do, and at his comminge back to confess the truth of all that to his remembrance he had any way offended in. I must needs give you thanks for the letter you writt from Linton. I will [*sic*] for your kindnes to them, if you gave me nother triall, yet I should confess you to be an exceedinge good Husbande and to deserve a better wife than my witt will serve me to be, but I will drawe as nigh to the high degree as I can, and so because it is late I will commit you without more circomstances to the lorde's best protection; my mother desires to be commended unto you, and so doth my selfe to all my Cossins, from Hackness this 6 of June, 1599. Your assured and Lovinge wiffe De MARGARET HOBY'.
From Sir Erskine Perry, *The Van den Bempde Papers* (1868/69), 17–18. These family papers were found mixed up, with many others, in an old box in a carpenter's shed.

grace, to w^(th)stand the Like' (31 December 1599). Lady Hoby indeed found her own means of expression, be it in the private sphere of correspondence or channelled through this daily record of spiritual endeavour.

Although we cannot determine the exact nature of her religious beliefs, it might be true to say that Lady Hoby was a first-generation Puritan who was learning through the doctrinaire approaches of Perkins and other divines to deal more strictly with the issues of discipline and leading a holy life. She must certainly have wished herself as one of the 'godly', like her former guardians the Earl and Countess of Huntingdon. Her confidence in God and Christ was absolute, and one regular feature of her daily life as recorded in the diary was her habit of self-examination. Here she found comfort in the knowledge of herself which was the central experience of her life in relation to God: 'I returned in to my hart, examenid my selfe and Craued pardon for my severall ommitions and Comitions' (7 October 1599). The Christian life consisted not in the achievement of perfection necessarily but in the attempt to desire to reach perfection: 'I praied priuatly and examened my selfe with what Integritie I had spent the day' (18 November 1599). Lady Hoby looked into herself to increase awareness of her failure, for this was the mark of her infirmity. With this in mind she sought knowledge of God's strength to hold her up: 'hauing no distractions or temptations felte more then ordenarie, so that I found great Cause to praise god who is the giuer of all true Comfort what soeuer' (27 March 1600). In assessing herself and finding herself guilty she could then turn to God knowing He loved her and would show her mercy. Realizing her own incapacity was necessary for her to keep faithful to God; she recognized that faith was freely given by grace, but only to those whom God had chosen to receive it. Her self-examination, therefore, was regarded as a means whereby she could not only check her outward religious observance but also assess signs of her election or damnation: 'by takinge an account what breaches I had made in my faith, since I found that I had itt, by reparinge those by repentance, as also medetating what grace I had, what benifetes godes spiritt ther did offer me' (22 December 1599). Her religious convictions were absolutely applied to her routine existence, and daily repentance lay at the heart of what she perceived as holy living. She believed in amending the mind of her sinful being: 'This day I went about the house: had temporall prosperitie but found inward Corruption' (27 June 1605) and 'I beseech the Lord pardon my seuerall defectes and restore me to my former Life, for thy mercies sake, with increase of his spiritt, and so much spirituall Comfort as now is a wantinge' (15 November 1599). Everything she did was carried out in the understanding of a beneficent providence, and her diary records a search for spiritual peace while at the same time rediscovering weaknesses and natural corruption. Generally the entries are straightforward, simply noting the routine of private and public prayer. Allusions to spiritual temptations are rarely identified in detail, but there are certain days when Lady Hoby allowed herself a more critical commentary, such as 'through corruption we vse not the blessinge of peace as we ought, so are we to expecte new temptations to humble vs for our former necclegence, and so I haue benne, this day, boffeted for better heed' (13 April 1601), followed some months later by 'all Crosses ought thankfully to be bourne' (22/3 October 1601).

One of the outstanding features of Lady Hoby's diary is the regular reference to her state of health: 'went to bed, god hauinge a Litle afflected me with sicknes for a great desart: the Lord grant me true repentance for all my sinnes'(19 December 1599). Lady Hoby's attitude to illness was typical of many with her religious belief. In the Scriptures a sinner was frequently compared to a sick person, and the figure of Christ the physician, the healer of the body as well as the soul, was an important image in the New Testament. The curing of illness was seen to be the curing of sin, and therefore Lady Hoby's physical illness was partly spiritualized, with God's providence easing any sickness: 'it pleased, for a Iust punishment to corricte my sinnes, to send me febelnis of stomak and paine of my head that kept me vpon my bed tell 5: a clock: at which time I arose, haveinge release of my sickness, according to the wonted kindnes of the Lord' (17 August 1599). One particular entry notes her sense of the body's proximity to the soul and its susceptibility to religion: 'I praise god I had health of body: how so euer Iustly god hath suffered satan to afflicte my mind, yet my hope is that my redemer will bringe my soule out of troubles, that it may praise his name: and so I will waite w^t patience for deliuerance' (6 May 1602). Her body was the instrument of her soul, and when she felt unwell she believed God was correcting her: 'being not well, partly through myne owne folly, which I humble praie the Lord to pardon' (25 October 1599).

During the six-year period of the diary Lady Hoby suffered from headaches and weariness, a sore foot and toothache, coughs and colds, sickness, colic and indigestion, general weakness and discomfort, and even a kidney stone. It is an impressive catalogue of real and possibly psychosomatic complaints. Her illness stirred up self-doubt, anxiety and guilt, and recourse was had to daily prayer as well as to curatives. A day set aside fasting (7 October 1603) was aimed at pleading with God to be

FOWRE BOOKES,

OF

THE INSTITVTION, VSE

AND DOCTRINE OF THE

HOLY SACRAMENT OF THE
EVCHARIST IN THE OLD
CHVRCH.

AS LIKEWISE, HOW, WHEN,
And by what Degrees the Maſſe is brought
in, in place thereof.

By my Lord PHILIP of Mornai, Lord of Pleſsis-
Marli; Councellour to the King in his Councell of Eſtate, Captaine
of fiftie men at armes at the Kings paie, Gouernour of his towne
and Caſtle of Samur, Ouerſeer of his houſe
and Crowne of Nauarre.

*The ſecond edition, reuiewed by the
Author.*

Margrett Hoby: 1600

Saint Cyprian, in the treatiſe of the Sacrament of the Cup of the Lord.

*We ought not herein to regard, what any man hath iudged meete to bee done; but rather, what he which was be-
fore all men, euen Ieſus Chriſt our Sauiour, hath done himſelfe, and commaunded others to doo : For we follow
not the cuſtome of men, but the truth of God.*

ALSO;

*If ſome one of our predeceſſors haue not ſo obſerued and kept it : God may haue pardoned him in his mercies: but
for Gt, from henceforth there will remaine no place for pardon, we hauing beene inſtructed and admoniſhed
by him.*

LONDON

Printed by IOHN WINDET, for I. B. T. M. and W. P. 1600.

The title page of Philip of Mornai's Doctrine of the Holy Sacraments . . . *(1600)
showing Lady Hoby's inscription.*

spared discomfort. When she was poorly Lady Hoby was confined to her room, but this did not discourage her from receiving visitors, and she regretted those times when her sickness cut short her devotions: 'I was not well, wch Continewed allmost all the day, so that I nether Could hear, praie, writt, or medetate as I ought' (10 August 1600). Belief in God's providence did not prevent her from having recourse to specialist help when necessary and she was in regular contact with her physician whom she was certain would work with God's blessing. She had her blood let, she took potions and medicines, suppositories and clysters. Sadness followed the death of old Doctor Brewer on whom she had so much relied, and this was only alleviated by her new physician, Master Lister. In the spring of 1600 she visited York for two weeks, mainly, though not entirely, for medical treatment. For a woman of her religious persuasion, however, the great physician was of course God Himself: 'therefore I may truly conclude it is the Lord, and not the phisision, who both ordaines the medesine for our health and orderethe the ministring of it' (31 August 1599). Any remedies given were subject to God's secret will as to whether they might work or not and her days of good health were therefore celebrated: 'I continewed well, and found godes mercie in vouchsaffinge me comfort euerie way' (6 May 1602), and: 'Hauinge my health, I thank god, I Continewed my accustomed exercises' (2 April 1601). Good health was of course a sign of God's favour, and being one that sought assurance in the every day occurrences of life that she was indeed one of the elect, the events of each day, including her state of health, took on a significance as indicators of God's decision.

To what extent Lady Hoby's physical condition was determined by rheumatics brought on by a damp house, by diet, by a sickly constitution, by her emotional state, or by anxiety about the state of her soul, cannot be determined. It is possible, however, to make assumptions about a sadness relating to her inability to have children. Significantly, the diary records that her stomach cramps and discomfort occur with some regularity in the third week of many months, and this might indicate that she had problems with her monthly cycle. It is tempting to suppose that by the time of writing, when she was nearing the age of thirty, she would have expected to have conceived and given birth to a child from at least one of her three marriages. Childbearing was after all the chief social obligation of married women – yet it was the one aspect of life in which Lady Hoby had experienced real failure. She spoke with both her chaplain and her physician about matters seemingly intimate to her state of health, body and soul, and it is again tempting to suppose that she may well have been wondering why she had been deprived of the one thing most assuring of God's grace. She never stated openly in the diary that she felt a particular loss, but there are at least two clear hints that she just might have longed for God's blessing in this respect: 'I talked a whill with Mr Lister of some of my greues' (30 September 1600) and 'this day I fasted untill Eueninge, eatinge nor drinkinge any thinge, begging of the Lord that blissne[49] wᶜʰ yet I want' (7 October 1603).

Certainly it was not unusual for women of this period to be in poor health and to experience problems with conception, pregnancy and childbirth. Evidence in the manuscripts of the Reverend Richard Napier, the seventeenth-century astrologer-physician, showed that women suffered more than men from sadness and anxiety, and that they were subject to a greater range of medical problems.[50] Nutritional deficiencies led to anaemia, infections were difficult to overcome, and there was a lack of understanding about gynaecological ailments. Many of Napier's female patients blamed their psychological distress on their inability to remedy disturbing situations at home as well as on marital problems, and it was recognized that maladies could well interfere with social and sexual satisfaction. Lady Hoby's reading of Timothy Bright's book on melancholy (12 October 1599)[51] is an interesting indicator of her frame of mind. There is evidence in the diary that she was sometimes quite tired and depressed, perhaps because of her excessive effort and exercise, socially, domestically, and religiously. Her emotional life was centred upon her family, the household at Hackness, and maybe there was indeed a sadness in the fact of having no children of her own. In their stead she superintended the education and training of young maids from other families, with a nephew whom she intended would inherit the riches left to her by her father. She was however prone to times of

---

[49]   *blissne*, blessing.

[50]   See Macdonald, *Mystical Bedlam* (1981). Further insight into attitudes towards the female body and sexuality is found in Keeble, *The Cultural Identity of Seventeenth-Century Women* (1994), 17–53.

[51]   Timothy Bright (1551?–1615), a physician who published *a treatise of melancholie, containing the causes thereof* (1586), said to have suggested to Robert Burton his *Anatomy of Melancholy* (1621); he also reinvented the lost art of shorthand and abridged Foxe's *Book of Martyrs* (1589). He became rector of Berwick-in-Elmet, Yorkshire (1594). In the old physiology, it was an excess of black bile humour that caused a disposition to melancholy. Associated with philosophical and intellectual thought as well as with sadness, sorrow and even mental disorder, it became a preoccupation of the time. It is not surprising, therefore, that Lady Hoby had an interest in it, and there are hints in the diary of her being of a melancholic temperament.

real grief and stress, not least when her mother upset her: 'dined at Newton with my Mother, wher I was much greued touchinge hir weaknes in receiung faulse reportes . . . sonme after I Came home, with teares and praires I went to bed' (3 October 1601).

One further specific indication of the perceived link between bodily and spiritual health can be found in Lady Hoby's attitude to the plague. Generally it was taken to demonstrate God's wrath and retribution and she did not miss the opportunity to make her own record. The latter part of the diary is interspersed with details about the plague of 1603 which was ravaging England, and particularly London where she was staying with her husband for the arrival of the new king. They had to move out to Kent and subsequently make their way back to Yorkshire, only to find that Newcastle, Hull, Whitby and Robin Hood's Bay had all become: 'greously veseted w^t a sore plaug' (24 August 1603). All the seaports were of course vulnerable, as the plague was carried by fleas riding on ship-board rats, and at one point the sickness even reached inland, touching them in their own village. As a precautionary measure, they moved out to stay with Lady Hoby's mother further into the countryside, for it was frightening that the plague had got so close. The miseries of a fearful death from such a destroyer could only be regarded as the vengeance of God, a punishment for allowing Satan to take a hold. Relief from the plague was therefore a counter suggestion of God's providence: 'thes day we hard from Hacknes that all there was well' (27 September 1603).

The main dramatic episode of the diary is the unwelcome visit in August 1600 of the younger members of two local families who did not enjoy good relations with Sir Thomas Hoby. The diary records briefly how they subverted the household's tranquillity and godly order with their unruly behaviour, and it became an event that seems particularly to have united the Hobys for the insults felt by each were shared with the other. Together they decided to lodge an official complaint against the abuse they and their household had endured. As noted earlier, friendship between Sir Thomas Hoby and his neighbours was often stretched to the limit by his litigious ways. William, son of Lord and Lady Eure of Malton, decided to take revenge, and, with a crowd of his friends, he organized a summer hunting party through the great Forest of Pickering. They deliberately headed far out to the wooded areas around Hackness, presumably to impose themselves on their devout neighbours. It was late afternoon, with a long return to Malton, and he conceived the idea of visiting the Hobys for the evening meal and requesting they might spend the night in their home. Eure sent one of

A TREATISE OF THE CHVRCH.

Wherein are handled the principall Que-
ftions mooued in our time concerning
that matter.

Margaritloby:

BY
PHILIP OF MORNAI,
Lord of *Plefsis-Marli*, Coun=
faylor to the King in his Counfell of Eftate,
Captaine of fiftie men at Armes of his Ordi-
nances, Gouernour for his Maieftie in the
Citie and *Iurifdiction* of Saumur, *and*
fuperintendent of his Houfe and
Crowne of Nauarre.

Reuiewed and Enlarged by the Author, and
the Authorities of the Fathers quoted in the
Margent, againft the common
flaunders of this Age.

Faithfully tranflated according to the laft French Copie.

Apocal. 18. 4. 5.
Goe out of Babylon, my people, that ye be not partakers of her finnes,
and that ye receiue not of her plagues: For her finnes by following
one another haue reached vp to heauen, and God hath remembred
her iniquities.

Jmprinted at London by L. S. *for*
George Potter, *dwelling in* Paules *Church-*
yard at the figne of the Bible. 1606.

The title page of Philip of Mornai's A Treatise of the Church *(1600) showing Lady*
Hoby's inscription.

his servants on ahead to order food and shelter for all the party, a gesture of hospitality that of course could not be refused, and he possibly planned to arrive even later than expected. Although Lady Hoby herself was unwell, she wrote in her diary that she had 'made prouision for som strangers that Came' (26 August 1600), and the house was made ready to receive the hunting party. Sir Thomas greeted them all and invited them up to the great chamber above the hall where a card game was soon noisily in progress. The host joined them for supper but refused to drink with them as it was not his custom, and he could not then persuade them to repair to their lodgings. They insisted that their game must continue a while longer. Public prayers, which usually took place in the great chamber, had to be transferred downstairs to the hall, where they were continuously disrupted by the noise and stamping of feet above. Meanwhile, Lady Hoby kept to her chamber, disturbed by the unfamiliar rowdiness carrying on nearby.

The normally tranquil routine of Hackness Hall was therefore deliberately upset by these raucous visitors clearly making every effort to show disrespect for its godly ways. With prayers mocked, and riotous singing interrupting the devout repetition of psalms, the peace of the evening was totally ruined – Hackness had, of course, never seen the like. The card game, dicing and drinking went on for much of the night and the Hobys longed to be rid of their unwanted, though welcomed, guests. At breakfast, William Eure and his friends carried on drinking each other's health with the beer and wine so generously provided for them, until such time as Sir Thomas allowed them no more. He asked them to leave quietly, having granted that they might spend the day hunting on his land, but the offer was followed by the greatest insult of the visit. Eure insisted on seeing Lady Hoby in her chamber before he would agree to leave, and realizing that the only way to get rid of them was to agree, she reluctantly gave in: 'I spake with Mr Ewrie, who was so drunke that I sone made an end of that I had no reasen to stay for' (27 August 1600). The young man then summoned his friends who were outside the door and they departed with glee. One of them, seeing stags' horns nailed to a screen, more or less called out that he wished Sir Thomas a cuckold, and they finally departed from Hackness, breaking windows and galloping around the freshly raked forecourt at the main entrance to the hall.

There is no question that both Lady Hoby and her husband felt themselves violated by this encounter and justifiably sought reparation. Although she did not write much about it in her diary (26–7 August 1600), Lady Hoby did note that she had 'talked with Mr Hoby about the abuse offered by Mr Ewere and his Companie' (28 August 1600), and she supported her husband throughout his call for redress.[52] He immediately lodged a formal complaint which was heard before the Council of the North on 26 September. Lord Eure, as Vice-President of the Council, used the occasion to defend his son and friends who claimed that they had themselves been ill-treated. The matter did not end there, however, for Sir Thomas, not unnaturally, was unhappy about Lord Eure's prejudiced intervention, and the result was that, in November, proceedings went to a higher court, that is, before the Privy Council sitting as the Court of Star Chamber in London.

Throughout the next few months the diary makes brief but significant references to the business of their 'bill' and to other legal matters. The Hobys had long discussions with a Master Jenkins in London, who may have been their lawyer and who seemed to know about the workings of the law. For example, he called one day with the news of a young man, presumably rather like William Eure, whose unruly behaviour had led to a fine and to his being 'expulsed the house, impresoned, bound to the Good behaviour, and inioyned to Confesse his fault and aske pardon' (29 November 1600). The Hobys met with a Master Gibson, 'the atturnie', on 9 December 1600, the lawyer who may have been in charge of their case in the Court of Star Chamber itself, and Lady Hoby wrote of a potentially embarrassing social encounter when William Eure happened to bump into them at Lord Burghley's house where they were invited to dinner: 'Came in Mr Ewry, so that we Came a way, rather giuinge place to him then our affections whic might haue bin prouoked' (25 January 1600/1). In February a Master John Mansfield, cousin of the Eures, tried to make them come to some kind of private agreement (23 February 1600/1), but the Hobys resisted such pressure, both throughout their London stay and later in York. Their welcome return to Hackness in March led only to a short recess, for by the first week of June members of their household, including Master Rhodes and various servants, were served to be examined by the Council of the North holding a special commission in Malton. The diary records Lady Hoby's anxiety and conference with her men on their departure and return. She also heard that her mother had to give evidence (5 June 1601), and she hurriedly visited Linton to discuss the matter with Mistress Dakins.

---

[52]   Letters and statements from both sides are to be found in the *Cecil Papers, Vol. X,* 302 ff, 325, 391; *Vol. XI,* 11–12, 456, 546; *Vol. XII,* 32, 105. See Appendix 2 (I).

Introduction

On 1 October 1601, over a year after the event, further evidence was still being ordered, this time from servants Robert Nettleton and John Wasse.[53] Nettleton's witness is a very succinct statement that clearly identifies Eure as the guilty party, but this did not prevent the father from continuing to press the innocence of his son. Eure's defence rested on the fact that any untoward actions on his part were prompted by the inhospitable welcome and lack of cordiality received from his surly host, and evidence was being called to prove or disprove his case. It was not doubted that Sir Thomas's Puritan disposition would naturally prejudice his attitude to the young men's boisterous behaviour, but the question was how far had they gone in their insults to the mistress of the house as well as to the master himself. In the period 5–10 October 1601, the diary records how the Hobys were further pressured by influential people, such as their cousin Lord Burghley, and their old friend, the Bishop of Limerick, to give up their suit and settle out of court. Still believing themselves wronged, however, they held to their position, feeling that to give in would not be to their credit in the long run. We cannot help but feel that it was very much a matter of pride at stake. Their own, as that of ordinary gentry, was too much involved for them to settle privately an affair that involved public humiliation at the hands of a proud and hostile aristocratic family.

Much evidence, therefore, went before the Council of the North in York and deliberations continued during the winter in London. In the end, the case was resolved in the Hoby's favour: 'Mr Hoby Came from London hauinge ended all his busenes there, I praise god' (17 February 1601/2), and a fine of £100 per annum was levied on the Eure family, to be paid in perpetuity, by way of compensation for the hurt caused.[54] In late May, Lady Hoby could hardly suppress her joy when the first payment was brought to Hackness by 'Lord Ewry his men . . . and so it fell out that, as it was done in the sight of our tenantes, so many of the tenants were bye when the mony was brought' (29 May 1602). The following day, Sunday, she recorded that she was 'truly thankfule', and rightly so, for at last she could see the back of a discomforting affair that had dragged on for some twenty-one months.

This dramatic episode dominates the middle section of the diary, and, although only briefly referred to, the reader can infer much about the

---

[53]   The evidence of Robert Nettleton, PRO STAC 5/H22/21. See Appendix 2 (II).
[54]   I am grateful to Lord Derwent for this information. Earlier this century an unsuccessful attempt was made to rescind the court's decision of 1602.

1

effect it had upon Lady Hoby herself and her life at Hackness. Apart from the raucous unpleasantness of the hunting party's visit, she had the upheaval of her own and her husband's various trips to York and London. There were the uncertainties of prolonged legal matters, with the anxiety of her mother, her chaplain and servants giving evidence in court. Above all, their relations with neighbouring families must have been further soured. The Hobys were up against a powerful local lobby, and we can assume that they felt vindicated in taking the case through to the end. There is a gap of two weeks until the next entry when Lady Hoby celebrated a general state of well-being: 'vntell this day, I praise god, I haue had my health, haue binn able to attend my busenes, and hard the exercises w^t profitt and quieet and peace from god' (13 June 1602). One might add peace from legal matters as well.

Such an episode demonstrates that this is a diary of action rather than abstraction. There is indeed very little intimate self-revelation beyond the constant anxiety about her health and her fear at the loss of God's love, but the texture of Lady Hoby's writing is rich even in the diary's minimalist detail. Other episodes hinted at, and thereby enriching what is present, pertain to such events as the arraignment of the Earl of Essex, the death of Queen Elizabeth, and the terrors of the plague; but, mainly, the diary is a simple record of religious activity, of daily prayer and attendance at church, of talk and of the study of godly texts. With our imaginative reading between the lines, however, it becomes much more than a simple record of a life of hard work and spiritual observance. Lady Hoby could not resist mentioning the routine that enfolded her devotions nor making reference to the stream of visitors and servants with whom she was in regular contact, and it is from this we can infer much about her plans, her aspirations and concerns. The diary possesses a fervent sense of self and soul – a state of being in relation to her family as well as to God. As a private document it is distinct from the writings of her contemporaries, such as the Countess of Pembroke, and in its way it pre-empts both the confessional Quaker diaries and the great autobiographical journals of the later seventeenth century. In the punctuation 'went to bed', 'sonne after to bed', and 'and then to bed', she even makes us think of Samuel Pepys.

The diary was intended as a vehicle for self-assessment, and as a help to Lady Hoby's memory of God's goodness to her. A pattern of doubt about the assurance of her salvation is easily distinguished through her daily routine, but she found consolation in God's love, using her writing as a way of expressing her recognition and thanks for His especial favours. When she looked back over what was written she demonstrated her sense of its value: 'in the readinge over some of my former spent time, I funde some profitt might be made of that Course' (1 April 1605). As readers we also can find profit, especially if we read the whole rather than its parts. Like Lady Hoby, we consider both herself and her diary important areas of concern.

This is an invaluable document, not only as an historical source for the Elizabethan period but also for the insight it gives into the life and thinking of an Elizabethan woman, whose Protestant piety and experience were structured in a culture which paradoxically both witheld and yet gave independence to those with property. Her own resistance and self-determination are there to be discovered in the text. Throughout the insistent religious preoccupations of the work her sense of self is paramount. Brief and repetitive may be these entries, but they nevertheless enable Margaret, Lady Hoby, confidently to assert the significance of her self and her inner world – an experience that can now provide us as readers with direct knowledge and understanding of the private life of an Elizabethan lady.

Note on the Text

The manuscript of the diary, written in Lady Hoby's neat italic hand, is now in the British Library Manuscripts Department, London (BL MS Egerton 2614). We cannot know if it is complete as the first two folios and the last have pieces torn out. The full text is included here. The author changed her pen several times, the writing varies in size, and there are blots, smudges, crossings-out and corrections, but it is generally easy to read. Lady Hoby managed to get thirty to thirty-three lines to a side, and wrote on both sides of the folio. The page measures 15 by 19 centimetres, and there are 59 folios giving 118 pages altogether. These were bound in May 1884 having been purchased from the Revd C. St B. Sydenham on 10 November 1883.

Lady Hoby's spelling is not consistent, the use of u/v is interchangeable, and there are duplications of certain letters and words. In an effort to address the needs of as wide an audience as possible, yet to retain the distinctive peculiarities and idiosyncrasies of her writing, the present edition retains the original spelling and capitalization, but contractions have been expanded and the long 's' is modernized. Full acknowledgment is given to the pioneering work of Evelyn Fox, who wrote on the diary for the Royal Historical Society (1908), and to Dorothy M. Meads, whose punctuation of the first edition (1930) is herein adopted. The biographical detail in the Introduction draws heavily on their commentary as well as on sources in the *Cecil* and *Fortescue Papers*. The notes and illustrations highlight Lady Hoby's life and times, not only in Elizabethan society but also in the everyday routine of her Tudor home. I have singled out those individuals I consider to be most important, and have aimed to provide a strong regional focus with extra information about Lady Hoby's Yorkshire. In addition to the normal scholarly notes, I have therefore added others that might interest readers wanting to know more about the area.

The diary commences on 9 August 1599, and continues until 21 July 1605. Lady Hoby's dating is often erratic, getting days and dates incorrectly matched. She did not always write the month and only sometimes did she refer to the days of the week, usually, but not always, counting Monday as the first day. She clearly wrote entries, even groups of entries, in retrospect, and often corrected the dates herself. I am indebted to Meads for her rigorous work on checking the exact dates of days during the period 1599–1605 and noting corrections as appropriate.

Chronology

1570/1   Margaret Dakins born at Linton, Yorkshire, only daughter to Arthur and Thomasin Dakins
10 February. Baptized in Wintringham church
Spends some of her teen years being educated and trained in the household of the Earl and Countess of Huntingdon where she meets Walter Devereux and Thomas Sidney

1589   Marries Walter Devereux
The Hackness estate is purchased for them

1591   8 September. Death of Walter Devereux at the siege of Rouen
2 November. Margaret goes to Huntingdons in London
22 December. Marries Thomas Sidney

1592   13 July. Death of Arthur Dakins at Hackness; buried in the chancel of Hackness church

1595   26 July. Death of Thomas Sidney; buried at Kingston upon Hull
Margaret sells manor of Kingston

December. Death of the Earl of Huntingdon
The new Earl of Huntingdon claims the Hackness estate as his own; Margaret faces suit in Chancery

1596   9 August. Marries Sir Thomas Posthumous Hoby in London
They go to Hackness

1597   The Hobys erect monument to Arthur Dakins in Hackness church

1599   9 August. Diary commences

1600   8–24 April. Hobys visit York

Chronology

26 August. The unruly Eure visit, starts the lawsuit
26 September. The Council of the North hears the lawsuit in York
9 October. Hobys go to London
November. Lawsuit becomes a case in the Court of Star Chamber

1600/1 [Arraignment of the Earl of Essex. 19 February. Trial; 25 February. Execution]

19 March. Hobys return to Hackness

4 June. Hackness servants examined for lawsuit at Malton
5 June. Lady Hoby's mother gives evidence

3–4 October. Hobys pressed to give up lawsuit

1601/2 Winter. Lawsuit continues in Court of Star Chamber
17 February. Lawsuit settled in Hobys' favour

1602 29 May. First payment of £100 by Eure family

1602/3 23 March. Death of Queen Elizabeth I
Accession of King James I of England, VI of Scotland

11 April. Hobys go to London for the queen's funeral

June. Plague spreads in London; Hobys leave

22 June. Lady Hoby kisses the new queen's hand at Ashby-de-la-Zouche

28 June. Hobys return to Hackness

Plague spreads to Whitby and surrounding area

1604 1 November. Hobys go to London

1604/5 7 March. Hobys return to Hackness

21 July. The diary ends

Chronology

1613 Death of Thomasin Dakins, Lady Hoby's mother;
13 November. Buried in the chancel of Hackness church

1632 July. Lady Hoby assigns all her lands to her husband

1633 Death of Lady Margaret Hoby; 6 September. Buried in the
chancel of Hackness church [Monument inside altar rail]

1634 Chapel of St Margaret, Harwood Dale, erected in her memory
by her husband

1640 30 December. Death of Sir Thomas Posthumous Hoby
Hackness estate bequeathed to his nephew, John Sydenham

1682 Monument to Sir Thomas erected in Hackness church by son
of his heir

1707 Hackness estate purchased by Mr John van den Bempde

1792 New Hackness Hall begun by Sir Richard van den Bempde
Johnstone

1798 Lady Hoby's home demolished. The new garden scheme
necessitates the moving of the village a few hundred yards
further westward

THE DIARY OF
LADY MARGARET
HOBY
1599–1605

1599

[Almost the whole of the first entry on this page is torn away]

Thursday
day was deadnes in praier, and my greatest offence was want of sorow for the same: the Lord of his mercie increase true and fervant mourninge vnto god that he neuer take his spiritt from me amen amen

Friday 10
After I was redie I betooke my selfe to priuat praier, wherin it pleased the Lord to Deall mercifully: after, I went about the house, and instructed Tomson wiffe in som principles of relegion, and then eate my breakfast,[1] and then walked abroad tell all most :11: of the Clock : and after I had read :2: chapters of the bible, I went to diner : after dinner I went to worke, at which *[page torn]* Contenewed tell :4:, then I took order for supper *[page torn]* went to praier and to writ som notes in my testament, from which I was Called to walk with Mr Hoby,[2] talkinge of sundrie busines, and so to supper : imediately after praer and Lector,[3] for the diligent attencion of which the Lord did heare my praier by remouing all wanderinges which vse to hvrt me so that I receiued much Comfort, I went to bed

[The entry for 11 August has disappeared completely, except the three words in the last two lines]

the Lordes day 12
after I was redie, I went to priuatt praiers, then to breakfast : then I walked tell church time[4] Mr Hoby, and after to dinner : after which I walked and had speech of no serious maters tell :2: a clock : then I wrett[5] notes into my

---

[1]   Lady Hoby wakes about 6 a.m. and breakfasts at about 8 a.m.
[2]   *Mr Hoby,* Master Hoby is the usual form of reference. Lady Hoby rarely calls him 'my husband', but see entry for 6 August 1600. She is always very loyal, although there is one entry that records discontent (19 July 1600).
[3]   *Lector,* the formal reading aloud of a given passage, probably from the Scriptures or a sermon. Any literate member of the household may have given the lecture at public prayers.
[4]   Lady Hoby refers to the parish church, originally St Mary's but dedicated to St Peter in 1567. The Catalogue of Hackness church library, dated 1701, still refers to the church as St Mary's. Lady Hoby has omitted 'with'.
[5]   *wrett,* wrote. We cannot know how far Lady Hoby's speaking and writing reflected her use of a North Riding regional dialect that would be recognizable today. In general, Yorkshire dialect vowels are mostly simple and 'broad', that is not rounded into dipthongs as in standard English. Consonants are pronounced with greater emphasis, and **I** is pronounced **ah**. Lady Hoby's spelling is often in accord with the dialect.

bible tell :3: and after :4: I came againe from the church, walk, and
medetated a Litle, and againe wrett som other notes in my bible of that I
had Learned tell :5: att which time I retourned to examenation and praier :
and after I had reed some of bond of the suboth,[6] I walked abroad : and so
to supper, after to praers, and Lastly to bed.

Munday 13

In the Morninge after priuat praiers and order taken for diner, I wrett
some notes in my testament tell :10: a clock : then I went to walk, and,
after I retourned home, I praied priuatly, read a chapter of the bible, and
wrought[7] tell dinner time : after I walked a whill with Mr Rhodes[8] and
Then I wrought, and did som things about the house tell :4: then I wrett
out the sarmon into my book preached the day before, and, when I had
again gone about in the house and giuen order for supper and other
thinges, I retourned to examination and praier : then I walked tell
supper time, and, after Catichisinge,[9] medetated awhill of that I had
hard, with mourninge to god for pardon both of my omition and
Commition wherin I found my selfe guilte, I went to bed.

Teusday 14

In the morning I praied priuatly and wrett notes in [*page torn*] tement[10]
tell :7: a clocke : then I took order for diuers thinges touchinge the house,
and, after I had brekfast [*page torn*], I wrought tell dinner time and hard
Mr Rhodes [*page torn*] tell dinner time : after dinner I walked with g

---

6   *bond of the suboth*, this book or tract about the sabbath has not been traced, but Lady
Hoby may be referring to John Bond (1550–1612), physician and classical scholar.
7   *wrought*, sewed or embroidered. Lady Hoby is engaged in needlework of some kind
or another most afternoons. Usually, though not always, she is in the company of her
women and listening to a reading.
8   Master Richard Rhodes, Lady Hoby's chaplain, often mentioned. See Introduction.
9   *Catichisinge*, the catechism became an instrument of instruction early on. It formed the
basis of a method of both teaching and learning about religious principles through
question and answer, in public or private. Instruction was provided in the short catechism
inserted in the Order of Confirmation in the prayer books of Edward and Elizabeth.
Edward issued an official catechism, and an unauthorized catechism by Calvin was also
used. The most influential catechism was prepared by Alexander Nowell and printed in an
authorized edition in 1570. This was the one used most extensively in private religious
instruction. Master Rhodes, the cleric most often in attendance on Lady Hoby, would have
assisted. See Green, *The Christian's ABC, Catechisms and Catechizing in England* (1996).
10   Probably 'my testament'. Where the pages are torn we can sometimes guess the entry.
Lady Hoby means that during prayer she is noting particular passages, possibly for
copying out later.

Painting of an inlaid chamber at Sizergh Castle by Joseph Nash (1808–78). (Water-colour on paper.)

[*page torn*] Younge tell 2: a clock, then I went to work tell [*page torn*] :after I had praied and taken order for supper, [*page torn*] walked abroad tell after. 5: at which time I retourned [*page torn*] examenation and praier, at which time it pleased the Lord to giue me sure testimonie of his fauor in christ, his [*torn*] name euermore be praised, who sendeth not his empty away : tell super time I was busie in the graniry[11] and, after supper and praiers, I went to bedd:

Wensday 15
In the morninge at :6: a clock I praied priuatly : that done, I went to awiffe in trauill of child, about whom I was busey[12] tell: 1 a Cloke, about which time, She bing deliuered and I hauinge praised god, returned home and betook my selfe to priuat praier :2: seuerall times vpon occasion : then I wrett the most part of an examenation or triall of a christian, framed by Mr Rhodes, in the doinge wher I againe fell to praier, and after continewed writing [*faded*] after 3: a cloke : then I went to work tell after 5, and then to examenation and praier : the Lord make me thankfull, who hath hard my praiers and hath not turned his face from me : then I taked with Mrs Brutnell[13] tell supper time, and after walked a litle into the feeldes, and so to prairs, and then to bed:

Thursday 16
After I was readie in the morning I praied priuatly and wrett out the rest of those possitions which I left vncopied the day before : then I went take order for dinner and went to work tell breakfast Came, and, after I had broken my fast, I examened that I had wreten with Mr Rhodes, read some thinge in the bible, and so to work tell Comringe[14] Cam for dinner

---

[11] *graniry*, Lady Hoby often works in the granary. She mentions both wheat and rye and she almost certainly grew barley for ale. She supervises the harvest and its storage; she weighs the grain, checks the level, and concerns herself with the autumn planting. There were several mills on the Hackness estate and the Hobys employed more than one miller. Rye was considered more beneficial than wheat for digestive problems and was one of the chief grains of the north, along with oatmeal, until the agricultural revolution and the enclosures of the eighteenth century. Rye bread and oatcake ('haverbread') were popular, and, apart from the more obvious uses in bread-making, wheat was used for salves and medicaments. 'Awm' is a traditional Yorkshire word for bread made without yeast.
[12] Attendance at childbirth is mentioned several times. This might have been emotionally demanding for Lady Hoby who so much wished for children of her own. She left no issue.
[13] Mistress Brutnell, possibly one of Lady Hoby's women.
[14] *Comringe*, later 'coueringe', perhaps the bailiff or steward. Other servants are mentioned later. They are not given the title Master or Mistress.

: then I went to pray and so came to dinner : after dinner I wrought and read tell 4, and then I walked a litle abroad and, after I Cam home, read and [*faded and torn*] tell all most 6: and then I went to praier and examenation: after which, I walked tell supper time : that don, I walked tell praiers, then hadd Mr Rhodes read a chapter, and so went to bed

Friday

After priuat prairs I went about the house and read of the bible and wrought tell dinner time : and, after dinner, it pleased, for a Iust punishment to corricte my sinnes, to send me febelnis of stomak and paine of my head, that kept me vpon my bed tell 5: a clock : at which time I arose, haveinge release of my sickness, according to the wonted kindnes of the Lord, who, after he had Let me se how I had offended, that so I might take better heed to my body and soule hereeafter, with a gentle corriction let me feele he was reconsiled To me : at which time I went to priuat praier, and praises, examenation, and so to work tell supper time : which done I hard the Lector and, after I had walked an Hower with Mr Hoby, I wente to bed

Saterday 18

After I was readie I praied priuatly, and, because I was weak and had paine in my head, I wret litle but wound yearne and walked tell dinner time : after which I went about the house, and did walke abroad, workinge litle all that day because of my weaknes, least I should be disabled to keepe the Lordes day as I desired and am bound : before supper, I praied and examened my selfe, not so perteculerly as I ought to have don, which I beseech the Lord to pardon for his christs sack, and giue me grace here after to be more carefull : then I walked tell supper time : after supper I taked[15] wth Mr Rhodes of the lordes praier, and, after lector, I medetated a litle of that I had hard, and so to bed.

The Lordes day 19

After I was redie I betooke me priuat praier: then, because Mr Hoby was not well, I kept him Kompanie tell the sarmon time, and did eate my breakfast : that done, I thank god who gaue him will and abelitie, we went to church, where we receiued the sacrementes : after I came home I praied and so to dinner, att which, and after, both my selfe did talk and heare of more worldly mattres then, by godes assistance, I will here after

---

15   *taked*, talked.

willingly doe : tell :3: a Clock I was with Mr Hoby, not so Care full, the Lord forgiue it me, as I ought, to medetate of what I hard, speakinge and thinking of many Idle mattres : then we went to Church and, after the sarmon, I walked tell 6: a clock, about which time I praied and examened my self, crauing pardon for these my infirmites : after, I went to supper : after which, tell praier time, I walked and, after repeticion,[16] went to bed:

Munday 20
After I was readie I praied priuatly : then I walked with Mr Hoby tell 8: a clock, at which time I brake my fast, and so to worke, and, at :11: of the Clock, I took a Lector of Mr Rhodes, and went to dinner : after dinner I wound yearn tell: 3, and then walked with Mr Hoby about the toune[17] to spye out the best places where Cotiges might be builded : after I Came home I wrought tell :6: and gaue order for supper, and then I betook me to priuat praier and examenation, in which I found my selfe a lackinge in performing my dutie I soune perceiued, and, therfore, besought Lord for pardon : then I went to supper, after which I walked a whill, and, because there [*torn and soiled*] not Mr Rhodes to pray publeckly, I praied priuatly, and, after I had helped Mr Hoby to Looke ouer some papers, I went to bed:

Teusday 21
after I was readie I praied, and then I went awhile about the house and so to breakfast, and then to work, tell coueringe came : then I went to priuat praier but was interrupted : after I had dined I went to work tell 6:, and walked a little abroad, and then Came to examenation and praier: after, I walked a litle, and so to supper : after which I went to praiers, and, Nut long after, accordinge to my wonted vse, to bed, saue only I did not so deligently think of that I had hard, which I beseech the Lord to pardon, for Christ sack Amen Amen

Wensday 22
after I was redie I praied, and, after I had gon a Litle about the house, I wrett out notes in my testement, and then brak my fast and walked

---

[16] *repeticion*, probably the repetition of psalms or the day's epistles, sermons and teaching. Sermons were important for they furnished both entertainment and intellectual exercise. Children and servants were catechized about the preacher's utterances and note-taking was usual. Lady Hoby kept a sermon book for future reference.
[17] The village of Hackness, so designated in Elizabethan times.

abroad tell dinner : before which I praied, according to my wonte, and, after dinner, I was buisie dispacting one a way to Linton[18] tell :3: a Clock : then I wret notes out into my bible, and after went a walkinge with Mr Hoby, and then returned into examination and praier : after, I reed of the bible, and walked alone, and then went into the kicthine, wher Mr Rhodes and my selfe had som speach with the poore and Ignorant of the som princeples of religion : and I had walked a litle after in the Court.[19] Mr Hoby came, and so to supper and after to lector and then to bed.

Thursday 23
In the morninge I praied : then I took order for thinges about the house tell I went to breakfast, and sonne after I took my Coach[20] and went to linton wher, after I had salluted my mother, I praied, and then, walkinge a litle and readinge of the bible in my Chamber went to supper : after which I hard the Lector and sonne after that went to bed

Friday 24
In the morninge, beinge readie, I praied, then brak my fast with Mr Hoby, and so reed[21] to church : after the sarmon I presently went to dinner, after which I passed the time in talk with some freinds, and then went to priuat praier : that don I took the aire in the Coach with Mr Hoby, and so cam in and walked in the garden, medetatinge of the pointes of the sarmon and prainge tell hard before I went to supper : and after supper went to publect praier and thence to bed:

Saterday 25
In the morning I praied and then I wreet a Letter to Doctor Brewer[22] and so to breakfast : after which I taked priuatly, with Mr Hoby, matters

---

[18] *Linton*, this was where Lady Hoby was born, her mother's home. They correspond regularly and visit each other. When she goes to Linton the normal pattern is to stay two nights; she is usually though not always accompanied by her husband and Master Rhodes. The house is later sold to a cousin and the Hobys can use it as a staging point on their way to York. See map of Lady Hoby's Yorkshire on p. viii.
[19] Lady Hoby may mean the earth and grass courtyard, or quadrangle, inside the main gate. See painting of Hackness Hall on p. xx.
[20] The covered carriage, or coach, was becoming very popular in London and the surrounding countryside by the end of the sixteenth century. The fact that Lady Hoby had a coach of her own in Yorkshire is evidence of her pragmatism, sense of fashion and wealth.
[21] *reed*, rode, but can be 'read'. In Yorkshire dialect **ee** can become the dipthong **ee–a**, giving two separate syllables. Lady Hoby often writes 'reead' for 'read'.
[22] Lady Hoby corresponds with her physician.

concerninge Conscience and our estates,[23] wch, beinge Concluded of betwene vs, I took my Coache and Came home to Hacknes, wher, after I was well Comed, I praise god, I went to praier and medetation : then I went about the house tell supper time : after supper I talked with Mr Rhodes in the garden,[24] and then to publect praiers, and sonne after to bed

The Lordes day 26
In the morninge, after priuat praiers, I taked a litle with Mr Rhodes, and then to breakfast : sonne after which, I went to church, and, when the seermon was ended, I medetated of that I hard, and praied, tell allmost diner : after diner I taked a while with Mrs Brutnell, and then hard a Chapter wher of Mr Rhodes spake, and so to church, wher, at Caticising and sermon, I staied tell 4 a clock : then I cam hom and took order for supper, and wret out notes in my bible, and then went to walke : and after my Comminge home, praied, after which I went to supper and, sonne after that, to praers and thence to bed : this day, as euer, the diuell laboreth to hinder my profittable hearinge of the word and callinge vpon god, but the Lord, for his mercis sach strengten, his children to rissist and ouer Come

Monday 27
In the morninge after priuatt praier I went a litle about the house, and then eate my breakfast, after which I wrett out a sermon that I was

---

23   Almost certainly Lady Hoby means their spiritual estate, but there is ambiguity here.
24   There would have been a flower, kitchen and herb garden, as well as an orchard. An important function of Lady Hoby's garden would have been to supply food and herbs for medicinal purposes. It may have featured a 'knot garden', which consisted of a rectangular arrangement of beds, each with compartments formed by an intricate geometrical design of close-clipped, low box hedging. Infillings included flowers, herbs, small shrubs and gravel. Lady Hoby writes of planting seeds in the spring and tending roses that bloom very late in a warm autumn. Garden tools have not changed much since early times and grasscutting in her garden would have been unknown; she would have played bowls on rough grass (see 7 September 1599). One of the problems of gardening in the north of England is coping with the cooler weather and strong winds. Lady Hoby would have benefited from the sheltered position of Hackness. The Yorkshireman gardener William Lawson was the first to write a book on gardening in the north, *New Orchard and Garden* (1615), in which he noted: 'What was Paradise but a garden, an orchard of trees and herbes full of pleasure and nothing there but delight'. He wrote the first book for women gardeners, *Countrie Housewife's Garden* (1617), and was also notable for giving full details and a plan of a terraced Elizabethan garden. See Amherst, *A History of Gardening in England* (1896) and Strong, *The Renaissance Garden* (1979).

behind with, then I walked, and, sonne after, to dinner : after which I talked a litle with Mr Cholmley,[25] and then dispached a messhinger to my mothers, and to York[26] to Mr Hoby,[27] and then wrett out another sermon in my book : and so walked abroad, and, retourning hom, betook my selfe to priuat praiers and medetacion : sonne after I went to supper, after which I walked a litle, and then to prairs : then I wret to Mr Hoby and so to bed:

Tewsday 28

In the morninge, after priuat praier, I Reed of the bible, and then wrought tell 8: a clock, and then I eate my breakfast : after which done, I walked in to the feeldes tell: 10 a clock, then I praied, and, not long after, I went to dinner:[28] and about one a clock I geathered my Apeles[29] tell :4:, then I Cam home, and wrought tell almost :6:, and then I went to priuat praier and examenation, in which it pleased the lord to blesse me : and besiech the lord, for christ his sack, to increase the power of this

[25] Either Henry Cholmley of Roxby, or his son, Richard, of Whitby. Neighbourly relations with the Cholmleys became fraught after the hunting party incident as Richard was one of those involved.

[26] York is an ancient city steeped in Roman and medieval history situated on the River Ouse in the centre of the fertile York plain. It is at a point where the three Ridings of Yorkshire meet, though it is not part of any of them, being a county in its own right (the Ainsty of York). In Lady Hoby's time it was the second city of England, with the seats of the Archbishop of the Northern Province and the Council of the North. It was therefore the major religious, legal and commercial centre for the whole of the north of the country. An old prophecy says: 'Lincoln was, London is, but York shall be, the greatest of the three'.

[27] Sir Thomas is regularly away, on matters of litigation, fulfilling his duties as Justice of the Peace in both the North and East Ridings of Yorkshire, and on various commissions. Later we hear of him collecting local taxes, or subsidies. He is also a parliamentary representative, first for Appleby, Westmoreland, then for Scarborough. His absences increase over the period of the diary as he takes on a more significant role in the region.

[28] *dinner*, Lady Hoby often runs two 'n's together, seeming to write 'm' for 'nn'. In Yorkshire dialect a double consonant is used to show a short vowel, eg: 'finnd' as in 'fit, 'watter' as in 'cat'.

[29] Apples have always been a great favourite. John Gerard found it impossible, in his herbal, to give the names of all kinds grown in his time, the varieties were infinite. In Elizabethan times they were served at the end of a feast with a little side dish of caraway seeds, and Lady Hoby would have made cider. The apple is easily digested and was said to be a cure for constipation; she may have recommended apple juice to heal small cuts, or even prescribed it for the red noses of those who drank too much. The pulp, mixed with swine's grease and rose water, was made into an ointment. See Gerard, *Herball* (1597), and entry for 17 September 1599.

spirite in me daly Amen Amen : tell supper time I hard Mr Rhodes read of Cartwright,[30] and, sonne after supper, I went to prairs, after which I wrett to Mr Hoby, and so to bed.

Wensday 29
after priuat praier I reed of the bible and wrought tell dinner time, before which I praied : and, after dinner, I continewed my ordenarie Course of working, reading, and dispossinge of busenes in the House, tell after 5:, at which time I praied, read a sermon, and examened my selfe : and then, goinge to super, it pleased god to send me ease of the tothache wher with I was troubled. Sonne after I went to praers, and, after som talk with some of the sarvantes of houshould mattres, I went to bed.

Thursday 30
After priuat praier in the morninge, I took order for dinner, and then wrought tell breakfast time : after that I walked, and then Came home and wrett of my Common place book:[31] then I praied, and so to dinner : after dinner I trifelde the time about the house and in the toune tell 2: a Clock, then I Came in, and wrought, and instructed som of my famelie:[32] at w[ch] time I found my mind much and altogether eased of sume trouble it had before : then I was busie and hard Mr Rhodes Read his Catechismie tell 5:, then I went to priuat praiers, medetation, and ordering some thing in the house, and so to supper : after that to Lector, and, no long after, to bed.

Friday 31
After priuat prairs I I[33] wrett notes in my testement after I had taken order in the house : then I eadt my break fast, and then wrought tell and walked

---

30   Thomas Cartwright (1535–1603), a learned scholar and popular teacher, imprisoned as a Puritan, 1590–2. He published exegetical and controversial treatises approved by Lady Hoby's mother-in-law, Lady Elizabeth Russell.
31   *Common place book*, a book in which Lady Hoby would have methodically noted worthy phrases, useful bits of information, metaphors and proverbs, references and favourite passages from the Bible and the classics. The Elizabethans regarded such compilations as instruments of instruction for rhetoric and thought. See Moss, *Printed Commonplace-Books and the Structuring of Renaissance Thought* (1996).
32   *famelie*, this means all the household as Lady Hoby had no children of her own. Apart from the servants there were maids in attendance for their education and training, plus widows given charitable hospitality.
33   Duplication such as this is not unusual.

tell dinner : then I praied priuatly, and, when I had dined, wrought tell :3: a clock : then I went a little about the house and reed of the diatt of the soule tell :5:, and then returned to priuat praier and medetacion, and so to readinge of the bible and walkinge tell supper : after which I hard of the sudden Death of Doctor Brewer, Procured by a medeson he minestred to him selfe to Cause him to sleep:[34] I was much greued for it, because of the familiaritie I had with him, and good I had receiued from, but, after better aduice, I found the mercie and power of god shewed in openinge his eies touchinge me, and shuttinge them against him selfe, by Causinge him to haue great Care of ministringe vnto me, and so litle for his owne saftie : therefore I may truly conclude it is the Lord, and not the phisision, who both ordaines the medesine for our health and orderethe the ministring of it for the good of his children, closinge and vnclosinge the Iudgmentes of men at his pleasure : therefore let euerie one phisision and pactente Call vpon the Lord for a blessinge:[35] and then, after Lector, I wen to bed:

September 1599, 1 *Saterday*
After praier in the morninge, I, beinge not well, did heare Mr Rhodes read of Gyffard vpon the songe of Sallemon:[36] sone after I went to breakfast, and so walked allmost tell dinner time : then I Came in, and praied, and so to dinner : after which I walked about the house, barne, and feeldes, and, when I Came home, I praied priuat with Mr Rhodes, wherin I had more comfort then euer I receiued in my Life before, I praise god : then I went to take my Beesse, and, after that, I returned to priuat praier my selfe and examenation : then I went to se my Honnie[37] ordered, and so to supper : after which I went to lector, and soone after to bed:

---

[34] Lady Hoby's physician is important to her and the death of Doctor Brewer is a great loss. She is delighted to find a replacement in Master Lister (see 21 and 22 September 1599) and goes to York in the spring for medical treatment (see 12 April 1600). She is herself a physician to her own household and tenants.
[35] For a Puritan like Lady Hoby, God is the great physician.
[36] George Gifford (d. 1620), Puritan divine and well-known preacher; deposed for nonconformity, 1584. He published theological works, including *Sermons vppon the Songe of Salomon* (1598). The book to which Lady Hoby refers was dedicated to the Earl of Essex, her brother-in-law by her first marriage.
[37] *Honnie*, honey was particularly important for culinary use and preserving fruit. In about 1600 it was discovered that fruit could be preserved in sugar, but some time before jam was made with it. Lady Hoby may also have made honey ale, generally known as mead. Books could give advice, eg: Sir Hugh Platt, *A Closet for Ladies and Gentlewomen, or, the Art of Preserving, Conserving and Candying* (1608, and 6 edns to 1636). Lady Hoby must have performed tasks such s this at the same time each year but she does not routinely mention them.

The Lordes day 2

After priuat praier I brak my fast before I went to Church, and, when I Came home, I praied priuatly, and so went to dinner: after which I talked tell :2: a Clock with som of my freindes, and then to Church : after I Cam home I wrett notes out into my bible, and then I went to priuatt praier and examenation and so to supper : sonne after which I went to praers and then to bed.

Munday 3

In the morninge, after priuat praier, I brake my fast : sonne after that I had hard som chapters of the bible read, I went abroad in to the feeldes in my Cotch, because my foot would not suffer me to goe : then I Came home and, hauinge praied a litle, went to dinner : after which I walked abroad and, at my Cominge home, I took order for supper, and went to praier, and sonne after to supper : after which Mr Hoby Came home and, for that night, when he had eaten som thinge, I went to praiers, hauinge no Lector, and so to bed.

Tewday 4

when I had praied priuatly I did read of the bible allmost vntell dinner time : after dinner I walked to the Church with Mr Hoby, and was then With him allmost tell :4: of the Clock : then I Came home an did studie my lector, and read a whill, and then, after talk wth him of many thinges, I went to priuat prair and examenation : after I went to supper, then to the lector, and so to Bed

Wensday 5

After priuat praier I wret to my Lady Ewre:[38] then I went about the house and, hauing taken order for dinner, I walked and kept Mr Hoby Compenie almost tel dinner time : then I reed a litle, and praied, and so to dinner : after which I hilped to read of the book for the placing of the people in the church to Mr Hoby,[39] and then we went to church : and after we Came home I taked with him, and Lay on my bed, not being

---

[38]   Mary Dawnay, Lady Eure, wife to Ralph, Lord Eure, of Malton. Her son William and friends make the unruly visit to Hackness that results in the lawsuit. Despite the delicate relations between Sir Thomas and his neighbours, Lady Eure is a friend of Lady Hoby, mentioned several times.

[39]   This was probably a pew book in which the Hackness congregation were allotted specific pew seats according to rank.

able well to goe for my foot that was sore, tell allmost supper time : and then I praied and examened myself and, after I had supped, I reed of grenhame,[40] and so went to bed :

Thursday 6
after I had praied I did goe about in to the house, and then eate my breakfast, and after did see my hunnie ordered, and then to dinner : after which I wrought, and walked about with Mr Hoby, nothinge reading nor profiting my selfe or any, the Lord pardon my ommitiones and Commitions, and giue me his spiritt to be watchfull to redeme the time : then I went to priuat praier and examenation, after to supper and lector, and so to bed:

Friday 7
After priuat praiers I wrett my notes in my testement, which I geathered out of the Lector the night before : then I did eate my breakfast, then I walked abroad and talked of good thinges, so that I found much Comfort : after I Cam hom I wrett my sermon that was preached the saboth day before, then I went to priuat praier and so to dinner : after which I taked a litle with some of my frendes, and exercised my body at bowles[41] a whill, of which I found good : then I Came home and wrought tell 4, then I praied with Mr Rhodes, and after walked abroad : and when I Came hom I praied priuatly, and sonne after went to supper : after which I went to the Lector, and then to bed:

Saterday 8
after praier I went about and then eate my breakfast and then walked abroad : after, I wrett notes in my testement and reed of the bible, then to dinner : after wch I talked a litle, and then I wrought tell 3 : then I walked with Mr Hoby tell 6 :, then I came and wrowght awhill, and so to praier and examenation, then to supper, after to lecor, and then to bed

[40]   Richard Greenham (1535?–94?), a learned Puritan divine, cited by Bishop Cox for nonconformity; his *Workes*, ed. Henry Holland, were published in four parts (1599) and went into four editions thereafter. His sermons supplied both spiritual guidance and practical advice.
[41]   Lady Hoby was probably playing simple bowls on a rough cut bowling green – a standard gentry game all over the country. In traditional Yorkshire games, however, the bowl (as in owl) is a hoop.

The Lords day 9

after priuat praier I did eate my breakfast and so went to church : after the sarmon was done, I praied priuatly and, after dinner, I kept Mr Hoby companie tell chuech time againe : after the sarmon I medetated a litle, and then I wrett out notes in my bible and, before supper, I praied, and, after supper and examenation, I went to bed:

Munday 10

After priuat praers I went about the house, an then eate my breakfast : then I walked to the church with Mr Hoby : after that I wrougt a litle, and neclected my custom of praier, for which, as for many other sinnes, it pleased the Lord to punishe me with an Inward assalte : But I know the Lord hath pardoned it because he is true of his promise and, if I had not taken this Course of examenation, I think I had for gotten itt : after dinner I walked with Mr Hoby and, after he was gon, I went to gett tithe aples :[42] after I Came home, I praied wth Mr Rhodes, and, after that, priuatly by my selfe, and tooke examenation of my selfe : and so, after I had walked a whill, I went to supper, after that to the Lector, and so to bed

Tewsday 11

After priuat praier I went about the house, and then wrett som notes into my testement : after, I walked and, when I cam home, praied With Mr Rhodes : then I wrought a whill and praied priuatly before diner : after, I walked, and took the aire in my Cocth, and when I Came home I wrought tell :6:, and then examened my selfe, and praied priuatly, and reed of Grenhame tell supper time : after supper I went to praers and, sonne after, to bed:

Wensday 12

after priuat praiers in the morning I, being not well, did walk a litle, and then eate my brecfast : then I wrought, and talked with such stragres[43] as as Came to me tell 5: a clock att night, at which time I praed and examened my selfe : sonne after to supper, then to lector, and Not long after to bed.

---

[42]   *tithe aples*, Lady Hoby is collecting the tenth part, used to support the church and clergy of Hackness.

[43]   *stragres*, strangers or visitors, people who do not live in the village of Hackness.

Thursday 13

In the morninge, after priuat praier, I wret some thinges touchinge Houshould mattres : then I did eate my breakfast, and did order diuerse thinges in the granirie : sonne after Mr Hoby Came home, and I kept him Companie tell he went away againe : after diner I went to Birstall, and se him, who was not well, and his aples tithed : then I wrought tell almost :6:, and praied with Mr Rhodes, and priuatly in my Closett:[44] after medetation, I went to supper : after, I had reed of the bible, after to lector, and then to bed

Friday 14

After order taken for the house, and priuat praers, I writt notes into my testement and then brak my fast : after, I wrought, and kept Mr Hoby compenie tell allmost diner time : then I praied and, after dinner, I walked awhill and went to church W^th Mr Hoby, and when I Cam home wrought tell 6:, then I examened my selfe and praied, walked tell supper time : then I hard the Lector, and after wrought a whill, and so went to bed : Lord, for Christs sack, pardone my drousenes which, with a neclegent mind, caused me to ommitt that medetation of that I had hard, which I ought to haue had.

Saterday 15

when I had praied I wrought tell 9:, then I did eate my breakfast : after, I walked to the church wth Mr Hoby, and was there tell dinner time : then I praied, and, after dinner, I wrought and went a litle about the house tell :6:, then I went againe to the church wth Mr Hoby and, after I came home, I examened my selfe, and praied : after supper I examened papers, when lector was done, with Mr Hoby, and so went to bed:

The Lordes day 16

After I had praied priuatly, I went to church and, from thence returninge, I praised god both for the inableinge the minister[45] so proffetably to declare the word as he had, and my selfe to heare wth that

---

[44] *Closett*, the closet was a kind of study, or office, for private devotions and business. It was a separate and more private room than the chamber in which Lady Hoby rested, slept and even entertained visitors. The custom of receiving in the bedroom long continued in England, but the closet was almost sacrosanct to the lady of the household.
[45] Probably William Ashton, parish priest at Hackness until March 1601.

Comfort and vnderstanding I did : after dinner I walked with Mr Hoby tell Catzhising was done, and then I went to church : after the sarmon I looked vpon a poore mans Legg, and after that I walked, and reed a sarmon of Geferd vpon the song of Salomon : then I examened my selfe and praied : after supper I was busie with Mr Hoby tell prair time, after which I went to bed :

Munday the 17
After priuat praier I saw a mans Legg dressed, took order for thinges in the house, and wrough tell dinner time : after dinner I went about the house, and read of the arball :[46] then I tooke my Cocth[47] and Came to Linton, wher, after I had talked a whill with my mother, examened my selfe and praied, I went to supper, and then praied publeckly, and so to bed:

Tewsday the 18
After I had praied priuatly I went to breakfast and, sonne after, took my Cocth, and wente to malton[48] to salute my Lady Ewre, with whom I staied about :2: howers : then Came to Rillington, and went to my Cossine Gates[49] house, and so home to Linton to supper : after that to prairs, and then to bed

[46]   *the arball*, a herbal was a compendium of plant folklore, containing the names and properties of plants. Information contained therein would help Lady Hoby with her work as nurse and physician. She may well be reading John Gerard's *Herball, or General Historie of Plants* (1597), a huge folio containing 1,392 pages of text and illustration. Gerard, a practical gardener and botanist, superintended the London gardens in the Strand of William Cecil, 1st Baron Burghley, and at Theobalds, Hertfordshire. The *Herball* was dedicated to his patron (see p. 19). Lady Hoby may have known his gardens through her husband who was related to the Cecils. Herbals were much copied one from another, and there were several from which to choose. Gerard drew on Dodoens, a great botanist, whose *Historie of Plants* (1554) was written in Dutch, then translated into French.There were over twenty printed books available on husbandry, gardening and herbals, though much of the knowledge would have been passed on through oral tradition. For the headaches particularly suffered by Lady Hoby, Gerard recommends the pulp of gourds (or courgettes) 'laid in the manner of a poultice'.
[47]   *Cocth*, coach.
[48]   Malton is a market town on the west bank of the River Derwent. Green fields separate New Malton from Old Malton, a quiet village 1 mile to the north-east.
[49]   Edward Gates, of Rillington near Malton, son of Sir Henry Gates of Seamer. A cousin on the Dakins side, and probably related to the Richard Gates to whom Sir Arthur Dakins refers in his will. Several branches of the family lived in the neighbourhood and surrounding district.

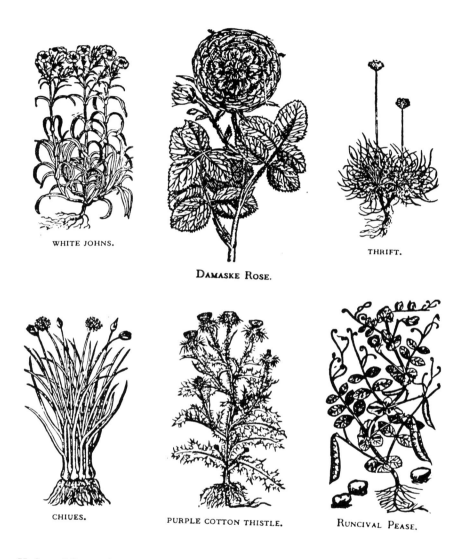

WHITE JOHNS.

DAMASKE ROSE.

THRIFT.

CHIUES.

PURPLE COTTON THISTLE.

RUNCIVAL PEASE.

Herbs and flowers from John Gerard's The Herball or Generall Historie of Plantes *(1597).*

The Private Life of an Elizabethan Lady

Wensday the 19

After praier I went to breakfast, and so tooke choch and Came to York, to Mr Skidmores house[50] their, wher, after much time spent their with some freindes, I went to priuat praier : and, hauinge supped, I was at publeck praers very sicke : the Lord pardon the sinne for which I was so punished, it beinge the will of god often to punishe one sinne with another, for I had Litle proffet by that praier, by reasone of my sicknes : yet, presently, I was well with meanes, and so went to bed

Thursday the 20

After priuat praier I went to the maner[51] to doe my dutie to my Lady Borley,[52] wher I hard Commune saruice, and diner : after which I had speech of some worldly matters, and then tooke Cocth with my Lady, and Cam home againe to supper with hir : before which we had saruice and, about ten a clock, I came to my Lodginge, and so went to bed

Friday the 21

After priuat praier I went to breakfast, and then I talked with a phesition which, I hope, the Lord hath prouided for me in steed of Doctor Brewer, and some other gentelmen : after dinner I had companie of many gentllwemen that came to me, and Mr Fuller, my Lorde Burleys chaplen, who seemed a godly and relegous young man : then I went to vesitte my Cossin Bouser[53] that lay ine, and thence returned to supper to Mr Skedmores, before which I praied priuatly : after supper diuers

---

50   This is Lady Hoby's lodging.
51   *the maner*, the manor house of the 'Lord's Place', later known as the King's Manor, York (see p. 23). Formerly the palace of the abbot, after the dissolution of the monasteries it was reconstructed out of the ruins of St Mary's Abbey. In 1541 Henry VIII visited York with Catherine Howard and stayed in the Manor. He there established his Council of the North under a Lord President, whose residence was the 'Lord's Place'. Further building work was done during the reign of Elizabeth and James enlarged it, fitting it up as a royal palace for his trips between London and Scotland. Over the principle entrance doorway, carved in stone, are the royal arms and the initials J R that we can still see today. As the official residence of the Lord President, in the late sixteenth century it was occupied by the Earl of Huntingdon, Lady Hoby's former guardian. She might therefore have lived there as a child as well as visiting it as an adult. It is one of historic York's most attractive and unusual sites, and, although leased by the University of York from the City Council, it is partially open to visitors.
52   Dorothy Neville, Lady Burghley, wife to Thomas Cecil, 2nd Lord Burghley, President of the Council of the North (1599). When in York, their residence was the King's Manor. Sir Thomas Hoby and Lord Burghley were cousins.
53   Possibly of the Bourchier family, cousins through Lady Russell, Lady Hoby's mother-in-law.

gentlemen cam in, who taried so late that we had no publeck praers, and so I went to bed, priuatly Comending my self to god

Saterday the 22
After a priuat praier I brake my fast and then talked with Mr lister : then I took my Cotch and went to Bisshopthorpe to the Busship:[54] their I dined, and talked with Mrs Hutten of relegion tell I Came from thence : then I Cam to York, to Mr Skidmors House, wher, after I had praied, I went to supper to my Cossine Bousers howse, wher I had Conferrance with a religious gintelwoman, and, thence Returninge, went to bed

The lordes day 23
After priuat praier I walked and did eate my breakfast : then I reed a chapter of the Bible to my mother, and repeted the Doctrins which from thence I had hard Mr Rhodes Colecte : then I went to the church, wher I hard Mr Pamer[55] speak, but to small profitte to any : thence I returned and priuately praied, lamentinge the misirie of godes visible Church, and praisinge his goodnes to my selfee about others : then, sonne after, I went to diner : after that, I talked with Mr Hoby, and so went to my Cossine Bousers child christininge, and hard a sarmon, somthing better then that in the morninge : which ended, with all Ceremones, I returned to my lodginge, and examened my selfe and praid : then I went to supper to Mr Neuells:[56] after, I went to my lodging, and so went to bed

Munday the 24
After I had praed, I went to breakfast to my Cosins bousers house : after that I went to Gremston, to my Cossin Stanopes,[57] wher I praied priuatly before supper, and sonne after went to bed

Tewsday the 25
After I had praied I walked in the garden tell break fast time : after

---

54   Matthew Hutton (1529–1606), Archbishop of York (1596–1606). His wife, Frances, was a friend of Lady Hoby.
55   William Palmer, Chancellor of York Minster (1571–1605).
56   Master Neville, possibly related to Lady Burghley.
57   Maybe Edward Stanhope who had been instrumental in Sir Thomas Hoby's courtship, or his brother John, both of whom were members of the Council of the North. They had another brother also called Edward. North Grimston is east of York at a point where the Yorkshire Wolds merge into the vales of York and Pickering. Lady Hoby stays overnight.

breakfast I Came to York, then I went to the manner after I had praied priuatly, and supped their, and took my leaue of my Lady Burley, Came to my Lodginge and went to bed

Wensday the 26
After I had praied I brake my fast and then went to se a house in Yorke :[58] and, after I had taken my leaue of Certaine freindes, I Came to Linton, wher I praied priuatly, went to supper, then hard a lector which Mr Neuill made, and so went to bed

Thursday the 27
After I had praied priuatly I went to breakfast : I took my Cotch and Came home to Hacknes safe, I thanke god, and, after I had praied priuatly and supped, I hard Mr Rhodes Caticize, and, sonne after, went to bed

Friday the 28
In the morninge, after priuat praier, I tooke order for thinges about the house, and at 8: I did eate my breakfast : then I hard Mr Rhodes read tell allmost dinner time : after dinner I talked with Tho: Adesone about the purchassinge his owne farme : then I wrought tell allmost supper time and, after I had priuatly praied, I went to supper : after that I walked tell Lector time, and after that I hard one of the men read of the book of Marters,[59] and so went to bed

---

[58]   Lady Hoby may be considering buying a house. There is a problem later over property in York. See 17 October 1600.

[59]   John Foxe (1516–87), *Actes and Monuments of these latter and perilous Dayes* (1563) also known as *The Book of Martyrs*, a history of English Protestant martyrs from the fourteenth century to his own day (see p. 25). Foxe had been prompted by a pious and patriotic desire to educate the public in Protestant church history and it became a sort of second Bible in the Protestant household. It was hugely popular, immensely influential, and the most famous of the prose collections of biography. Every literate family owned a copy and they would have been very familiar with it. The original work, in three volume folio editions, proved too bulky and expensive for ordinary readers, so abridged versions were produced, the first by Timothy Bright (1589). In the Hackness church library there are to be found later purchases, Volume I dated 1610, inscribed with Sir Thomas's name, and Volume II dated 1631. Lady Hoby often mentions the *Book of Martyrs*, probably reading from it, or hearing it read, several nights concurrently. The stories vary in length and some would have lasted over more than one evening. She would have known it since a child, for the Countess of Huntingdon was influential in campaigning for its use in Protestant education. There was also a personal link: one account of martyrdom was that of her second husband's great-aunt, Lady Jane Grey, celebrated for her learning and Protestant faith. Other stories about women are of more ordinary folk, eg: 'The trouble and martyrdome of a godly poore woman which suffered at Exeter', complete with a woodcut of her 'cruel burning', *Book of Martyrs* (1596), 1861.

The entrance doorway to the King's Manor, York.

Saterday the 29[60]

After priuat praier I did take order for thinges in the house, then I brak my fast and went to church : then I Came home and priuatly praied : after I had dinned I wret to my mother and Mr Hoby, and dispacted one away to him, then I sawe some thinges done in the house : after, I wret notes in my bible, then I praied with Mr Rhodes, and then walked tell all most supper time, and then examened my selfe and praied

The Lordes day 30

After priuat praier I went to church wher I hard the word preached, and receiued the sacrementes to my Comfort : after I had giuen thankes and dined, I walked a whill, and then went to church, whence, after I had hard Catcizising and sarmon, I returned home and wret notes in my bible, and talked of the sarmon and good thinges with Mrs Ormston : then I went to praier, after to supper, then to repetecion of the wholl daies exersice and praiers, hard one of the men reade of the book of marters, and so went to bed

Munday the :1: *of October* 1599

After priuat praier I wrought a whill and hard Mr Rhodes read : then I brake my fast, then I walked : when I Cam in, I took a Lector, praied, and went to diner : after that I walked abroade, then I Cam in and wrought, hard Mr Rhodes read, then I praied with Mr Rhodes, then I went about the house and examened my selfe, praied, and studied my Lector, then to supper : after the Lector I hard Helurn read of the Book of marters, and taked with Mr Rhodes, and so went to bed

Tewsday the 2

After priuat praier I wret notes into my testement, then I went to church : after I came home, I praied, and so went to dinner : after, I talked with Mr Bell and his wiffe : when they were gon, I gaue out Corne, wrett more notes in my testement, took order for supper, took a lector, and then went to medetation & praier : then I went to supper : after which I hard the sarmone repeated, and M. Rhodes read a sarmon of the Reuel:[61] and so went to bed.

---

[60] This is Michaelmas Day, or Quarter Day. See Tuesday 9 October.
[61] *Reuel*, Book of Revelations. We cannot know exactly which Bible Lady Hoby possessed, but it seems to have been complete, with Old and New Testament, and she often made notes in it. As the Authorised Version did not appear until 1611, she may have had a copy of one of the following: Coverdale's text (1535), published in Cologne, but printed in English; *Matthew's Bible* (1537), printed in England; or the *Geneva Bible* (1560), a translation produced by English Protestant exiles during the reign of Mary. The *Bishop's Bible* (1568), though too large for personal use, became the official version of the Church until the Authorised.

The title page of John Foxe's Actes and Monuments . . . *(1554).*

Wednesday the 3

After priuat praier I wret some of a sarmon tell diner time, then I praied : then, after dinner, I walked, and hard Mr Rhodes Read, then I wrought a whill, and then went about the house and took a Lector, and after praied with Mr Rhodes : then walked a whill, and so went to examene my selfe and praier, then to supper after to Lector : then hard Mr Rhodes read, and so went to bed:

Thursday the 4

After I had praied I wrett notes in my testemen, then I walked abroad, then I Came home and dined : and after diner I went againe awalkinge : then I wret in my sarmon book, then I went about the house with Mrs Ormston, then I went to examenation and praier, then to supper : after, to the Lectore, and then hard one of the men read of the book of marters, and so went to bed

October 1599. *Friday the* 5 *day*

After priuat praier I went about the house, then I wrett notes in my testement : then Mr Hoby Came home, with whom I talked tell diner time : after diner I was busie about presaruing quinces,[62] and, a Litle before supper time, I walked about the house : then I examened my selfe and praied, then I went to supper : after to the lector, and, sonne after that, to bed

Saterday the 6 *day*

After priuat prairs I did walke about and eate my breakfast : then I went abroad with Mr Hoby : then I Cam home and dined : after, I wret notes in my testement, then I went into the Granerie, and other places in the house, and so came to examine my selfe and praied : and then I went to supper, and so to lector, and then to bed.

*The lordes day :*7

After priuat praers I did eate my breakfast, and then to the church, wher, after the hearing of the word and receauinge the sacrementes, I Came

---

[62]   *quinces,* an ancient, hard fruit, like pears, but with a distinctively different flavour. Often used in preserves, they made the original marmalade. Peeled, quartered and pipped, they were boiled in red wine, honey and added spices. These were of course the days of home industries: of preserving, of confections, of decoctions from herbs, of brewing, curing, baking and distillation. Lady Hoby may well have had a copy of Thomas Dawson, *The Good Huswifes Jewell; Rare Devises for Conseites in Cookerie* (1587) which not only gave cookery hints but also approved points of husbandry and various medical formulas.

home and did praie : and so to diner : after which I walked and talked with Mr Rhodes : then, sonne after, I went to church againe, and, after the sarmone ended, I Came home, where I did litle good but talked of many maters, litle Concerning me, with Mrs Ormston, to whom I read a whill of the Bible : and after I returned in to my hart, examenid my selfe, and Craued pardon for my severall ommitions and Comitions : the Lord stringten me with his grace that I may sinne no more in the Like sort, amen : then I went to supper, after to the repetition and praers, and so to bed

Munday the 8: day

After praers I went about the house, then I did eate my breakfast : after, I was busie tell diner time : after dinner I was busie and did talke with Mr Rhodes touchinge diuerse thinges : then I wret notes in my testement, and then examened myselfe and praied, then went to supper : after, talked with Mr Rhodes of good thinges, and so went to bed.

Tewsday the :9 day

After priuat praers I did eate my breakfast with Mr Hoby : then I walked abroad, and tooke a lector : after, I Came in and praied, and then went to diner : then I went about and deliuered corne : then I Came into my Chamber, & wret notes in my testement, and after receiued Rentes,[63] and walked awhile : and then examened my selfe and praied : after, I walked a while, and read of Babington,[64] and then went to supper and, sonne after, went to bed, Mr Hoby Cominge home late

Wensday the :10: day

After priuat praers I went about and did eate my breakfast : then I wret some notes in my bible, then went to diner : after, I walked and presarued some sweet meat:[65] then I wret notes againe in my bible, then

---

[63] Quarter Day began each quarter of the year, and was generally the day on which it was contracted that rents should be paid and houses or lands entered upon or quitted. Lady Hoby is running a little late in collecting rents and paying wages.

[64] Gervase Babington (1550?–1610); Bishop of Llandaff (1591), of Exeter (1595), and of Worcester (1597); author of many theological treatises and sermons. Lady Hoby may have known him through her second husband's family, for he was often at Wilton and assisted the Countess of Pembroke with her translation of the Psalms.

[65] Sweetmeats included delicacies such as fruits and nuts preserved in honey and spices. Also, turnips, carrots, parsley and fennel roots were chopped up and cooked, then preserved in honey, cinnamon and pepper.

I walked, and then came in and examened my selfe and praid : then I went to supper, and, after, paied seruantes wages, and so went to bed

Thursday the :11: *day*
After praers I wret awhill some notes in my testemente, then I did eate my breakfast : then I walked tell allmost dinner time, then I wret a whil some notes in my testement, and then dined : after, I walked with Mr Hoby, and then againe wret some notes in my testement : then I went about the house and taked a whill with Mr Rhodes, and, sonne after, Came vnto priuat praier and examenation : then went to supper, and, sonne after, to the Lector, and then to bed

Friday the 12
After priuat praier I went about the house and did eate my breakfast : then I wrett some notes in my testement, and then walked about : then I praied and read of the bible, and so went to dinner : after, I walked a broad, and, at my Comming home, I tooke a Lector, and wrett a whill : and, after I had gone about the house, I returned to praier and examenation, my selfe, and then reed of Bright of Mallincocolie,[66] and then went to supper : after, to praers, and so to bed.

October Saterday the 13
After priuat prairs, I did writ a Letter : after, I did breake my fast, then I went about the house and, after, read of the bible : then I went to dinner, and after walked abroad with Mrs Ormston : then I was busie in the kitchine and about the house tell 6:, then I praied and examened my selfe : then I walked tell supper time and, after supper, to prairs, and so to bed

The Lordes day 14
After priuat prairs I did eate my breakfast, and then I did read of the Testement, and so went to church : after I Cam from thence, I medetated a while of that I had hard, and then praied, and so went to dinner : after, I walked tell church time and then, after the sarmon, I walked, and read and talked with Mrs Ormston of that was deliuered : after, I examened my selfe and praied : after I went to supper and, after that, to praers, and lastly to bed

---

[66] *Mallincocolie*, melancholy. Timothy Bright (1551?–1615). See Introduction, n. 51.

Munday the 15 *day*

After priuat prairs I did take my leave of Mr Hoby and, sonne after, went to church wher, a child beinge Babtised, I hard a sarmon : after, I Came home and wrett to Mr Hoby and my Mother, and sent away a messhinger to Linton : then I praied, and then to dinner : after, I wrett notes in my testement and walked, and, at 6: a clock, I examened my selfe and praied : then I hard Mrs. Brutnell Read of the Herball tell supper time, after which I praied, and so went to bed:

Tewsday the 16

After priuat praier, and order taken for the house, I did eate my breakfast, took a lector, walked, and praid, and so went to dinner : after, I talked with Mr Measse, then I wret in my sarmon bood,[67] and walked, talking with him, and then examened my selfe and praied : then went to supper, after to the lector, and so to bed

Wensday the 17

After I was readie, and had praied priuatly, I tooke order for the house and so went to breakfast : then, soone after, I tooke my Cotch and went to Linton, wher, I aftor salutinge my mother, praied, and so went to supper : after, I hard a good lector and, after that, talked with Mr Wilsone, a godly Preacher, and so went to bed

Thursday 18

After I had praied with Mr Rhodes, I did eat my breakfast and so went to the Church, wher I hard Mr Wilson preach : then I Came hom to dinner, neccltinge[68] my Costomarie manner of praier by reason of my Lord Ewrie and my lades being there : after dinner we talked a whill and then went to church, whor I hard Mr Rhodes preach : after I Came home and praied before supper, and, after supper, talked, and so went to bed

Friday the 19

After priuat praier I took my leaue of diuerse, then hard a Lector and went to breakfast : after, I took my leaue of Mr Wilson, and then walked abroad, and then I Came home and talked of many good thinges with Mr Rhodes and, after priuat praied, I went to supper, and, aftor supper, I hard a Lector, and so went to bed

---

[67]   *bood*, book.
[68]   *neccltinge*, neglecting.

Saterday the 20
After priuat praier I did eate my breakfast, and so hard a Lector : then I went to dinner and, after, took my Leaue of Mrs Gower that Came to se me, and so Came to Hacknes, wher I praied and then went so supper : after which I hard a Lector, and so went to bed

The Lordes day 21
After priuat praier I did eate my breakfast and then I went to church : after, I cam home and praid, then dined and after went to Catezisme and after none sermon : and then Came home, and wrett somthinge, then praied, and so went to suppr : after, I hard praers and, not long after that, hauinge talked with the workime,[69] I went to bed

Munday the 22
After priuat praier I did write : then I did eate my breakfast : then I went about the house and then I wret out my sermon : after, I praied, and so went to dinner : after dinner I walked about and had a Lector, and then Came to priuat praier and medetation : after, I wret some notes in my testement and then went to supper : after, to the Lector, and then I wret a letter to my mother, and so to bed

Tewsday the 23
After priuat praier I did walk a bout the house and then write note in my testement : after, I went to brakfast and, after, talked awhile with Mr Langdall[70] of his sonne, and then went to Skabye[71] to visitt Mrs Bell : then, after 2 howers, I Came home and took order for thinges in the house, and then examened my selfe and praied : after, I walked a while and then went to supper, after that to the Lector, and, whan I had despacthed some to York and Skarbraugh, I went to bed

Wensday the 24
After priuat praier I went about the house a while, then I wrett notes in my testement, and, after I had eaten my breakfast, I went abroad : after I Came home I praid, and, sonne after, when I had reed of the Bible, I

---

[69] *workime*, workmen. Lady Hoby occasionally records the times she has talked with her servants and tenants. Later she draws an interesting distinction between her own workmen and those of her husband.
[70] George Langdalle, sometime churchwarden of Hackness.
[71] Scauby, now Scalby, between Hackness and Scarborough.

dined : after, I despacthed[72] some busenes in the house, then I tooke a Lector : after, I wrett in my Comun place book, and then praied with Mr Rhodes, and went about the howse a whill, and then returned to medetation and priuat praier : then I stoudied a while for my Lector, and, after, went to supper : after I hard a Lector, and then I read of the book of marters and so went to bed

Thursday the 25

After priuat praier and breakfast I did read a whill for beinge not well, partly through myne owne folly, which I humble praie the Lord to pardon : I went to dinner : after, I wrett some notes in my testement and then took a Lector : after, hard Euerill[73] Read, and then praied, so went to supper, after to prairs, and then to bed

Friday the 26

After priuat praier I did eate my breakfast, Read a Longe Letter and wret an other, then praied, and after went to dinner : after which I hard a great disputation betwen 2: preachers, then took a lector : after, talked with one that Came to se me, and then went to praier and examenation : after, I went to supper, then to the Lector, and so to bed:

Saterday the 27

After priuat praier I wret to my Lord Ewre, then I took leaue, with some Conferance, of some that Came to se me, then I did eate my breakfast, and walked about tell diner time : after dinner I went about the house, and then tooke my Cotch and went abroad: after I Cam home and took order for supper, I praied priuatly & examened my selfe : then I Looked and wret in the houshould book, and so went to supper, after to Lector, and then to bed

The Lordes day the 28

After priuat praers I wret notes in my testement, and did eate my breakfast : then to church, after I Came honne[74] to praier and so to

---

72   *despacthed*, despatched.
73   Probably Everill Aske, one of the young women being educated and trained in the Hoby household. She was the eighth daughter, by his second wife, of Master Robert Aske of Aughton, High Sheriff of Yorkshire in 1588. She became the third wife of Master Thomas Ricard of Hatfield.
74   *honne*, home.

dinner : after which, I talked wth a woman that was to be deuorsed from hir Husbande with whome she liued inceasteously: then I went to Church and, after Catezising and sermone, I walked abroad : then I medetated of the sarmons, and raed and spoke to Mrs Ormstone of the chapter that was read in the morning, and so went to priuat praier : after, to supper, then to praers, and sonne after to bed:

Munday the 29
After priuat praier I did eate my breakfast, then I did go about the house tell allmost diner time, then I praied and then dined : after I had rested a while, I wrett my sermone, and then took a Lector, and, after, I hard praier and a Lecttor, because, in regard of mens dullnes after meat and being winter, it was thought more conuenient to be before supper : after, I praied priuatly and then of the testement and so went to bed:

October Tewsday the 30
After priuat praier I did eate my breakfast, then I was busie to dye wooll[75] tell allmost diner time, then I praied and dined : then I walked, and took a Lector, and read tell Lector time : then I hard that, and so went to supper : after, I was busie a whill and then praied and examened my selfe, and, after, reed a whill, and so went to bed

Nouember 1599: *Wensday the first*[76]
After priuat praier I talked a while with Mr Rhodes, then I did eate my breakfast, and went a while about the house : after, I answered a Vaine Letter, then I went to dinner : then I walked about the house and wret in my testemente : after, I walked abroad and, when I Came hom, I talked with Jousha, and so went to priaut praier and medetation, and then to supper : after, to praiers and so to bed

---

[75] *dye wooll*, very much a home industry, alongside spinning and weaving. Lady Hoby probably grew plants for dyeing in her garden, and may have brought dyestuffs back from London, such as saffron, woad, madder and cochineal. Blue was the commonest colour for wool, and alum was used to fix the dyes. In the area between Scarborough and the Tees, the red of alum shale can occasionally be seen. Alum mining was established in the sixteenth century and became an important part of the local economy during this period.
[76] More erratic dating. Wednesday was 31 October, not 1 November, and the dates continue incorrect until 16 November, when Lady Hoby puts herself right by giving this same date to two consecutive days. I am indebted to Dorothy M. Meads for her work on the dating of the diary. See p. 33 for this entry and following in folio 13v of the original manuscript.

[1599]

ewsday the 30: After privat praier I did eate my breakfast then I was busie to dye woll tell almost diner time then I praied and dined then I walked and took a lector and read tell Lector time then I hard that and so went to supper after I was busie a whille and then praied and examened my selfe and after red a whille and so went to bed

November 1599 Wensday the first: After privat praier I talked a whille with Mr Rhodes then I did eate my breakfast and went a while about the house after I answered a vaine letter then I went to diner then I walked about the house and wret in my testem: euen after I walked abroad and when I came home I talked with Jonsha and so went to privat praier and meditation and then to supper after to praier and so to bed

Thursday the 2: After privat praier I did eate a litle and so took ... chork and went to Seamer to se my Cosine Bousfas with whom I dined and then came home wher after I had walked a whille about I went to privat praier and meditation then I went to supper after to praier and so to bed:

Frisday the 3: After I privat praier I did breakinge fast then I wrought tell allmost diner time then I praied after diner I walked about the house and did pray with Mr Rhodes then I did read a while to my workwomen and then to the Lector after to supper and after that I did walke a whille and then I praied privatly and examened my selfe and so to bed.

Saterday the 4: After privat praier I red a whille the Bible then I tooke a Lector after I praied and then went to diner after that I performed som bussines for a frend and one of my servantes after I praied with Mr Rhodes and some after that went to praiers then to supper and after that to privat praiers and so to bed.

A page from Lady Margaret Hoby's diary, f. 13v ms Egerton 2614.

Thursday the 2

After priuat praier I did eate a Litle, and so took my Choch and went to Seamer[77] to see my Cosine Bousers wiffe, wher I dined : and then Cam home, wher, after I had walked a while about, I went to priuat praier and medetation : then I went to supper, after to prairs, and so to bed:

Friday the 3

After I priuat praier I did break my fast, then I wrought tell allmost dinner time, then I praied : after dinner, I walked aboute the house, and did pray with Mr Rhodes : then I did read a while to my workwemen, and then to the Lector : after, to supper, and, after that, I did walke a whill, and then I praied priuatly and examened my selfe, and so to bed.

Saturday the 4

After priuat praier I reed a while of the Bible, then I took a Lector : after, I praied, and then went to dener : after that I performed som Biusines for a freind and one of my seruantes : after, I praied with Mr Rhodes and, sonne after that, went to prairs, then to supper, and after that to priuat prairs, and so to bed :

The Lordes day 5

After priuat praier I did eate my breakfast, and so went to church : after, I prared, then went to dener : sonne after, to Catecizisege, and then to the sermon : after, I reed of the Bible, and spock of Certaine Chapters to Mrs Ormston and John douson, and then went to priuat praier : then to supper, after to the Lector, and so to bed :

Munday the 6

After priuat praier I did eate my breakfast : then I walked abroad : after, I wret a Letter by John Dousone to Richard Hodgsone,[78] then I wret in my testemente, praied, and wento to dinner : after, I walked forth, recieued in Corne, wret in my testement and Bible, praied priuatly with Mr Rhodes, hard the Lector before supper : after supper, hard Mr

---

[77] Seamer, 4 miles from Scarborough on the Malton road. In former times there was a large lake to the south-west, hence the name 'Sea-mere'. The village had a yearly fair of six days which interfered with that of Scarborough, leading to constant litigation.

[78] Lady Hoby could mean that she sent the letter with John Dousone or is writing on his behalf.

Rhodes read, and then went to priuat praier and examenation, and so, sonne after, to bed :

Tewsday the 7
After priuate praers I did eate my breakfast, and so wente to the Church wher I, vpon occasion, hard a sermon : after, I Came home and was busie vntell dinner time : after dinner I walked abroad and did se some thinge in the house ordered : then I praied with Mr Rhodes and so went to supper : after, I hard the repeticion of the sarmon and prairs, and, sonne after, went to bed

Wensday the 8
After priuat praier I talked with Mrs Brutnell tell breakfast time, then I took my Cotch and went to vesitt Mrs Dannie, wher I praied awhill : and then, Comminge home, I found Lettres that gaue me occasion to writ diuers waies : then I went to supper, after to prairs with the Houshould : after, I praied priuatly, and so went to bed :

Thursday the 9
After priuat praers I did eate my breakfast : after that, I praied with Mr Rhodes, then I tooke a Lector, and so went to dinner : then I walked abroad, and dispactched some busenes in the house, wret a medetation made by Mr Rhodes, praied with him, and so went to supper : after, hard him read, then praied, and so went to bed :

Friday the 10
After priuat praier I was busie about the house tell dinner time : after, I took a Lector, then I went to doe Certaine thinges about the house tell night, then I praied with Mr Rhodes and reed tell supper time : after, I hard publect prairs, and Reed of the testement, and, after, praied priuatly and examened my selfe, and so went to bed

Saterday the 11
After priuat praier I was busie about the house tell dinner time : after, I had A Lector, then I walked, then I Came home and praied, then I tooke order for thinges in the house, and went to suppor : after, I hard the Lector : after that, praied and examened my selfe and, sonne after that, went to bed :

The Lordes day 12
After priuat praier I did eate my breakfast and so went to church : after I had dined, I went to catezising : after, to the sarmon : then I Came home

and reed to Mrs Ormstone:[79] then I went about the house and, after, went to priuat praier and examenation, after to supper, then to praiers, after to priuat praier, and so to bed :

Munday the 13
After priuat praier I beused my selfe about the house tell dinner time : after which I went aboute againe, and wrought tell allmost supper time : then I examened my selfe and praied, and so read tel suppr Came : after, I walked and talked touchinge houshould mattres, and then praied and so went to bed

Tewsday the 14
After priuat praier I went about the house tell some strangers Came, whom I accompaned tell dinner time : then I praied : after, I was busie all the day tell allmost supper time, and then I examened my selfe and praied : then I went to supper, after I wrought, then I praied, and so went to bed.

Wensday the 15
After priuat praier I wrought tell dinner time : after, I wrought and did buesenes in the house tell allmost supper time : then I praied and examened my selfe, when I found what it was to want the Contineuall preachinge of the word by my Couldnes to all sperituall exercises : but I beseech the Lord pardon my seuerall defectes and restore me to my former Life, for thy mercies sake, with increase of his spiritt, and so much more spirituall Comfort as now is a wantinge : after supper I walked tell bed time, and then I praied, and so went to bed :

Thursday the 16
After priuat praier I did read of the Bible and then eate my breakfast : after, I goe about tell dinner time : then I dimed, and talked with some strangers that Came to visitt me, and after, being not well, I slept a while and then reed a while, and so praied and examened my selfe, and then supped : after that I went sonne to bed

Friday the 16[80]
After priuat praier I did busie my selfe tell dinner time : after, I kept

---

79   Mistress Ormstone and Mistress Brutnell may be widows charitably housed at Hackness. They are mentioned several times.
80   This is the correct date of this Friday in November. See p. 37 for folio 15v of the diary.

Friday the 16: After privat praier I did busie my selfe all dinner time after I kept companie with my mother and other strangers tell supper time after supper I hard publeke praiers and because I was not well I went straught to bed

Saturday the 17: After privat praers I did eate my breakfast and so went to church after I dined and then went againe to church there tell allmost supper time I kept Companie with strangers and then as it pleased the Lord to restore my health I returned to examenation and privat praiers then went to supper and then hard praers and repetition of both the sermons and after I had brought all to there Chambres and taken order for dinner the next day went to privat praers and so to bed

the Lords day 18: After privat praier I went to church and when I came home I praised god for his mercies ther offered me then I dined I went to church againe and hard Cate=ings and sermon then I talked and song psalmes with diverse that was with me and after that I praied privatly and examened my selfe with what neglegenc I had spent the day and then went to supper after that to publeke examenation and praiers and so to bed

Munday the 19: After privat praers I have a sarmon then I dined all the afternone I did little being in paine after supper I have Lecter and so sonne after that I went to bed

Teusday the 20: After privat praers I did break my fast and then went to church and after to dinner after I took my Cotch and went abrode then I came home and examened my selfe and praied then went to supper after to the Lector and so to bed

A page from Lady Margaret Hoby's diary, f. 15v ms Egerton 2614.

Companie with my mother and other strangers tell supper time : after supper I hard publecte praiers and, because I was not well, I went straught to bed

Saterday the 17
After priuat praers I did eate my breakfast and so went to church : after, I dinner, and then went againe to church : then, tell all most supper time, I kept Companie with strangers and then, as it pleased the Lord to restore my health, I Returned to examenation and priuat praiers, then went to supper : and then hard praers and repetition of both sarmons, and, after I had brought all to ther Chambres and taken order for dinner the next day, went to priuat praers and so to bed

The Lordes day 18
After priuat praier I went to Church, and, when I Came home, I praised god for his meries[81] ther offered me : Aftr I dined, I went to church againe and hard Catezisinge and sermon : then I talked and song psalmes[82] with diuerse that was with me, and, after that, I praied priuatly and examened my selfe with what Integretie I had spent the day, and then went to supper : after that, to publeck examenation and praers, and so to bed

Munday the 19
After priuat praers I hard a sarmon, then I dined : all the Afternone I did Litle, beinge in paine : after supper I hard A Lector and so, sonne after that, I went to bed

Tewsday the 20[83]
After priuat praers I did break my fast and then went to church, and after to dinner : after, I took my Cotch and went abroad : then I Came home, and examened my selfe and praied, then went to supper : after, to the Lector, and so to bed

---

[81]   *meries*, mercies.
[82]   The singing of Psalms was very important to Lady Hoby. Her sister-in-law (by her second marriage), Mary (Sidney) Herbert, the Countess of Pembroke, completed a translation of the Psalms, begun by her brother Sir Philip Sidney, for Queen Elizabeth I (1599).
[83]   On this day Sir Thomas Hoby was appointed one of the High Commissioners for the province of York.

Wensday the 21

After priuat praier I went into the garden and, after I had walked, I wrought and talked with some strangers that Came to se me tell dinner time : after dinner I wrought and hard Mr Rhodes Read tell all most supper time, then I tooke a Lector, medetated and praied, and so went to supper : after, I hard a Lector, and then walked a whill, and then went to praier and so to bed :

Thursday the 22

After priuat praier I wrett in my sarmon booke, then I walked, and dined : and after that, tell night, I wrought, then I praied with Mr Rhodes and then hard a Lector and so went to supper : after, I wret a Letter to my Cossine Isons,[84] and praied priuatly, and so went to bed :

Friday the 23

After priuat praier I wrett notes in my testement and then eate my breakfast : after, I praied and then dined : after that I did sundrie beusenesses, and then I took a Lector and, after that, praied and examened myselfe : after that to supper, then so to the Lector, and so to bed :

Saterday the 24

After priuat praers I did eate my breakfast, and then wret of my sarmon book : then I walked, reed of the bible, praied, and so went to dinner : after dinner I tooke order for thinges about the house, paied billes, medetated and praied, and so went to the Lector, then to supper : after, I walked and talked with Mr. Rhodes, Reed of the bible and, after, praied, and then went to to bed :

The Lordes day 25

After priuat[85] I went to church : after, I praied, then to dinner : then, sonne after, to Church : then I talked with my maides of that was their deliuered, and then I hard Margeret Rhodes reed of Mr Grenhm, and, after that, I examened my selfe and praied, and, sonne after that, to supper : then to publeck prairs, after that to priuat, and so to bed :

---

84   Edward Isons of Troutsdale, related by marriage on the Dakins side. Lady Hoby sees much of him and his wife.
85   Lady Hoby has omitted 'prayers'.

Munday the 26
After priuat praers I did read of the bible, then I went to publeck, after to work, then to breakfast : and so about the house : after, to dinner : after dinner I did se Lightes[86] made allmost all the after none, and then I took a Lector and went to medetation and priuat praier : after, I went to the lector, then to supper : after, I hard Mr Rhodes Read of Grenhame, and then I praied and so went to bed :

Tewsday the 27
After priuat praier I went to the church : after, I praied, then I dimed, then I walked and did se a sicke man : when I Came home I receiued diuerse thinges from Londone : after that I went to priuat praier and medetation, and from thence to publecke praers, so to supper : after, I wrought, and hard Mr Rhodes read of Mr Grenhame, and so praied priuatly and then went to bed :

Wenday the 28
After priuat praers I did write in my sarmon book and, after, I did walk : then I Cam home and praied, then went to dinner : then I took a Lector and to work, after that to praier with Mr Rhodes, then to publeck praers and Lector : after, to supper, then to work, and hard readinge of the bible : then I praied priuatly and so, Lookinge of my Lector, went to bed

Thursday the 29
After priuat praers I did walke and eate my breakfast : after I wrought, reed of the bible and praied, and then went to dinner : after, I wrought, and dispatched some beusenes and, befor 6 aclock, I went to priuat praier and examenation : after, I supped and, after that, praied, and not Long after that went to bed :

Friday the 30
After priuat praers I did break my fast, then I wrought and reed tell dinner time : after, I walked and talked with Mr Rhodes, then I took order for some thinges in the house and hard Auerill reed of Grenham, and then praied : then I hard a Lectore, after supped, then wrought, and priuatly praied, and to bed

---

[86] *Lightes*, rush or wax candles from the bees.

1599 *Saterday the* 1 *of December*

After priuat praers I did eate my breakfast, then I wrough and reed of the bible tell dinner time : after, I wrought, and did my deutie in the house tel alMost 6 a clock, and then I praied priuatly and examened my selfe, then I went to supper : after, I disharged houshould billes and, after, praied : then reed a whill of perkins,[87] and so went to bed :

The Lordes day 2

After priuat praers I eate my breakfast, then I went to church, wher it pleased the Lord, his mame[88] be praised, to assist me with his spiritt in Callinge vpon him, and hearinge his word : then I Came home and praesed him and praied : after, I dined, and then went to caticizing and sarmon, then I Came home and hard Mr Rhodes read of the bible : after, I talked with a good Christiane, and then returned to priuat praers and examenation : after, to supper, then to publeck praers, then to priuat, and Lastly to bed.

Munday the 3

After priuat praier I break my fast, then I wrought : After, I wrat, praied, and then dined : after dinner I wrought, took a Lector, went a litle about the house, then praied and, after, went to supper : then I reed a hard readinge a whill, and publeck praers, and after praied priuatly, and so went to bed

Tewsday the 4:

After priuat praiers I did eate my breakfast, then reed of the bible and wrought : after, I took a Lector, then I dined : after, I talked and wrought, stvide[89] my lector, examened my selfe and praied priuatly, then I hard the Lector : after I went to supper, and then walked a great while tell bed time : then I praied privaly and so went to bed.

Wensday the: 5 *day*

After priuat praier I did eate my breakfast, then I walked, then I took a Lector, after praied, and went to dinner : after, I wrought a while, then I walked, after that I went about the house, took a Lector, praied with Mr

---

[87] William Perkins (1558–1602), the great Puritan teacher. See Introduction, n. 45.
[88] *mame*, name.
[89] *stvide*, studied.

Rhodes, hard one read, and then went to priuat praier, then to the Lector and publeck, after to supper : then I walked, after to priuat praiers, and Lastly to bed

Thursday the :6:
After priuat praier I did eate my breakfast : then I reed of the bible : then I wrought, praied, and after went to dinner : after dinner I was befowe[90] with my maieds busie, and then stveded my Lector : after, I took a newe Lector and then praied priuatly, and examened my selfe : then I went to supper : after, to publeck praers, then I talked and song a psalme with diuers that were with me, and, lastly, praied priuatly, and so went to bed

Friday the :7:
After priuat praers I took a glester:[91] after, I talked, and hard Mr Rhodes Read, then I went to dinner : maters after dinner I wrought, took order for thinges in the house and, towardes night, I examened my selfe and praied, then I hard the Lectore : after, went to supper : then I talked of good maters with Mr Maud:[92] after, dispacthed som beusenes in the house, and then praied and so went to bed

Saterday the 8:
After priuat praers I tooke a glester, for which Cause I kept my chamber tell the after none : then I hard one read of ardentons book,[93] and after I talked with Mr Rhodes, then praied priuatly, and after Came to publecke praers and Lector, then went to supper : after, I Conferred with Mr Maud of feelinge, and then, after som priuat Conference betwene Mr Rhodes and me of som thinges that Concerned vs both nearly, I went to bed

The lordes day 9:
After priuat praier I did eate som thinge, and so went to the church : after, I cam home and praied, and so dined : then I went to church

---

[90] *befowe*, below.
[91] *glester*, clyster or suppository. Note next entry, 8 December.
[92] A young divine, resident in the Hoby household. Lady Hoby enjoys her discussions with him almost as much as she does with Master Rhodes.
[93] This book has not been traced. Master Ardington is one of the visiting clerics.

againe and, when Caticizinge and sarmon was done, I Came hom and wrett some notes in my testement, and then Conferred of that was ther deliuered, and of other good maters, and then Came to priuat praers and examenation : after supper, I hard the Lector, and then praied and so went to bed :

Munday the 10

After priuat praier I did eate my breakfast, then I wrought and went about the house tell all most dinner time, then I praied and, After, dined : after dinner I talked a whill, and then wrought and hard Mr Maude read of a sermon : after, I praied with Mr Rhodes : after that, examened my selfe and praied, and so went to the Lector, after to supper : then talked a good while of good thinges with the Compenie, after praied, and so went to bed :

Teusday the :11:

After priuat praiers I did eate my breakfast, then I reed of the bible and write in my table book,[94] and so went to dinner : after, I made an end of my table, and went about the house : after praied with Mr Rhodes, and then wen to supper : after, I hard publeck praers, and then took order for some thinges, and talked of good matters with Mr Rhodes and Mr Maude, a younge deuine, a exceedinge good Christian : I went to priuat examenation and praier, and so to bed :

Wensday the :12:

After priuat praers I did work awhile, and then eate my breakfast : after, I hard Mr Maud read of a sarmon book, then I praied, after dinned : then then I wrought, and hard Mr Maud read againe : then I dispacthed some busenes in the house after supper, then praied publeckly, and talked with Mr Hoby, and so Ccame to examene my selfe and praier, and so went to bed

Thursday the 13:

After priuat praier I went about the house, and reed, did eate my breakfast, then I reed againe tell dinner time, then praied : after diner I

---

[94]   *table book,* this was a note-book composed of tablets on which Lady Hoby made memoranda. It was usual to keep a household book which contained lists of things in the house and garden, with works completed, new acquisitions and exchanges made.

was busie tell I walked abroad with Mr Hoby, then I went about amonge my maides[95] tell allmost supper time, and then I praied and examened my selfe : then I went to supper, after to priuat praier, and so to bed :

Friday the 14:
After priuat praier I was beusie about the house tell dinner time : after dinner I did read of a good book, and then went about the house : then I reed againe : after, wrought awhill, and then returned to examenation and priuat praier, then to supper : after, to the Lector : after that to priuat praier, and so to bed :

Saterday the :15:
After priuat praier I did eate my breakfast, goe abowt, read of the bible, pray, and after dime:[96] then I talked a while, reed, went about, and took order for Houshould affares, walked and Conferred of diuers thinges with Mr Hoby, and after returned to examenation and priuat praier : then to supper : after, I talked a good whill and then praied priuatly, and so went to bed :

The Lordes day :16:
After priuat praier I did eate my breakfast and went to church : after I Came from thence I was not well : after dinner I talked with diuers tell Church time, and, after the sarmon, I talked, not beeinge very well, tell supper time : after which I hard the exercise, and then praied priuatly and examened my selfe, and so went to bed

Munday the :17:
After priuat praers I Reed tell dinner time : after, I wroughte tell 5 a clock, then I examened my selfe and praied, went to supper, after to the Lector : then, hauinge talked with Mr Rhodes and som others, I praied priuatly and then went to bed

Tewsday the :18:
After priuat praier I did write in my sermon booke : then I praied : after, I dinned : all most all the afternone I was busie makinge ginger

---

95 *maides*, Lady Hoby refers to the young women under her tutelage.
96 *dime*, dined.

bread[97] and other thinges : thene I examened my selfe and praied, and after reed a while, and so went to supper : then to publeck praers, after to priuat praers, and then to bed

Wensday the 19:
After priuat praers and Doing som thing in the house, I brak my fast : after, I wrett in my sarmon book, then I praied, then dined : after, took the aire in my Cotch : then supped : after, praied priuat and examened my selfe : after, hard the Lector and then went to bed, god hauinge a Litle afflected me with sicknes for a great desart : the Lord grant me true repentance for all my sinnes, amen, amen :

Thursday the 20:[98]
After priuat praers, I did eat my breakfast : then I wrett in my sarmon booke : after, I praied, then I dined, and almost I wrett in my bible all the after none : then I dispacthed some beusenes in the house, and then praied and examened myselfe : then I went about the house and, in talke with Mr Rhodes, I understood thus much, that, wher as graces are of 2 sortes, some generall, belonginge to euerie christian, others speciall, as Contenancie and . . .,[99] for the better preuailinge against a temptation, it is not sufficient only to haue faith, wherby I know that I shall nether yeald vnto it, nor be ouer come by it : but I must Likewise pray especially for that vertue which is opposed to that vise wher vnto I am

---

[97]   This would have been similar to a traditional French spice-bread, consisting of equal quantities of breadcrumbs and honey, with colourings such as saffron for yellow. Spice was used for flavouring – not always ginger, perhaps cinnamon and peppercorns. It made a kind of stiff dough, hardened in moulds. Nowadays, Yorkshire gingerbread is better known as *parkin* and is often found in the shape of a pig. A traditional recipe states:

   225g fine oatmeal, 1 teaspoon baking powder, 225g flour, 3 teaspoons ground ginger, 225g brown sugar, 1 cup milk, 1 large egg, 225g dark treacle, 112g butter.

   Sieve flour, baking powder and ginger together, add oatmeal. Put treacle, butter and sugar into a saucepan, melt slowly. Beat egg with milk. Add treacle mixture to flour, beat well, add egg and milk. Mix thoroughly, pour into tin (25 × 15 × 8 cm), well greased, lined with greaseproof paper. Mixture should be very soft before cooking in moderate oven (170°C, 350°F, Gas Mark 3) for half an hour, then at 150°C, 350°F, Gas Mark 2 for a further half hour. Test centre before taking out. A good, spicy, sticky cake, best left a few days before cutting.

[98]   This is one of the longest entries with its record of an important lesson from Master Rhodes.

[99]   This word is indecipherable; Meads suggests it might be 'pretching'.

then tempted, because, though faith be the Fondamentall Cause of ouercoming sinne, yet oppretiuely[100] the seuerall graces of god work:[101] after, I supped, then I hard the Lector, and then praied, and so went to bed

Friday the :21:
After priuat praier I ded a litle, and so went to church : after the sermon I praied, then dined, and, in the after none, was busie tell 5 a clock : then I returned to priuat praier and examenation : after supped, then hard publeck praiers and, after that, praied priuatly, hauinge reed a Chapter of the bible, and so went to bed

Saterday the 22:
After priuat praier I did eate my breakfast, dispacthed diuerse buesenes in the house, praied, and then read of the bible, and so dined : after, I was busie about the house preparing diuers thinges against the holy daies, and, att 5 a Clock, I returned into my Closett vnto priuat examenation and praier : then I went to supper, after to the Lector, and Lastly to priuat praers and preperation to the supper of the Lord by takinge an account what breaches I had made in my faith, since I found that I had itt, by reparinge those by repentance, as also medetating what grace I had, what benifetes godes spiritt ther did offer me, if I Came rightly, and worthyly, both of person and vsag:[102] and so I went to bed :

The Lordes day :23:
After I was readie I was Called away to the Church, for which Cause I was dreuen to prepare my selfe, in parte, as I went to the holy exercises : after the sarmone and sacrementes, I came home and praied : after dinner I talked a whill, and then went to the after none sarmon : after that I was busie tell all most supper time, then I praied and examened my selfe, then went to supper : after, to publeck praers and examenation of the sarmons,[103] and, after that, talked a Litle and, when I had priuetly praied, went to bed

---

[100] *oppretiuely*, operatively, meaning the graces of God work effectively.
[101] Lady Hoby gives a rare longer commentary about herself.
[102] *vsag*, usage.
[103] *examenation of the sarmons*, this was a religious exercise for all the household.

Munday the 24:

After priuat praers I did eate my breakfast : then I reed of the bible, praied, walked a litle abroad, dinned : after, serued diuers poore people with wheet and beeffer,[104] then was busie in the kitchin Vntell .5 a Clock, and then examened my selfe and praied : after, I went to supper, then hard the Lector, and so to bed

Tewsday beinge Christes day :25:[105]

After priuat praier I reed of the bible, eate my breakfast, and went to Church : then I Com home and praied : after dinner, I went a while about the house, then I Caused one to Read vnto me and, beinge not well, I did omitte my orderarie exercise of praier tell after supper : then I hard repetition and praers and, after I had talked a whill to Litle purposse, I went to examenation and priuat praers, and so to bed :

Wensday the :26:[106]

After priuat praier I wrett notes in my bible, then I brake my fast, and after went to church : after, I dimed, then I talked with Mr Cholmley of diuerse thinges, and, towardes night, I betooke my selfe, after order giuen for the house, to priuat praier and examenation : after, I went to supper, then to publece praers and, after that, to priuat, and thence to bed :

Thursday the :27:

After priuat praers I reed of the bible, then brake my fast and walked abroad, then I praied and then dinned : after dinner I talked with diuers

---

[104] *beeffer,* beef broth or beef-ham? (beef cured like ham, by salting or smoking). It is Christmas Eve and this could be a special charitable gesture.
[105] Christmas Day. Lady Hoby noted on 22 that she was making preparations, but there is no mention here of rejoicing, nor evidence of festivity in the 14 days till Epiphany. She spends the evening talking 'to Litle purposse', which could imply intolerance of whatever Christmas celebration was allowed to take place in the Hackness household. Maybe there was some leniency for the less zealous. Puritans did not like merriment at this time, on the grounds that it was a heathen festival. In 1644 they would forbid celebration along with religious services by Act of Parliament and order it to be kept as a fast. In the Yorkshire dialect Christmas is **Kersmass** or **Kessamas**. The traditional festival pie, which could be enormous, consisted of an elaborately decorated crust containing an assortment of goose, chicken, pigeon and partridge with spices.
[106] St Stephen's Day was the first of four festivals that stressed man's folly and worldliness. Biblical readings urged patience in adversity and the festival was normally celebrated by granting hospitality, especially to the poor.

of good thinges and then songe spsalmes with some of my Cosins : then I walked and talked with Mr Hoby, took order for Househould mattres, and then went to examenation and praier : after, to supper, then into the kitchine wher beinge and with good talke spent the time tell :10: a Clock : then I praied and so went to bed :

Friday the :28:
After priuat praers I did eate my breakfast, then I went to church : after I Came home I was busie tell dinner time, then I tooke the Aire abroad, and, after my Cominge home, I went about the house, talked a whill, and then I examened my selfe and praied : then I went to supper : after, to the publece praers and examenation of the Morninge sarmon : after, I wrett to my mother, then I praied, and so went to bed :

Saterday the :29:
After priuat praers I went about the house and then did eate my breakfast : after I was busie tell dinner time, then I praied and after dimed : in the after none I was busie about the house, and Conferred with Mr Rhodes of diuers thinges and, att :5: a cloke, I returned againe to examenation and praier : then I reed a whill and, after, went to supper, then to the Lector : after, I was busie in the house tell. 10 a clock, then I praied, and so went to bed:

The Lordes day :30:
After priuat praers I did read of the bible, brake my fast and then went to church : after, I praied and then dined : after dinner I, with Mr Hoby, talked with som tenantes that dined with vs : after that we went to the afternone sermon and from thence came home and reed of Grenhame, and hard Megg Rhodes read : then I walked and Conferred with Mr Hoby, tooke order for supper, and then went to priuat examenation and praier : after, to supper, then to publece praers and, because I was not very well, I went to bed.

Munday the :31:
After priuat praers I wrought : then did eate my breakfast : then, tell dinner, I kept companie with neighbours : after, I walked, then I was busie in the Kitchine tell 5 a clock, and then returned to examenation and priuat praier : then I went to supper, after to the Lector, wher many sundrie distractions withdrwe my mind from so profitable hearing as I ought, which I humble pray the Lord to pardon, and grant me here after strength, by grace, to w[th]stand the Like : after, I praied priuatly and so went to bed.

1600

Jeneuarie 1599[107] *Tewsday the* 1:
After priuat praier I did eate my breakfast and then went to Church : after, I Came home and praied, then I dimed and, when I had talked a whill with some of my Neighbours, I went againe to Church : and, after the sarmon, I went about the house and took order for diuerse thinges which were to be done iny[108] absence, and, at 5 a Clock, I returned to priuat praier and medetation : After I went to supper, then to Lector, and so to bed

wensday the 2:
After I was readie, I went about the house takinge order for all thinges tell my returne from Linton : then againe I praied and, after breakfast, I tooke my Cotch and Came to Linton : there, after I had saluted my mother, I praied priuatly and then I supped : after supper, hard a Lector, and so went to bed

Thursday the :3:
After I was readie, had praied and broake my fast, I reed of the bible, kept Companie with diuerse ther tell dinner time : after dinner, I walked and Confered of good mattres with Mr Rhodes : after that, I hard him read tell all most night, then I praied priuatly, and so went to supper : after supper I hard a Lector and, sonne after that, I went to bed

Friday the :4:
After priuat praers and my breakfast, I reed of the bible : then I kep Companie with diuers that came to me : after, I praied and then dined : after dimed, I took my Cotch and Came to Eberston,[109] to Mr Etheringtons house, wher I was kindly, with Mr Hoby, receiued : after I was in my Chamber, I praied priuatly, reed of the Testament, and then supper : after, I praied publeckly, and then went to bed

Saterday the 5:
After I was readie I had Conferrence with Mr Hoby of diuers matters and, when I had praied, I went, within short time after, to Breakfast : after, I took my Cotch and so Came hom saiffe, I thank god : after I was

107 Lady Hoby is dating her diary according to the English calendar of the time. For most purposes, New Year was reckoned to begin at the Feast of the Annunciation in March.
108 *iny*, in my.
109 Ebberston is an attractive village at the foot of Netherby Dale, east of Pickering, with views over the vale of the River Derwent. Master Richard Etherington was lord of the manor.

att home, I went about and did eate somthinge, and, after that, was busie about the house tell night, at wch time I examened my selfe, both of this daies work as of all the rest, and praied priuatly, and so went to supper : after, to publece praers, then to priuatt and so to bed :

The Lordes day :6:
After priuatt praers I did eate my breakfast and went to Church : after I came home I praied, then dined : after dinner I talked a whill with a Cosine of mine, & then, when I had praied and craued a blesing, I went to Church againe : when I Came home I tooke order for supper, and, about 5 a cloke, I returned to priuat examenation and praer, and so to supper : after, to publece, and then to priuat, and after to bed :

Munday the :7:
After I had praised god for my rest and was readie, I went about the house, then I returned to priuatt praier : after, I did eate my breakfast, and againe was busie tell all most dinner time : then I praied, dined, and, after, went into the toune about som busines : then I was in the granerie receiuing Corne, and againe took order for supper and hard one of my wemen read of perkins, and, after that, returned to priuat praier and examenation : then, soune after, I went to supper, after that to the lector, then to priuat praer, and so to bed :

Tewsday the :8:
After praer and that I was readie, I went about & tooke order for diuers thinges, then I praied and, after I had eaten a litle, I went to church & hard a sarmon. after I Came home, I praied, dined, tooke my Leaue of Mr Hoby, and so went againe about the house tell 5, and then went to publece praers and examenation of the sarmon : then I pupped:¹¹⁰ after, hard mr Rhodes read praies, and went to bed

Wensday the 9:
After I had praised god for my rest and was ready, I did some busenes about the house, then I praied, and after wrett some thinges in my Comune place booke : after, I did eate some thinge, and then was busie in the house tell night : then I went to priuat praier and examenation, then I went to supper : after, to the Lector : after that I had taken order for some thinges, I went to priuat praers and so to bed

---

¹¹⁰ *pupped,* supped.

Thursday the :10:
After I had praised god for my rest, I went about the house and walked whill abroad : then I Came home and Kept Companie with some strangers tell all most dinner time : then I praied : after I had dined, I talked with the Companie tell they departed : then I was busie receiuing things that Came from London, bought by Mr Hoby : after, I praied with Mr Rhodes, then I took a Lector, wrought a whill and went to supper : after, I wrett to my Mother, Mr Hoby, and hard publece praers and, after, examened my selfe and praied priuatly, and so went to bed :

Friday the :11:
After I was vp I went to doe some beusenes about the house : after beinge not well, I did eate my breakfast : after that, I went a litle a broad, praied, then wrett, and after dined : then I did ouersee som thinges done about the house, and againe wrett some medetations in to my book framed by Mr Rhodes : then I took order for supper, and so returned to priuatt examenation and praier : after, I went to supper, then to publece praers, after that to priuat, and so to bed:

Saterday the :12:
In the Morninge I went about the house and after did pray, break my fast, walked abroad, and then dimmed : after dinner I was busie about reconinges and other thinges tell night, at which time I returned to examenation and priuat praier : then I went to supper, after to publece praers, then to priuat, and so to bed :

The Lordes day :13:
In the morninge I, beinge not well, was driuen, to the discomfort of my hart, with short praier and preperation to goe to church : after I Came home I dined and, though I were not well, I went againe to church wher I hard a good sermon, wher, I praise god, I was both Comforted, moued, and instructed : after, I passed the afternone with Litle readinge because of my secknes, then I went to supper, after that to the Lector, and then to priuat praier and examenation, and Lastly to bed :

Munday the :14:
After I was readie I went downe and was busie with my maieds tell 10 a clok, then I returned to priuat praier, did eate a Litle, reed of the bible, studeed my Lector, and so dined : after, I went to se the work in the Garden, and after that I Came In and did writt notes in my bible : after, I went about in the house tell allmost :5:, and then returned to priuat

praier and medetation : after, I praied with Mr Rhodes, then went to supper, after to the lector, and Lastly to bed :

Tewday the :15:
After I had praied priuatly I did eate my breakfast and went forth : then I returned and wrett in my sarmon booke after, and, after that, was busie all the day about mendinge and sortinge linan:[111] before supper I took order for diuerse thinges in the house, hard a Lector, and then went to supper : after, I talked a whill, and then wrett to Mr Hoby and dispatched a messhinger to him : after, I returned to priuat praier and examenation, and then went to bed :

Wensday the :16:
After I was readie I praied with Mr Rhodes, then I walked forth to workmen : after I Came home I praied, reed of the bible, and dined : then I went againe forthe : after, I wrett in my sermon book, then I went about busines tell 6 a Clok and then priuatly praied and examened my selfe : then I went to supper, after to the Lector, after that I did sum busenes, and then pread and so went to bed :

Thursday the :17:
After priuat praers I tooke order for diner and then reed of the bible : after, wrett in my table book and did eate my breakfast : then som strangers Came which held me tell Diner time, and after, tell 3 a cloke : then I went forth to some workmen, and after dispatched busenes in the house tell night : after I went to priuat examenation and praier, then I went to the Lector, after that to supper, then to priuat praers and so to bed :

Friday the :18:
After I was readie I went about the house dispatching some busenes : then I brake my fast : after, I praied, and againe went about sunderie thinges and then dined : after dinner I was bused in Houshould maters tell night, at which time I returned to priuat examenation,

---

[111] Lady Hoby also mentions sorting linen with her mother in London, where it may have been purchased. It was of course necessary to check the linen and protect it against the dangers of damp and mildew. Much attention was given to cupboards to keep them free of moths, fleas and flies. At least once a week, cloth was aired, shaken and brushed, using a soft brush. Bitter but sweet smelling herbs were laid, including bay leaves.

how I had spent the day, and praier, After I had hard Mr Rhodes Read of a good mans book, who proueth against Bis : Bilson[112] that Christ suffered in soule the wrath of god and that he desended not into hell : then I went to heare the Lector : after, I did eate some thinge and, after I had talked a whill and hard Mr Rhodes Read of the same book, I priuatly praied, reed a Chapter of the testement, and so went to bed

Saterday the 19
After priuat praers I did eate my breakfast, take order for diuerse Houshould matters, and read tell diner time : after, I was busie tell all most night, at wch time I talked of some thinge not so as I ought, when I had considered of them, but I find what is in man if the Lordes spiritt doe neuer so Litle hide it selfe from presaruinge vs from outward and inward daungers : but this is my Comfort, that my harte is setled to be more watchfull hereafter that I so grossly offend not my god : then I praied priuatly and, after, talked with Mr Hoby tell supper time : after, I hard the lector and so, when I had praied priautly, I went to bed :

The Lordes day .20:
After priuat praier I reed a whill and then did eate my breakfast : after, I went to the church, then I Came home and praied, after dined : then I reed in perkins tell I went againe to the Church, wher I found the Lord to assiste me most graciously from the malice of my enimie : after, tell night, I kept Companie with Mr Hoby who reed a whill of Cartwrights book to me, then I went to priuat examenation and praier : then I went to supper, after to publech praiers, then I talked a whill and after praied priuatly, and so went to bed :

The first day of the weeke. 21:
After priuat praier I went about the house and did ouersee the doinge of sundrie thinges : after, tell dinner time, I was busie with Mr Hoby, and, after, I wrought, hearinge Mr Rhodes Read of a booke against some newe spronge vp herisies : then after I went about the house and after Came to priuat examenation and praier ; then I reed a whill, after I went

---

[112]   Lady Hoby refers here to Thomas Bilson (1547–1616), Bishop of Winchester, opposed to much Puritan thought. See Introduction, n. 44.

to supper, after to the lector, then sonne after that I priuatly praied, and so went to bed :

The second day of the weeke 22: *of Ianuarie* 1599:
After suplecation and thankes giuinge vnto god I went about the house : after, I wrett in my sermon booke after that I had broken my fast, then I praied, then dined : after none I was busie tell all most night with my maieds, then I went to priuat medetation and praier : after, I went to supper, then to the Lector, after to priuat praers and so to bed :

The 3 day of the week 23:.:
After I had praied I brake my fast and then I went to ouersee some thinges in the house : after, I wrett Certaine thinges in my sermon book and did read of the bible, praied, and then dined : after I writt a whill, and wrought tell 4 of the Clok : then I went about the house, took order for supper and for the next day at dinner : after, I was busie in my Chamber tell allmost 6 : at what time I betooke me to priuat praier and examenation, after to supper, then to the lector which I had don other nightes : I wrett the cheffe doctrines in my testement and then, because I was not Verie well, I went to bed :

The 4 day in the week the 24:
After priuat praers in the morninge I reed of the bible, and so dined : after dinner I hard Mr Rhodes read, and was busie in my Clositt tell all most 4a Cloke : then I went about the house and, beinge not verie well, did litle but satt with Mr Hoby tell 6 : then I went to priuat examenatione and praier, and to Read of the Testement : then I went to supper : after, to the lector, then talked a whill and wrett a Letter, and, after, praied priuatly and so went to bed :

The 5 day of the week :25:
After I was readie I went about and was busie tell all most :11: a cloke : then I praied, read of the bible, dined, and after kepte Companie with a kinsman of mine that Came to se me : after that I bused my selfe in the House and in my Closett tell all most :6:, and then I went to priuat praier and examenation : then I went to supper, after to publect praers, then to priuat, and lastly to bed :

The 6: day of the week the 26:
After priuat praers I went about the house and then I reed of the bible

tell dinner time : after diner I dresed vp my Clositte and read and, to refreshe my selfe being dull, I plaied and sunge to the Alpherion:[113] after, I tooke order for supper and the next day, and then, after I had Conferred a whill with Mr Hoby I went to priuat examenation and praier

The Lordes day :27:
After I was readie and had praied, I did read of the testemente and bible : after, brak my fast and went to Church : after, I praied, then dined, and after dinner talked with Mr Hoby tell I went againe to church : and, after, Hard Mr Hoby read of perkins tell all most 5 a Clok : then I took Order for supper, and after went to priuat examenation and praier : after, I went to supper, then to publect praier : then to priuat, and so to bed.

The first day of the weeke :28:
After priuat praier I went about the house, then brake my fast : after, reed of the bible : after, took a lector and then went to dinner : after dinner I was busie presaruing, and wrought, and hard Mr Rhodes read of Mr Cartwright and the Bushoppe of Canterberies booke : after, I took order for thinges in the house and so Came to priuat praier and medetation : after I went to supper, then to the lector : after, I talked with Mr Hoby and Mr Rhodes of orderarie thinges, and then went to priuat praier and so to bed :

The 2: day of the weeke 29:
After priuat praers I went about the house, did break my fast, tooke a lector, praied, and then dined : after, I wend downe vpon occasion of busenes and, after, came vp and wrett in my bible notes, then wrought and hard Mr Rhodes read tell 4 acloke : then I took order for supper, and went about the house and, after I had a whill Conferred with Mr Hoby, I

---

[113]   *Alpherion,* orpharion, a flat-backed, stringed instrument of the Bandora family, of similar scalloped shape but smaller and tuned like the lute (see p. 57). It was larger than the popular cittern, having eight double strings of wire rather than four, and it had to be gently played with a plectrum, quill or fingers. It became very popular and was played almost as widely as the lute. Queen Elizabeth was skilled at the instrument, and music was specially written by William Barley, *A Newe Booke of Tabliture for the Orpharion* (1596). There are now only two of these instruments extant. See Sadie, ed. *The New Grove Dictionary of Music, Vol. 13* (1980), 869–70.

An orpharion.

went to priuat praier and examenation : after that I went to supper, then to the lector, then talked a whill, and then to priuatt praier and so to bed :

Ianur The 3 *day of the week* 30: 1599:
After I had praied priuatly I dressed apoore boies legge that Came to me, and then brake my fast wth Mr Hoby : after, I dressed the hand of one of our seruants that was verie sore Cutt,[114] and after I wrett in my testement notes Vpon James : then I went about the doinge of some thinges in the house, paiynge of billes, and, after I had talked with Mr Hoby, I went to examenation and praier, after to supper, then to the lector : after that I dressed one of the mens handes that was hurt, lastly praied, and so to bed :

The 4: *day of the weeke* 31:
After I was readie I praied, then I went about the house and dressed :2: that was hurte : after, I had talke with Mr Rhodes touchinge him selfe, wherin the Lord was mercifull to me : after I took a lector and then went to diner : after, I was busie in the house vpon an extreordenarie occasion tell all most night, and then I went to writ to Megy Rhodes and to priuat praier and examenation : after, I talked with some of my neighbours that Came to super to me, and after I hard the lector and so went to bed :

The 5 *day of the weke Feb*: :1:
After I was readie I went about the house and then praied, brake my fast, dressed a poore boyes legge that was hurt, and Jurdens hand : after took a lector, read of the bible, praied, and so went to dinner : after, I went downe a whill, then wrought tell 4 : a Cloke and tooke order for supper, and then talked a whill W^th Mr Hoby, and after went to priuat praier and medetation : after to supper, then to publect praers, and lastly to bed :

The 6 *day of the weke* 2:
After I had praied I dressed the sores that Cam to me : after, I dined and talked with som of my neighbours the afternone tell about 3 a Cloke : then I rede of the arball, went a bout the house, and returned to priuat praers : after, to supper, then to publeck praier, and lastly to priuat

---

[114] Lady Hoby refers below to dressing Jarden's hand. He was one of their more important servants. She now begins to write more regularly about tending her patients' wounds and ailments.

Feb. The Lordes day :3:

After priuat praers I did eate my breakfast, and then dresed the sores that I had vndertaken : after, I went to the Church : after, I praied priuatly and then dined : in the after none I went againe to church : after I Came home I reed of the testement, and wrett notes in itt and vpon Perknes, and then went about the house and, at my accustomed hower, Came to priuat examenation and praier, and then to supper : after, to the repeticion and, when I had dressed some sores, I went to priuat praier and so to bed :

The :1: *day of the week* :4:

After I had praied I went about and dispatched the former busines I was accustomed : after, I studed my lector and dined : after dinner I talked a whill with Mr Hoby and then, all the after none, I was busie in the kitchen and about som other thinges : at 5 a cloke I dressed my patientes, and then returned to priuat praier and examenation, then to supper, after to the lector : after that, to my Closit, wher I praied and Writt som thinge for mine owne priuat Conscience, and so I went to bed

The 2: day of the week :5:

After priuat praers I went to dresse my patientes and did eate my breakfast : then I wrett in my sarmon book tell diner time : after diner I walked abroad, and, when I Came home, I mad an end of writing my sermon, then reed of the bible, dressed my patients and, after I had taken order for the house, I returned to priuat examenation and praier : then to supper, after to publeck praers, and thence to bed :

The 3 day of the week :6:

After priuat praier I went about the house and dresed my patients, then I praied, took a Lector, and dined : after diner, I talked a whill with Mr Hoby and then went to the church and hard a sermon : after, I Came home and was busie in the kitchine all the afternone, and then I took order for supper, dresed my patient, and so came to priuat examenation and praier : after, to supper, then to publeck praers and, after I had talked a whill, I went to priuat and so to bed :

Feb: 1599 *The 4 day of the week 7: day*

After priuat praier I went to breakfast with Mr. Hoby : after, I dressed my patientes and wrett in my testement tell 12 : a Cloke : after, I did eate a litle, and then was busie about the house tell all most : 3: then Mr Rhodes reed to me tell 4, and then I took order for supper, dressed my patient and, after I had talked a whill Wth Mr Hoby, I returned to priuat examenation and praier : after, to supper, then to the Lector, and, because I was not very well, I went to bed

The 5 day of the week 8 : day
After my priuat praier I dressed my patientes, took a lector, studeed that a whill, praied, and then dined : after, I walked abroad, took order for houshould mattres, dresed my patient, and so returned to priuat praier and medetation : after that to supper : then, after talk a whill, to the Lector and, Lastly, to priuat praier, and so to bed :

The 6 day of the weeke 9 : day
After priuat praier I did break my fast and then dressed my patientes : after, I took a lector, then I reed of the bible : after, I praied and so dined : after dinner Mr Hoby, Mr Rhodes, and my selfe, talked of maters Concerninge the good of the paritioners : all the afternone I went not out of the chamber, by occasion any : yet, thouge I were with all the Companie, it pleased god to fre me from sunderie temptation wher Vnto I had before benne subiect : then I took order for supper, and, when I had dressed one of my patientes, I went to priut examenation and praier

The Lordes day the :10:
After priuat praiers I did eate my breakfaste, then went to Church : after I Came home, I dresed my patientes, then dined : after dinner I talked with some of my neighbours, that Came to me, tell church time : then, after the sarmon, I dresed other poore folkes, and then, after order taken for supper and some talke with Mr Rhodes touchinge some of his flock, I went to priuat praier and examenation : then to supper, after to the lectors, and so to bed :

The first day of the week :11:
After priuat praers I dressed my patients, took order for some thinges, and after went to breakfast wᵗʰ Mr Hoby : then I went about the house, took a lector, hard Mr Rhodes read, then made Mr Procter some meate, went to the lector and publect praers : after, dressed my patients, then went to supper : after, talked with Mr Rhodes of deuinetie, and so went to priuat praers and lastly to bed, with a good Conscience, I thank god, who hath this day giuen me much Comfort by his spiritt, to whom be all praise, amen

The 2 day of the weke 12: day
After I had priuatly praied with Mr Rhodes I did eate my breakfast and then did writt notes in my bible tell sarmon time, to which I went after I

had dressed my patients : after I Came from the Church I praied, dined, and allmost all the afternone, I hard Mr Rhodes read : then I took order for supper, and so returned to priuat medetation and praier : after, I went to supper, then to the lector, and, sonne after that, to bed, being not verie well in my head.

The 3 *day of the week* 13: *day*
from priuat praers to breakfast : then I dresed my patients : after, I reed of the bible, praied, and lastly dined : then I walked a whill, and hard one read : then I wrett in my testement : after, gaue order for supper, dressed my patient, and then exemened my selfe and praied : after went to supper, then to the lector, and lastly to bed :

1599. *The 4 day of the week Feb : the* :14:
After priuat praers I did break my fast, dresse my patients, write in my testement, took a lector, praied, and then dined : after dinner I wrought, talked with some that Came to me, hard Mr Rhodes read, took order for supper : after, talked with Mr Hoby and then went to priuat medetation and praier : after, I went to supper, then to publeck praers : after, to priuat, and lastly to bed :

The 5 *day of the weeke* :15:
After praier and breakfast and dressinge of my patiencs, I went to church : then, from the sarmon, I went to work : after, to praier and so to dinner : after diner I talked with an neighbour touching the misdemenors of a kinsman of mine, then I wrought some trifle I had to doe tell night, so the afternone was spent without any sperituall profetinge extraordenarie:[115] then I dressed my patientes, and after returned to priuat praier and medetation when I had taken order for supper : after supper, I hard publecke praers and, sonne after, I went to bed:

The 6: *day of the weeke* : 16:
After praier I ded eate, then dressed my patients : after, took a lector, praied, and so dinned : after, I wrought by Mr Hoby, hard Mr Rhodes read, conferred with him Vpon some thinges touchinge himselfe : after, tooke order for supper, and then returned to priuat medetation and

---

[115] Lady Hoby is put out that her routine affairs have left her little time for her devotional pursuits.

praier : after, I went to supper, then to the lector, after that to private praier and readinge, and so to bed:

The Lordes day :17:
After priuat praier I did eate, and so went to Church : after I returned I praied and then talked with a Cossine of mine tell dinner : after, I kept Companie with Mr Hoby tell church time, and, after that, I reed of perkins, hauinge som further Conference with my Cossine : then I took order for supper, dressed my patients, and returned to priuat medetation and praier : after, I went to supper, then to publeck praers, and lastly to bed :

The 1⁰ day of the week :18:
After priuat praers I did break my fast, then I walked : after, I wrought, and hard Mr Rhodes read of the bible tell diner time : then I wrought, and walked a whill, and after hard him read : then dressed my patients, one of which, I that[116] god, was wholl : after, I praied with Mr Rhodes and, sonne after that, went to the lector, then to supper : after, I looked of the Houshould book, and then went to priuat praers and so to bed :

The 2 : day of the wekke :19:[117]
After priuat praier I brak my fast, then dressed my patientes : after, wrett in my sarmon book, and, after I had praied, went to dinner : after, I talked with a neighbour, then wrought a whill and hard Mr Rhodes read : after, I went about the house & ouersawe some besenes, dressed my patients, and then went to the lector, after to supper : wret a Letter to my mother : after walked a while, and then went to priuat medetation and praier, and so to bed :

[118]After praier, breakfast : then, soune after, to the church : then to dinner : after, I wrought, was busie in the house, wrett in my sermon book and, after order taken for supper, I praied with Mr Rhodes : then I hard publeck praers and so went to supper : after, I walked a whill, and talked of no cerious mater, and then went to priuat examenation and praier

---

116   *that*, thank.
117   Lady Hoby has written in the margin here: 'This day the diuell would have brought in to question the truth of gods word which by the certefecate of godes spiritt in my hart wch had heretofore wrought in the same was sonne vanquished'.
118   These next two entries are undated.

After priuat praier I did break my fast, dressed my patients, went to my workmen, wrought, and after praied and then dined : after, I walked to Mr procters who was not well:[119] after, Came and wrett in my sermon book, wrought, dresed my patients, took order for supper, praied, went to the lector, then to supper : after, walked a whill, and lastly to priuat praers and so to bed :

Febb 1599. *The 5 day of the week* 21: *day*[120]
After priuat praers I did make an ende of my work, break my fast, walked to a neighbour of mine, and, after, I did eate some thinge : then I went to my Garden, and about the house, talked with a stranger, and wret to my Mother : after, dresed my patients, went to the lector, then to supper : after, walked a whil, and so to priuat examenation and praier

The 6 day of the weeke :22: *day* :[121]
After priuat praier I did break my fast, read of the bible, walked to my workmen, and then was busie in the house tell Mr Hoby Came home : then I kept him Companie tell diner time and after, all the day goinge about sundrie thinges and talkinge of diuers maters : after supper I went to publeck praier, and then to priuat examenation and praier, and so to bed :

The Lordes day. 23:[122]
After priuat praier I did eate my breakfast : then I went to the church, and, after I Came home, I praied, then dined : after, tell church time, talked with some of my neighbours, and then I went to church : after, I kept with Mr Hoby tell night when I went to priuat examenation and praied, and after did eate a litle, and so went to bed

The first day of the week 24:[123]
After priuat praier I did eate, then dressed my patients, reed of the bible, and then saluted some strangers : after, praied and then dined : after, I

---

[119]   Lady Hoby mentioned visiting the poorly Master Proctor on 11 February. He dies two years later and she attends his burial, 6 August 1601.
[120]   The fifth day of the week is correct, but Friday was 22 February, not 21.
[121]   Incorrectly dated, this should be 23 February.
[122]   Should be 24.
[123]   Should be 25.

kept Companie tell they departed and, after, reed and talked with a yonge papest maide:[124] and when I had giuen order for thinges in the house, I went to priuat examenation and praier, and, after that, to supper : then I talked with Mr Hoby, and then went to priuat praers and so to bed

The 2 day of the weke 25:[125]
After priuat praers I did eate my breakefast, dressed my patients, took order for dinner, reed of the bible, walked abroad, praied and dined : after, I walked forth wth Mr Hoby and then I wrett notes in my testement : after, I wret a letter to my Cossine Dakine and, after I had taken order for supper, I returned to priuat praier and examenation : then I walked a whill and so went to supper : after, talked with Mr Hoby and then priuatly praied, and so went to bed :

The 3 day of the weeke 26:[126]
After priuat praier I did eate, then I dressed my patients, reed, talked with a neighbour, praied, and then dined : after, I was busie weyinge of wooll[127] tell all most night and then, after talke with Mr Hoby and order for supper, I went to priuat exercises in my Closet : then after I supped and, after that, praied and so went to bed

The 4: day of the week 27:[128]
After priuat praers I brak my fast, dressed my patients, praied, and after

---

[124]   Lady Hoby is attempting her own conversion of the young woman. The Hobys were fervent Puritans in an area where many recusants lived. The Council of the North had been urged by the queen to search them out and Sir Thomas Hoby considered this to be one of his most important duties. Not unnaturally, it made him very unpopular in the region. See Introduction.

[125]   Should be 26, not 25.

[126]   Should be 27, not 26.

[127]   Wool was a significant source of income and Lady Hoby would have owned many hundreds of sheep. Apart from wool and meat, the flocks also gave milk for a Rocquefort-like cheese. She later mentions their sale and purchase, and the gift of sheep from her mother. In the sixteenth century, as the wool trade flourished and better breeds of sheep were introduced, great attention was given to their grazing and to the improvement of pastures. Parts of the outlying moors and wastes were fenced or walled in for the first time, to form restricted pasture easier to control. Most of the summer sheep were kept on the moor, although they could be put on the lower pastures in winter. Heather on the moor was burned only in the late winter, to produce young shoots for the sheep to eat. Yorkshire still carries more sheep per acre/hectare than any other county.

[128]   This was the 28.

talked with sundrie strangers tell diner time : after, I kept them Compaine and talked with a kinsman of mine : after, walked abroad vith Mr hoby, tooke order for supper, and then Came to my Chamber to rest, beinge not well, wher I talked with Mr Hoby tell supper time, and, after that, went to bed :

The :5: day of the weke :28:[129]
After priuat praers I did eate, went about diuerse thinges in the house with some paine of the toothach : after diner I talked a whill with an neighboure, but, beinge in great paine, was forced to vse diuerse medesons that did litle profett, for, all the next day and all the week after, I to goe out of my chamber, nor the lordes day after, which was the 9 of March I durst not goe to the Church, which was much greffe vnto me, beinge by that means depriued of the word and Sacramentes : and, though I know the Lord is powerfull And hath promised to keep his Children without the meanes, when he doth not afford them vnto them, yet, when he depriueth them of the ordenarie Instrumentes wherby he hath promised to Conuaye his graces vnto His people for their sinnes, there is great Cause of sorowe and greffe, tell it please the Lord, by his spiritt, to Certefie agan that their sinnes are pardoned : which Confort I had vpon the lordes euen, when, after ernest Inuocation, I had my paine taken away, and assurance of godes Loue:[130] and, from that time, felt no more paine

The Lords day 9:
After which time I returned to my accustomed order of praier, and then, vpon the Lordes day, I praied priuatly, and gott Mr Hoby to Read some of perkines to me, and, after diner, I red as Longe as I Could my selfe : after supper I praied publeckly with Mr Rhodes and so went to bed

The day following :10:
After priuat praier I brak my fast with my mother : after, I hard Mr Rhodes Read, and wrought, took order for supper, and then returned to

---

[129] This was the 29.
[130] Lady Hoby draws a connection between toothache and sin, demonstrating the Puritan link between illness and God's providence. Troubled by her toothache for over a week, she refers to diverse medicines, and might have eased the pain with her head covered, leaning over steaming water steeped in sage and other herbs. Gerard recommends crowfoot: 'tie a little of the herbe stamped with salt vnto any of the fingers' and 'purslane leaves eaten raw, taketh a way the paine'.

priuat medetation and praier : after, I went to supper, then to the lector &, after that, to bed :

The 2 day the 11: *day*
After priuat praier I did break my fast with Mr Hoby : then I was busie presaruinge : after, I walked abroad, took order for supper, then dressed my patients, and lastly went to priuat praier and medetation : after, I wrett in my testement some notes, then went to supper and then to the lector, and so to bed

The 3 day the :12:
After priuat praier I did read of the bible, then wret in my sermon book : after, dined : then was busie about diuerse thinges tell all most night, at which time took order for supper, and then I went to priuat examenation and praier : after that, to the lector and then to bed, when I had taken order for diner the next day

The 4 day the 13:
I was this day so ill with Could as I kept my Chamber, and had some of my neighbours, with whom I took ocasion to speak of diuers nedfull dutes to be knowne : as of parence Chousinge for their children,[131] of the charge of godfathers, and of the first instetuting of them : after they were gone frome me I praied, went to supper, and then hard the lector : after, I talked with Mr Rhodes touchinge his match[132] and so went to bed, takinge order for sundrie thinges to be don the nect morninge

The 5: the :14:
After I was readie I praied, then brak my fast : after, wrett in my testement, then dined : after, went about busenes tell 4 a clok, and then went abroad to workmen and, after, Came in and went to priuat examenation : after, to supper, then to the lector, and lastly to bed

The 6: the :15:
After I was readie I praied with Mr Rhodes, then I brak my fast : after, I went to my workmen, then to diner : all the after none I was busie, and,

---

[131] Lady Hoby writes of arranged marriages. Her first husband, Walter Devereux, had been chosen for her.
[132] Perhaps this refers to Master Rhodes' marriage to Rebecca.

at night, to priuat praier, then to supper : after, to publeck praers, then talked and, lastly, to priuat, and to bed

March 1599 *The Lordes day* :16:
After priuat praers I did eate, read, and then goe to the church : after, I praied, then I dined and, when I had talked a whill, I went to church againe : after, I went to visite a neighboure, then I walked : after, I vret notes in my bible and, after I had dressed my patients, I went to priuat praier, and so to supper : after, to publeck, and, when I had taken order for diner the next day and praied priuatly, I went to bed

The next day the :17:
After priuat praers I did eate, heare Mr Rhodes read, dressed my patients, praied, went to my workmen, and then dined : after, I wrought, walked abroad, took a lector, reed of the testement, praied with Mr Rhodes and, before supper, examened my selfe and praied priuatly : after, went to supper, then to the lector, and lastly to bed :

The 2: *day the* :18:
After I had praied with Mr Rhodes I did eate, then I went to walke : after, I talked with a stranger, then praied and, after, dined : after diner I went with him to my workmen, and sonne after Mr Hoby Came home with whom I kept Companie tell almost night : then I examened my selfe and praied, after went to supper, then to publecke praers and so, after I had taken order for diner the next day, went to bed :

The 3 *day the* :19:
After priuat praer I did read, break my fast, and then went with Mr Hoby to the Garden : after, I did goe about to diuerse places wher I find that buseneses hindereth wanderinge Coggetation : after, I dressed my patent and then dined : the afternone was almost spent in talke with a gentlewoman my freinde, and, after, I walked abroad and talked with Mr Rhodes, and then returned to priuat examenation and praier, after to supper, then to the lector, and lastly to bed :

The 4 *day the* :20:
After priuat praers I was much releced from a temptation and so went about busenes, brake my fast, took a lector, and, after praier, dined : all the afternone I was busie about som Huswiffrie tell night, when I went to priuat praier and medetation : after, to supper, then to the lector, and, after I had some good talke with Mr Rhodes, I went to bed :

The 5 day the :21:

After priuat praers I brake my fast, was busie in the ketchine tell diner time, then I praied, after dined : all the after none I ws buseed about takinge of accountes and other thinges so that through Idlenes, distractions had no aduantage, and at night I betook my selfe and to priuat examenation and praier : then I went to supper, after to pudleck[133] praers, then to priuat, and so to my Chamber, with much Comfort, I thank god.

The :6: day the :22:[134]

After I had priuatly praied I brak my fast wth Mr Hoby and Mr Vrpith : then I dresed my patiente : after, I praied and lastly went to diner : the after none I spent about the house tell towardes night and then I went to priuat examenation and praier : after, I went to supper, then to the lector and lastly to bed

The Lordes day :23:

After priuat praier I did eate and went to the church : after, I praied and dined : then I talked of god thinges with the Companie I praied and dined : then I talked of god thinges with the Companie tell it was againe church time : after I Came hom I talked with some of the house of the sarmon, and then took order for supper, dressd my patients, medetated of both the sarmons, reed a whill of another good book, and then went to priuat medetation and praier : after, to supper, then to the examenation of all the daies exercise, and so to bed

The day after the Lordes day the 24:

After priuat praier I went to the Church : after, I praied, dined, and then kept Companie with a Kinswoman of mine : then I took order for supper, dispatched som busienes, and, after, went to priuat praier : then to supper and, after one a Cloke after midnight when I had praied priuatly, went to bed : Mr Hoby that night went to search a house for papests

The :2: day the :25:

After priuat praier and reading of the bible I did eate : then I hard M. Doman read : after, Mr Hoby Came home, and then I went to dinner,

---

[133] *pudleck*, public.
[134] Lady Hoby has written in the margin: 'a christian shall find great ease in buseing himselfe in his ordernarie callinge: the divell then hauing Lesse advantage against him'.

and I wrought, walked abroad, and then Returned to priuat praier and medetation : after, to supper and, lastly, to bed

The 3 day the :26:
After priuat praier I took my leaue of Mr Hoby, paied Lutter 26ᴸⁱ,[135] and then wrought, reed, and wrett tell diner tim : after, I praied and dined, then talked a whill, took a Lector, and after went a bout the house : after, I came to priuat medetation and praier : after Mr Hoby Came home I went to supper, then to publeck praers and so to bed :

The 4 day the :27:
After priuat praier I did eate, read, and obsarued mine accustomed exercises tell night, hauing no distractions or temptations felte more then ordenarie, so that I found great Cause to praise god who is the giuer of all true Comfort what soeuer

The 5 day the :28:
After priuat praier I did eate, receiue munie of Steuen Tubley the last paiement for his land 60ᴸⁱ:[136] after, I reed of the bible, went about the house, praied, and after dined : then I took order for supper and reed abroad with Mr Hoby : after I Came home I medetated and praied : after, I went to supper, then to publeck praers, and so to bed :

The :6: *day the* :29:
After priuat praers I did eate, tooke a lector, reed of the bible and testement, and then dined : all the after none I was with Mr Hoby busie aboue nesesarie busenes and then, taking order for supper, I wen to priuat medetation and praier : then I went to supper, after to the lector, then I dressed my patients and so went to priuat praier, and, after order taken for diner the next day, I went to bed :

The lordes day the 30:
After priuat praier and breakfast I did goe to the Church and after I Came home I went to diner, with short medetation, beinge not well : then I talked with some of my neighbours tell is[137] was all most church

[135]   26 pounds sterling.
[136]   60 pounds sterling. The acquisition of a long lease gave the substantial yeoman farmer a secure economic and social position.
[137]   *is*, it.

time againe : then I hard the sarmon and after reed of a good book tell supper time : after supper I hard the examenations and publeck praers, and so went to bed, the lord pardon all my wantes in hearing and omitions in practisinge those Christten dutes which this day I am guiltie of, amen

The day following 31: *day*
After priuat praier I did eate, read, and was busie deliueringe some monie : then I dined and after diner I talked with a Gentlewoman, wrought tell all most night and then praied, went to supper, after to the Lector, and so to bed

The :2: *day The* :1: *of Aprill* :1600:
After priuat praers I did eate and was busie about dyinge of stuffe tell diner time, sauing I had some Conference with Iohn browne vnto whom I gaue the best aduice I Could : after, I praied and then dined : after, I was busie as I was before times and so, at 5 a Cloke, I went to priuat medetation and praier : After I went to supper, then to publecke prers, and then to bed

The 3 *day the* 2:
After priuat praers I did eate, dresse my patents, worke and pray : then dined : after, I wrought and hard one read of the book of Marters : then I went abroad and, after that, wrough tell nighte, and then priuatly praied and examened my selfe ; then I went to supper, after to publeck praers, and lastly to bed

The 4: *day the* 3:
After I had praied I wrought, hearinge Mr Rhodes read tell dinner time : then I praied : after, I did the like tell night when, after order taken taken for supper, I went to priuat medetations and praier : and then I reed of the Testemente and so to supper, then to publeck praers, and so to bed

The :5: *the* :4:
After praers I did goe about the house and, hauinge dune som busenes, I did eate a litle, read and lastly dined : after, I was busie about needfull thinges as preuented temptation, yet was not Cerious, so that, tell Mr Hoby Came home, I was not Idle : sonne after I went to supper, and, after the lector, dressed my patients, then examened my selfe and praied and so went to bed : haue wreten the notes of the lector in my testement :

The Lordes : day the 5[138]

After priuat praers I did eate and then was busie tell diner time : after, I praied, dined, and was in needfull thinges bused tell tell night, at what time I praied and so went to supper : after, to publecke praers and then to bed, hauing taken order for diner and supper the next day

The lordes day the :6:

After priuat praers I did read, eate, and went to the church : after, I praied, dined, and then, hauinge talked a whill with some of my neighbours, I went to church : and then tooke order for some thinges for my Iurnie that I had forgotten to doe the night before,[139] and, after, I went to priuat praied : after, I went to supper, then to publeck praers, and lastly to bed :

The first day of the week the 7: day:

After priuat praers I was buseede about my remouinge to yorke tell breakfast time : after, I took order for sundrie thinges in the house and sent Mr bell :40ˢ: for parte of litle kat's boord, and then tooke my Cotch and went to Linton : after I Came thether I praied and then went to supper : after supper I had a litle talke with Mr Measse, and then went to bed

The 2: day :8:

After priuat praier I Came to breakfast, and, not long after, I took my Cotch and Came to Yorke:[140] then I praied priuatly and, not long after, I went to supper : after, my Cossine Neuils wiffe Came to me, and and, when she was departed, being verie wearie, I went to bed

The 3: day :9:

After I had praied I went to heare the lord Archbushoppe preach : after I Came home I praied, then I went to diner, and, after diner, I went to the manner, and when I Came back I went to priuat medetation and praier, after that to supper, and, lastly, to bed

---

[138]   This day was a Saturday, not Sunday.
[139]   Lady Hoby is preparing for a two-week stay in York, during which she will see her new physician, meet friends, and attend religious services.
[140]   The last time Lady Hoby came to York she lodged in Master Skidmore's house. This time she and her husband are considering the purchase of a house.

York Minster viewed from the south-east.

The 4 day after the lordes day the :10: of Aprill :1600

After priuat praers I went to the Minster[141] wher I hard Mr Smith defend the truth against the papest, The question beinge whether the regenerate doe sinne : after I Came home I went to diner : I went to the church wher I hard Mr Stuard handle this question betwene the papests and vs[142] – whether we were Iustefied by faith or workes:[143] after, I Came to my lodginge, and, after I had praied, I went and talked with my Cossine bouser : then I went to Mr Doctor Benets, and after supper I praied publeckly with Mr Rhodes, and so went to bed

The 5 : The :11:

After I had praied and reed, some of my freindes came, with whome I talked, and so went to diner : after dinner I went to the Manner and then I walked with my ladie wansworth, and then went to my lodginge to priuat praers and medetation : after, she, with diuerse, Came to me and so, after A whill, I went to supper : then I talked, tell I it was late, with those that Came to me, and so I went to bed

The :6: The :12:

After priuat praers I reed, talked with my phesition[144] and som other gentlewemen, and so went to dinner : after, I walked to the manner garden and from thence to my owne lodginge, wher I had some speaches with Mrs fearne of Mr Rhodes, and how much she had mistaken him : then Mr Hoby reed to me and an other gentlewoman Came to me, with whom I talked tell 5 a Clock, at which time I went to priuat praier, then to supper, and lastly to Bed

The lordes day: 13:

After priuat praers and eatinge som thinge, I went to the Minster wher

---

[141] York Minster, cathedral and the pride and glory of York. It is one of the greatest medieval churches in Europe north of the Alps (see pp. 72, 74). In the 1570s the York High Commission had bound over recusants to hear sermons there. By the 1580s the city, under pressure from the President of the Council of the North, began financing its own civic preachers based on the city churches. During this period, however, the Minster remained more of a concern of the Yorkshire gentry than York city folk. See Aylmer and Cant, *A History of York Minster* (1977), 208–11.

[142] *vs*, us, ie. Protestants.

[143] Lady Hoby is stimulated enough by these two sermons briefly to note their subject. Sin and the regenerate, and salvation by faith rather than by works, were contemporary preoccupations. Also, see entry for 16 April.

[144] Master Lister is now Lady Hoby's physician.

The nave of York Minster looking west.

I hard Mr Gregorie prech : then I went to the manner to diner : after I had seene my lord and my lady[145] I went to Mr Harwoodes sermon, in which he deliuered this faulse possion,[146] that, for necessetie, a minester might buye church Liuinges, for necessetie had no lawe : thence I went to the manner, after I had been at my lodginge, wher I staied praers and supper, and then Came home, praied, and went to bed :

The first day after, the :14
when I had praied, I took a litle phesick and then I reed of Mr Browghtons book : after, I went to diner and then kept Companie with diuers tell allmost night, at which time I praied, then I went to supper : after, to priuat praers and so to bed

The 2 day the :15:
After priuat praers I tooke my phesick of Mr Lister and then I walked awhill, and after reed of Mr Broughtons booke : then I went to diner : after that I went to see a house that Mr Hoby should buy and then, tell supper time, kept Companie with gentlewemen that Came to se me : and then I went to priuat medetation and praier, so to supper, and, after, to priuat praers and then to bed :

The :3: *the* :16:
After I was awake Mr lister Came with phisecke which I tooke presently and lay after it a whill, which Continewed me ill all most all the day that I omitted my ordenarie exercises of praier : in the after none A freind of mine Came to me with a godly preacher, Mr wilson, of whom I learned this, among other Conferences – that relegion consisted of 2 princepall heades, which, who so euer did denie, Could not be saued : the one was Iuestefecation by and in christes Righteousnes : the other, of life touchinge the true worssheppe of god, so that, who so euer were ether Idolaters, or grounded their Iustefecation on workes, did denie so farr the truth in the foundation of christian religion : after they were gon I went to priuat praier and examenation : after, I went to supper, then I talked with Mr lister and, lastly, went to bed

---

[145]   Lord and Lady Burghley, previously mentioned.
[146]   *possion*, position.

The 4: *The* :17:
After I was readie I praied, then reed of the bible and an other good book, and, after 10 a cloke, I priuatly praied and so went to dinner : after, I talk first with a godly preacher of Mr braughtons[147] booke : then , after, wth diuers others that Came to me tell towardes supper time : then I priuatly praied and examened my selfe : after, supped : then I talked with Mr. Lister touchinge sundrie thinges that Concerned more others then my selfe and so, when I had praied, I went to bed

The 5: *The* :18:
After I was awake and had praised god for my rest, I got vp and was lett blood:[148] then I made me readie and went to priuat praier and reeadinge of the bible, as I was wonte : after, I walked, praied, and then dined : after, I talked with Mr fuller and diuers that Came to vesitt me, and, at night, I went to priuat praier : after, I went to supper and then went to publeck praers and so to bed

The 6: *The* :19:
After I was readie and had praied, I talked with Mrs stillington tell dinner time : then I praied, dimed, and, in the after none, I took a glister : after, I went to super, then to priuat praier and so to bed

The 20: *day the lordes day*
After I was readie and had praied, I brake my fast and then went to the minster : after the sarmon I Came to my lodging and lay downe, beinge not well, and, in the after none, I went to the Manner, wher I hard publeck praers, supped, and, after I had taken my leaue of my Lady, I Came to my Lodginge, and and, when I had praied priuatly, I went to bed

The 1: *day after* :20:[149]
After priuat praier I went to my Cosine bousers to dinner : after, I Came home and, when thinges were packd vp for goinge into the Contrie, I

---

[147] Hugh Broughton (1549–1612), published *Explication* (1599) of article respecting Christ's descent into hell. See Introduction, n. 43. Broughton wished to revise the translation of the Bible, and Lady Hoby may have known of his *Epistle* (1597), addressed mainly to Lord Burghley, in which he promoted his project. He was disconcerted not to be chosen by King James to work on the new Authorized Version.
[148] Bloodletting was used as a cure for almost every known medical condition.
[149] Monday was in fact 21 April. Lady Hoby's dates are incorrect until 1 May.

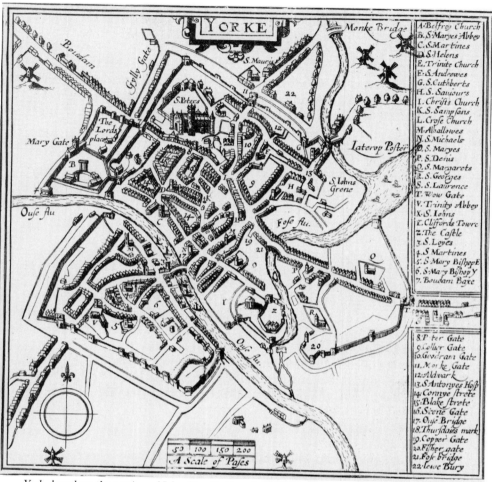

York, based on the version of John Speed's plate from 1610 which was the first-known plan of the city, Frans Hogenberg, Civitates Orbis Terrarum *(1618).*

kept Compani with diuers gentlewemen that Came to me : after, I went to Alline pinckstone, and, from thence, to Mr Blackcollers house wher I supped, and, after, Came home and, beinge not well, I went to bed :

The 2: *the* :21:
After priuat praers I brak my fast, and, after, my lady wansworth Came to me with whome I talked tell I went to my Cotch : and about 6 a cloke I Came to Linton wher, after priuat praier, I went to supper and after that to bed

The :3: *the* :22:
After priuat praier I dinned, then I walked about with my mother and reed, tell towardes night : then I praied priuatly and went to my booke againe : after, I went to supper and lastly to bed

The 4: *the* :23:
After priuat praers, I reed of the bible and walked about before diner : after, I praied, dinned, and then reed out a book that was lent me : then I talked with Mr Rhodes of sundrie thinges, and walked abroad tell towardes night, and then went to priuat praier and medetation : after, to supper, then walked : after, praied publeckly and then went to bed

The 5 *day the* 24:
After I had praied I did eate, then went to church : after, I Cam home and dinned : then I took my Cotch and Came to Hacknes,[150] wher, After supper, I hard a lector, took order for diner the next day, and so went to bed :

The 6: *the* :25:
After priuat praier I did eate, walke about, praie, and then dined : after, I was busie in the house, and walkinge and reading tell supper time, at which time I praied and so went to supper : after, to the lector, and lastly to bed

The Lordes day :26:
After I was readie I walked and praied tell I went to the church : after I was returned I walked tell diner time : after diner I kepe Companie with

---

[150]   Lady Hoby has been away from Hackness more than a fortnight, 8–24 April.

Mr Rhodes and other neighbours a whill, then with Mr Hoby : after, I reed of the bible tell all most Church time, and then I went to priuat praier : After, I walked abroad and then Came in to supper : after, I hard the lector and then, after I had walked a whill talkinge of no great matters, I went to priuat praier and so to bed

The :1: *day after* :27:[151]
After priuat praier I did read, eate, and so went to the Church : after I came home I dined and then went downe, where I remained all the after none : after order taken for supper, I went to medetation and praier, and then talked with Mr Hoby and so went to supper : after, to the repetition of the sarmon : after, I dressed one that was hurt and so, after priuat praers, I went to bed

The :2: *the* :28:
After I had praied with Mr Rhodes I did eat, and, sonne after, went to a sarmon : after, I praied, then I dined : after diner I went to Iosuas house : after, I kept Companie with Mrs Bell, and, towardes night, I went to priuat medetation and praier

The 3: *the* 29
After I had praied I went about the house, dressed my patient, walked to Garden and there medetated : after dined : then I went to talk with my olde wemen, and then I kept Companie with Mr Cholmely tell allmost night : and then I went downe to take order for suppr, and, after, returned to priuat examenation and praier : after, I went to supper and lastly to bed

The 4: *the* :1: *of May* :1600:
After priuat praier I did eate and then took my Cotch and went to Eaton,[152] to Mistress DauNies[153] Labour : there I dined, and, at 2 in the after none, I returned home, & and, after I had taken order for diuers thinges, I went to priuat examenation and praied : after, to supper : then I went about a whill, and reed praier, and then went to bed

---

[151] Lady Hoby has written in the margin, 'I wret to Mr Lister'.
[152] Ayton, on the east bank of the River Derwent, at the foot of the picturesque Forge Valley.
[153] Mistress Dawnay was related to Lady Eure. Young William Dawnay was a member of the Eure hunting party.

The 5 day 2:
After priuat praier I went to work, and then kept my Cosine Boucher Companie : after I had dined I went into my Garden, and was their busie tell 5 a clok : then I Cam in and went to priuat medetation and praier : after, I went to supper and then I walked abroad a whill : after, I came in to publeck praers and then went to bed:

May 3: 1600:
After priuat praers went about and so to diner : after, I was busie in the house a whill, then I walked abroad : after, wrett to Mr lister,[154] then I returned to priuat medetation and praier : after, I went about tell supper time and reed of the Testement : after supper, praied publeckly and then went to bed

The lordes day the 4:
After priuat praer I went to the church, and, after the sarmon, I Came home and praied : after, dined, and, tell Church time, I Confered with my Cosine Isons, then I went to the sarmon and then walked abroad and talked of itt : did eate som thinge before supper beinge verie emptie, which, of purpos, I vse to doe, that I may be the fitter to heare : and then I went to priuat praer and medetation : after, to supper, then to publeck praers and lastly to bed

The:1: day The 5:
After priuat praer I went about the house and after Came to dinner : then I went abroade, and was busie dyinge of stuffe tell allmost night, and then I went to priuat medetation and praier, and I walked, tell supper time : then I went to supper : after, I walked abroad, then went to priuat praer and reed a whill, and so went to bed

The 2 day the :6:
After priuat praers I did eate some meate wth Mr Hoby, and so took horsse and rede to Hurwoodall, to see our farme we bought of Tho : Calsone:[155] then I Came home and went to diner : after, I was busie in

---

[154]   Lady Hoby maintains regular contact with her physician.
[155]   Hardwick Farm in Harwood Dale is a welcome purchase. It is mentioned several times and Lady Hoby takes her mother to see it. In the village is a church built in 1862 to replace the smaller, now derelict chapel erected by Sir Thomas in remembrance of his wife, 1634. There is a tablet commemorating the chapel and the Hobys. See n. 386. The carefully preserved ruins are to the north surrounded by fields. You can spot them from Reasty Hill Top where there are magnificent views over the dale.

the house and talkinge with Mr Daunie, who inuited me to be a witnes at his childes baptisinge, which I refussed, in regard that my Conscience was not perswaded of the charge I was to vndertake, nor Throughly taught touchinge the paruartinge[156] the ende of witnesses from a christiane instetutione . . . siuell pollicie : but I will inquire more of this matter, god willinge, with the next faithfull deuine, beinge loth to denie, if I may, any freind such a Curtesie:[157] after, I went about the house and took order for supper, and after returned to priuat examenation and praier : after, I went to supper, then I reed, and lastly went to bed :

The 3: day :7:
After priuat praers I went about the house and, after diner, I was busie in my Chamber tell 5 a cloke, about which time I went to priuat praers : after, I went to supper, then to publeck praers, and lastly to bed

The 4 day 8:
After priuat praers I went about the house : after, I praied and dined with diuers that Came to me : then I, after they were gone with whom I kept Companie, tell allmost 5 a Clok I went to priuat praers, and was busie in the house tell super time, and after I I went to bed

The 5 day the :9:
After priuat praers I did eate a litle and then walked abroad with Mr Hoby : after, I did diuers thinges in the house and then went to diner. After, I was busie tell towardes night, about wch time I walked with Mr Hoby and Mr Rhodes, and talked touchinge baptismie : then I went to priuat examenation and praier, hauinge had a long rest now, I thank god, who, of his mercie, I pray to stringten me so in this releese that I may be prepared for new assaultes : after that I went to supper, then to the lector, and so to bed

The 6 day the :10:
After priuat praier I went abroad with Mr Hoby, and, after I Came in againe, was busie tell diner time : after I was busie about the house tell some of my freind Came wth whome I kept Companie tell supper time : after supper I went to the lector, and so to bed

---

[156]   *paruartinge,* perverting.
[157]   Lady Hoby does not tell us if she agrees to become a godparent. See entries for 9 and 13 May.

The lordes day :11:
After priuat praers I did eate, and then went to the church and, after, I praied and dined : then I kept Companie with my freindes ther tell church tim : after the sarmon, I walked a broad and, sonne after my Coming hom, I went to priuat examenation and praier, then to supper, after to the lector, and so, when I had talked a whill, I went to bed

The first day after :12:
After praier I did eate and then went to the church : after I Came hom I praied and then went to dinner : after, I went in to the faire[158] and bought diuers thinges : then I went to the church againe and, after I had talked a whill with my Cossins, I went to supper : after, I walked abroad and then Cam home and went to publeck praers and, after that, to bed

The 2 day :13:
After praers I did eate, and then took my Cotch and went to Mr Dannes : after dinner, and all Ceremones ended, I Came hom and walked abroade, and, after I had gonne about the house, I went to priuat medetation and praier : after, to supper, then to publecke praers and, after I had talked a good time with Mr Hoby of Husbandrie and Houshoulde matters, we went to bed :

The 3 day 14
After priuat praers I went about the house when I had reed of the bible : and then I praied priuatly, and so went to dinner : after, I was busie about the house and did work tell all most :6: a cloke, and then I went to priuat examenation and praier : after to supper, then to the lector and, after, went about the house and reed a whill, and so went to bed

May : The 4 day the 15:
After priuat praers I went about the hous : then I wrought tell dinner time and, after dinner, I wrought tell all most 5 a cloke, and hard Mr Rhodes read : then I went to priuatt medetation and praier : after, I walked into the feeldes wth my maides, and after Came home and went to supper, then to the lectour, and after that to bd

[158]   Lady Hoby may refer to a market for goods and livestock. All over the county there are ancient fairs, sometimes called 'feasts' or 'tides'. Country fairs and markets are still a distinctive feature of Yorkshire life.

The 5 day after the :16:
After I was readie I tooke a medeson and then walked after it, and, for exercise, boweld awhill : then I Came home and praied priuatly and reed of the bible : after, I wrought and then went to dinner : after, I talked a litle with a Gentlewoman, and then wrought and hard Mr Rhodes read of the princples of poperie out of one of their owne bookes:[159] then, it beinge time, I went to priuat examenation & praier : then to supper, after to the lecture, and so to priuat praier and then to bed :

The 6: day the :17:
After I had priuatly praied I tooke my medeson and after walked : when I Came home, I read of the bible, wrought, and after dined : then I dispatched som worke and so went about the house, takinge order for diuers thinges, and, at my time, went to priuat examenation and praier : after, to supper, then to the lecture and, when I had praied, I went to bed

The lordes day the :18:
After priuat praier I went to walk and medetate : then I did eate, read, and after went to the church : then I Came home and praied, then dined : after, I kept Companie with some of my freindes, after praied priuatly, and then went to the Church : after, I walked, Came home and went about, and, before supper, went to priuat examenation and praier : after, I went to supper, then to the publeck exercises, and after to bed

The :1:day the :19:
After priuat praere I did read to my wemen : after, I eate, then I wrough a whill and went about the house with my Cosine Isones wiffe : after, I praied and went to dinner : after, I wrought and hard Mr Rhodes read of a popeshe booke and after, towardes night, I went to priuat examenation and praier : after, to supper, then to publeck praers, and, when we had talked a whill to no great purposse, I went to bed

---

[159] An interesting insight into the Hobys' need to keep themselves well-informed and even with 'the enemy'. They had a real interest in protecting the reformed faith against the old. In the Hackness church library is a book with Sir Thomas Hoby's inscription: Thomas Morton, Bishop of Durham, *A catholike appeale for protestants, out of the confessions of the Roman doctors; particularly answering the mis-named Catholike apologie for the Romane faith, out of the protestants: manifesting the antiquitie of our religion, and satisfying all scrupulous obiections which have bene urged against it* (1610).

The 2: day after :20:

After priuat praers I talked with a good christian touchinge sundrie infirmetes that our humaine nature is subiect vnto : after, I brak my fast, wrought, hard Mr Rhodes Read, took a lector and, when I had praied, I went to dinner : after, I wrought a whill and then walked a fisshinge:[160] after I Came home I went to priuat medetation and praier : after, to supper : then I walked abroad and then Came to the lecture : after, I went to priuat praers and so went to bed

The 3 day the :21:

After priuat praer I went to break fast and, sonne after that that, took horsse and went to Trutsdall wher I spent allmost all the day : after I Came home I went to priuat medetation and praier : after, I went to supper, then to the lecture : after to priuat praers and so to bed

The 4 day the :22:

the lord hath freed me a long time from any temptation grious,[161] though the body haue benn a litle Iustly punished

After priuat praers I did eate, and then I went to Eaton to Mrs Dannie wher I dinned : and then, in the after none, I Came home wher, when I had gone about a whill, I went to priuat medetation and praier : after, to supper, then to the lecture, and, when I had praied, I went to bed :

The :5: day the :23:

After priuat praier I took a medesone, then I went about, praied, and dined : after, I wrought a whill and walked abroad and took a lector : after, I wroug and hard Mr Rhodes reead : then I went to priuat examenation and praier, then to supper, after to publeck praers : after, I talked with Mr Hoby, then I went to priuat praers and so to bed

---

[160] Lady Hoby would have gone fishing, for crawfish or trout, either in the river or in the old ponds constructed by the monks who occupied Hackness in earlier times. The River Derwent rises within the eastern moorlands a few miles from the sea. It weaves its way inland, through the village of Hackness, and then heads towards Malton and the Vale of York. It forms the boundary between the North and East Ridings for part of its course. Forge Valley, about 1½ miles (2 km) in length, is the most picturesque portion, popular with tourists. It is named after a forge anciently erected here for the manufacture of iron. The river itself is still well stocked with trout, strictly preserved.

[161] *grious*, grievous.

The 6: *day the* 24:
After priuat praer I went About the house, and, when I had reed a whill, I went to dinner : after, I wrought and hard Mr Rhodes reead of the testement and other good bookes, and vhen I had taken order for supper, I lay downe, being not well : after, I did eate, and then went to the lecture, and, soune after that, went to bed

The Lordes day :25:
After priuat praers I did eate and then went to the church : after, I Came home and praied, and then went to dinner : after, I praied and went to the church, and then I came home and took order for supper : after, I talked with my freindes that were with me, and then I went to priuat examenation and praier : after, I suppe and, when the publeck exercise was done, I went to bed :

The :1: *day after* :26:
When I had praied I walked about, brake my fast, and then went to the church : after I had dinned, I went abroad, and was busie in my garden[162] all the day allmost and then, towardes supper, I went to priuat examenation and praier : after, to supper, then to the publeck exercise, and then I reed a whill and praied, and so went to bed

The :27:
After priuat praer I did eate, went about the house, and wrett in my testement : after, I dined : then I kept in my Chamber workinge tell allmost night and hard my Cosine Isons Read, and, after, went about the house tell I went to priuat examenation and praier : after that I went to supper, then to the lector and, when I had talked a whill, I went to priuat praier and so to bed :

The 28:
After priuat praer I did eate, walke, work, and then pray, and after went to dinner : then I dispatched a messhinger to my Mother : after, I walked abroad to se fishe taken, and, when I Came home, I went to priuat examenation & praier : after to supper, then to publeck praers, and lastly to bed

---

[162]   See p. 86 for a contemporary recommendation as to what should be grown by the housewife in her garden.

Of huswifry.

¶ A digreſſion from huſbandꝛie: to a point oꝛ two of huſwitrie.

Now here I think nedeful, a pawſe foꝛ to make:
to treate of ſome paines, a good huſwife muſt take.
Foꝛ huſwiues muſt huſbande, as wel as the man:
oꝛ farewel thy huſbandꝛie, do what thou can.

In Marche and in Apꝛill, from moꝛning to night:
in ſowing and ſetting, good huſwiues delight.
To haue in their gardein oꝛ ſome other plot:
to trim vp their houſe, and to furniſh their pot.

Haue millons at Mihelmas, parſneps in lent:
in June, buttred beanes, ſaueth fiſh to be ſpent.
With thoſe and good pottage, inough hauing than:
thou winneſt the heart, of thy laboꝛing man.

'Of huswifry', *Thomas Tusser,* Five hundred pointes of good Husbandrie *(1580).*

May the 29:
After priuat praer I went to take some order in the house and then I brake my fast : after wch I took my Cotch and Came to Linton to my Mother, wher I was not well, and, therfore, after I had taken some meat, Mr Rhodes praied in my Chamber and then I went to bd

The :30:
After I was readie Mr Rhodes praied in my Chamber : then I did eate and after walked abroad with my Mother : after, I praed and so Came in to diner : after diner I went to Malton to se my lady Ewre, wher I staied tell allmost night : then I Came hom to Linton, and, when I had praied, I went to supper : after, I hard publeck praers and then went to bed

The :31:
After I had praed I walked with Mr Hoby and Mr Rhodes : then I Came in to breakfast, and, when I had talked a whill with some of my Mothers saruants, I took Cotch and Came hom to Hacknes, wher, after I had praed, I walked abroad with my Mother and my Cosine tell supper time : after which we walked againe and then Came in to publeck praers, and, after all was gone to their Chambers, I went to priuat examenation and praier : then I took order for the next day and so went to bed

The Lordes day June :1:
After priuat praer I did eate and then went to the church : after, I Came home and praed, then I dined : after, I talked tell church time and, after the sarmon, I walked abroad and talked of the sarmons, and after returnede to priuat examenation and praier : after, to supper and then to bed

The 2 *day of the Month*
After priuat praers I did eate and then went about the house and was busie tell dinner time : after, I praed, dined, and after talked with a freind of mine : then I went about busenes, and after walked a fisshinge with a freind that Came to me for that purposse : after, I Came home and did goe to priuat examenation and praier : after, I went to supper, then walked abroad and, after I had hard the lecture, I went to bed

The 3 *day*
After I was readie, had praied and taken a medeson, I walked : then I Came home and was busie vntell dinner time : then I went among Mr Hobes workmen and wrought tell I went to priuate examenation and praier : then

I went to supper, and, after I had walked a whill, I went to the lecture, and after that I tooke order for the next day and praied, and so went to bed

The 4 day
went Stp : and hall away[163]

After I had praied I tooke a medesone and went about the house tell breakfast : when I had eaten with Mr Hoby and my Mother, and they both gone, I returned busenes, goinge about all the day tell night : after, I went to priuat examenation and praier : after, I went to supper, then to publeck, and, when I talked a whill, I praied priuatly and after went to bed

The 5 day
In the Morninge I praied and then went about the house : after, I reed, praied, and went to dinner : then I staied and whill with the worke men, wrett notes in my testament and then walked abroad : after, I returned to priuat examenation and praier, then I went to supper, after to the lecture : then, when I had walked a whill, I praied priuatly and so went to bed

The :6: day:
After priuat praier I was busie about the house and with workmen tell allmost dinner time, then I praied and went to dinner : after, I was like wise busie about the house tell :5: a cloke and then I went to priuat examenation and praier : after, to supper, then to the lecture, and, after I had wrough a whill, I praied and went to bed :

The :7: day
in the Morninge, Mr Rhodes Cominge vp to me, I desired him to pray with me : after, I brake my fast and then walked abroad : after I Came in I reed, praied, and then went to dinner : all the followinge I went about and hard Mr Rhodes Read tell my time of priuat examenaiton and praier : after, I walked about tell supper time and then I to supper, after to the lecture, and, when I had taken accountes, I praied, took order for the next day, and so went to bed :

The lordes day :8:
After priuat praers I reed, walked, and, medetated, and then went to the church

---

163   This may refer to two servants who have departed from Hackness.

: after I had hard the sarmon I praied, then dined and, after, I Conferred of diuers thinges tell church time againe : after the sarmon I talked with one of my maides, walked with Mr Hoby abroad, and then returnedto priuat examenation and praier : after, I went to supper, then to the repeticion of the sarmons, and, when I had praied and praised god, I went to bed :

The 9: day

After I was readie I was Called to some busenes, which done I went to priuat praier and readinge : after I went about the house, took a lecture, praied, and then went to dinner : after, I talked a whill with Mr Hoby and then I went to busenes, in which I Continewed tell 5 a clok, and then I went to priuat examenation and praier : after, I went abroad & then came to supper, and then went to publick praers and, after priuat, to bed :

The :10:

When I was readie I was Called to some busenes, and, when I had don, I praied priuatly : after, I reed and went to the church : then, after the sarmon, I praied, dined, and went about busenes a whill : then I wrought and hard Mr Rhodes read of Grenhame, and, when I had gon about a whill, I went to priuat examenation and praier : then I with my Cosi walked into the closes,[164] and, after I Came in, had supped and hard the exercise, I went to bed

The 11: day

After I had gone about some busenes I praied priuatly, and after reed and took a lecture : after, I praied and then dined : all the after none I wrought tell towardes night, and then I walked abroad, and, when I Came in, I reed a litle of humanitie,[165] and then went to priuat examenation and praier : after, to supper, then to the lecture, and so to bed.

---

[164] *closes*, enclosures of grassland, on the other side of the river from the manor house; names later included 'Long Field Close' and 'Home Close', as can be seen on the old Hackness estate map. There is occasional evidence in the monastic cartularies of the early walling of fields and enclosures. Monks walled with stone in several places, or there were ditches, banks, and even fencing. Different pastures were allocated to cows, ox, horses, and poultry. See pp. 90, 92 for details from estate maps.

[165] It is tempting to wonder what such reading meant to Lady Hoby. To comment on reading 'a little of humanity' implies a distinction between that and her religious study, and judging from her religiosity she must have read these books with some sense of guilt. If she knew Latin she might have read Virgil, or Tacitus and Livy in translation, or, later, Chapman's translation of Homer (pub. 1609).

'The Mannour House', detail from a late seventeenth-century map.

The :12: day

After I was readie I praied, then I went about busenes till I break my fast : after, I took a lecture and went to dinner : after, I walked with Mr Hoby, and then I went to work and hard Mr Rhodes read : after, I walked a litle and then returned to priuat examenation and praier : after, to supper, then to the lecture, and lastly to bed

The :13: day

After I was readie, I praied, went about the house, took a lecture, reed of the bible, praied, and went to dinner : after, I walked a whill with Mr Hoby, then I talked with a goldsmith and bought some thing of him : after, I went about the house and then wrett in my sarmon book tell I went to priuat examenation and praier : after, I went to supper : after, I walked, hard publeck praers and, when I had praied priuatly, I went to bed

The :14: day

After I was readie I praied priuatly, went about the house, and then dined : after, I wrought and went about the house, and after returned to priuat examenation and praier : after, I went to supper, then to the lecture, and lastly praied and went to bed

The Lordes day :15:

After priuat praier I wrett notes in my testement, reed a whill, and went to the church wher it pleased the lord to blesse me in hearinge : when I Came home I praied, dined : after dinner I Conferred of the sarmon with the Gentlewemen that were with me, and then I praied and went to the church : after I Came home I was busie and talked a whill with a freind that was wth me, and then I went to priuatt examenation and praier : after, to supper, then walked and, when I had hard the publeck exercise, I praied and so went to bed

The :16:

After priuat praers I reed, went about and, afte, Came to work, then dined : in the after none I went to Harwoodall with Mr Hoby, and when I Came home, I went to priuat pra:[166] after, I went to supper, then to publeck praers and so to bed :

---

[166] *pra*, prayer.

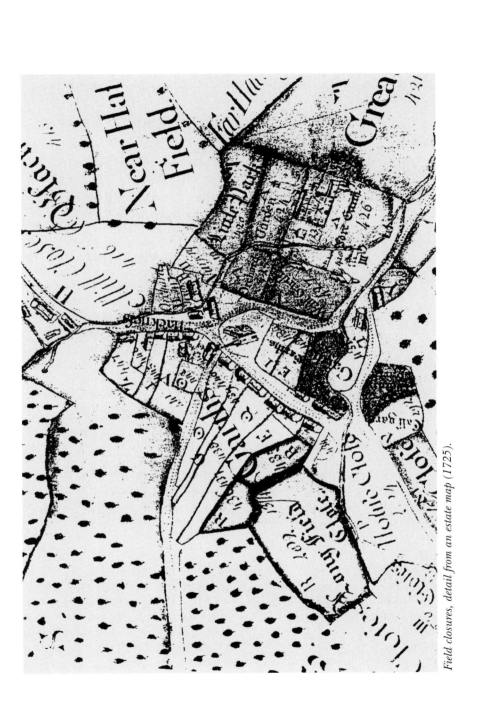

Field closures, detail from an estate map (1725).

The 17: *day*

After I had praied I went about the house, and then I made an end of a dressinge I was doinge before : then I reed of the bible, after praied and so went to diner : after, I went to linton where I praied and went to supper, and after that to bed

The 18: *day*

After priuat praers I reed and walked abroad, and after praied and dined : after, I went into the feeldes and, when Came I home, I praied, then went to supper, then to the lecture, and after to bed

The 19: *day*

After priuat praier I brake my fast and walkked : then I praied, and, after, went to dinner : after, I took horsse and Came home to Hacknes wher, after I had praied, I went about the house, then to supper : after, I walked abroad and, when I Had praied bubleckly and priuatly, I went to bed

The 20:

After I was readie I praied, then I wrett to Megy Rhodes : after, I went a whill about and so went to dinner : after dinner I talked with som strangers that Came to Mr Hoby, wrought, reed a sarmon, and, when I had taken order for thing in the house, I went to priuat examenation & praier : then to supper, after to the lecture, and so to bed

The :21: *day*

After priuat praier I did read of the bible and then went about the house, wrought, praied, and then dined : after diner, I went about a whill, wrought, hard Mr Rhodes Read, and then I went to priuat examenation and praier : after, to supper : then I walked with my freindes that were come to me, and, when I had hard the lecture and praied priuatly, I went to bed

The lordes day :22:

After priuat praier I did eate, read awhill, and then went to church : then I, returninge home, praied, dined, and after kept Companie with my freindes, talkinge some what of the sarmon : after, I praied and then I went to the church : after the sarmon I walked and, when I Came home, I praied and so went to supper : then, sonne after, I went to the examenation of that which had been deliuered, and so, after priuat praier and order taken for the next day, I went to bed :

The 23:
After priuat praier I went about the house and then kept companie with diuers gentlewemen that were with me : after, I withdrew my selfe and reed of the bible and praied, and then went to dinner : after dinner I, with them, went to Skarbrowgh,[167] and when I came home I went to priuat medetation and praier : then I wente to supper : after, to priuat praer and so to bed :

The 24:
After priuat praier I kept companie with my Cosines and led them about the house : then we went to diner and, when they were gone, I reed and wrett in my sarmon booke : after, I went about the house and then I went to priuat examenation and praier after, to supper, and, when I had praied priuatly, I went to bed

June 25:
After priuat praers I went about the house and then I wrought tell diner time : after, I went abroad with Mr Hoby, and after wrought tell 5 a cloke : then I went about the house, and, when I had finished my work, I went att :6: to priuat examenatione and praier : after, I went to supper and then, being not well, I went to bed :

The 26:
After priuat praier I wrett in my sarmon book, and then I walked and so went to dinner : after, I went abroad with Mr Hoby and, when I Came in, I wrought and reed tell 5 a cloke, and then I went to priuat examenation and praier : after, to suppe : then I walked with my Cosin and, after I had praied priuatly, I went to bed

The 27:
After priuat praier I went about : then I wrought and was busie with a gold smith that brought me home some thinge I had to mend : after, I praied, then I dined : after, I walked with Mr Hoby, and after I wrett in my sermon book and walked a litle, & then went to priuat examenation

---

[167]   In Lady Hoby's time Scarborough was a fishing port and a refuge in times of storm for coastal traffic. It was developed as a watering place about 1626 when mineral springs with supposed medicinal properties were discovered. It was not until the late seventeenth century, however, that it came to prominence as a health and holiday resort. Scarborough had an ancient fair that originated in a charter of 1161. It is commemorated by an old cross in the harbour and in the folksong 'Are you going to Scarborough Fair?'

and praier : after, I went to supper : after walked and then, when I had praied priuatly, I went to bed

The 28:
After I had praied I spent all the forenone in ordringe thinges in my Clositt and sorting of papers : after diner I was busie in the house tell 6 a clok, and then I went to priuat praier and examenation : after, I went to supper, and, when I had walked a whill, I went to publecke praier and, not longe after, to priuat, and so to bed

The lordes day :29:
After priuat praier I wrett a litle and then made me readie : after I reed a whill and so went to the church : after, I praied and then dined : then I Conferred of that that was deleuered, and, when I had a whill walked and praied, I went to the church againe : after, I wrett a litle and then I went to priuat examenation and praier : after, I went to supper, then I walked abroad and, when I came in, I went to the publeck exercise and after that to bed :

The 30:
After priuat praier I wrett in my sermon book, and after reed and praied, and then I went to dinner : after diner I went to work, and hard Mr Rhodes read of a sarmon booke, and, after, I walked, and then I came to priuat examenation and praier : after, I went to supper and then, hauinge walked a whill, I Came in to the lecture : and so, after priuat praers, I Reed a whill and so went to bed :

The :1: *day of July* : 1600:
After priuat praers I did read, then I wrought a peece of work for a freind : after, I went about, and then praied and so dined : after, I walked a whill and wrought and, towardes night, I walked againe, and then Came in to priuat examenation and praier : after, I went to supper and publeck praers, and they I went to priuat after a whill, and so to bed

The :2: *day*
After priuat praers I wrought a whill, praied wth Mr Rhodes, and after I walked abroad & was at my work tell all most diner time : then I praied, and dined, and, after, tooke my Cotch and went abroad : then I Cam home and wrought, and after went to priuat examenation and praier : after, I went to supper : then, after a whill, to the publeck exercise and, when I had praied priuatly, I went to bed

The 3 day:
After priuat praers I made me readie, and then went to work and hard Mr Rhodes read of Latimers sarmons[168] and some other thinges : after, I praied and, sonne after, went to diner : then I went to the workmen a whill, and then to worke, and, after I had taken a lecture, I went about the house & so returned to priuat examenation and praier : after, I went to supper, then to the lecture and, after, to priuat praers and so to bed

The :4: day
After priuat I stoudied my lecture and, after, I I took a newe, wrought, and hard Mr Rhodes read of the bible : before diner I praied and, after, I wrought tell 4 a cloke, and then I went about the house, and, after I had sitt a whill with my wemen talkinge of som princeples vnto them, I went to priuat examenation and praier : after, to supper, then to the publecke lecture : after, I talked with my Cossins, and then I went to priuat praier and so to bed

The :5: day
After I had praied I went about the house, then I hard Mr Rhodes Read, took a lecture, praied, wrought, and went to diner : after diner I went a walkinge and, after I Came home, I was busie about diuerss thinges, and then I went to priuat examenation and praier : after I sett an order for diuers thinges, and so went to supper : after, I walked, then went to the lecture and, after a whill, to priuat praier, and lastly to bed :

The lordes day :6:
After priuat praers I went to the church and, after, I praied and dined, and then I talked with my Mother and reed to hir : after, I went to the church, and, after that, walked a whill about, and then returned to priuatt examenation and praier : after, I walked a whill and then went to publeck praers : after a litle time, I went to priuat and so to bed

---

[168]   Hugh Latimer (1485?–1555), Bishop of Worcester, a theologian and writer who encouraged Puritanism in his diocese. He was committed to the Tower after Mary I's accession (1553) and finally condemned as a heretic and burnt at Oxford. Lady Hoby would have read about his disputation there in Foxe's *Book of Martyrs*. His sermons were published in *Fruitfvull Sermons, preached by the right Reuerend Father, and constant Martyr of Iesus Christ, Master Hugh Latimer* (London, 1596).

The :7: day

After priuat praier I tooke order for sunderie thinges in the house and then went to breakfast, and, after, took my Cotch and went to Seamer : after diner I Came from thence, and, when I was Come home, I went to priuat praers : after, to supper : then I walked and hard publeck praers, and after went to bed

The 8: day

After priuat praier I went about and tooke accountes and paied billes : after, I reed, praied, and dined : after, I was busie, wrought, and after took my Cotch and went in to the feeldes, wher I did eate my supper with my Mother and other freindes,[169] and then Came home and hard publeck exercise : and then, after that, I went to priuat examenation and praier, and so to bed

The 9:

After I was readie and had praied, I took order for the house, and then went to breakfast : after, took my Cotch and, wth my Mother, went to Linton : after I Came thether I praied, and then walked with a stranger with whom I hard litle good talke, and therfore the time, as ill bestowed, I greeued for : after, I went to supper and, when publeck praers was donne, I went to bed

The :10:

After I had praied I brake my fast : after, I hard Mr Rhodes read, and wrought tell allmost dinner time : then I praied and dined and, after, wrought a whill and talked with some that Came to me : and then I tooke my Cotch and Came home, and so went to supper : after, I walked a whill and hard publeck praers, and, after a litle time, I went to priuat examenation and praier, and so to bed :

The ::11:

After I had praied I went about the house & gott all out to the hay, and I returned to work : after, I praied and dined : then I went to work againe and then went a walkinge : when I Came in Mr Hoby Called for supper, and, after that, I walked a whill and then went to the lecture : after, I dispacthed a litle Huswiffrie and so, hauinge praied, I went to bed

---

[169]   This is probably a hay-making supper. In Yorkshire this is known as 'Hay-timin'. Also see entry for 11 June.

The :12: day

After I was readie and had praied, I went about the house, wrought a whill, reed, and praied : after I dined and, all the after none, I was busie about such thinges as were needfull : and, att 5 a clocke, I wrett in my testement, and went to priuat examenation and praier : after, I went to supper, then to the publeck praers : after, I made readie a purgatione[170] for my Cosine Isons woman and, when I had praied priuatly, I went to bed

July 1600: *The lordes day* 13:

After priuat praers I reed and then went to the church : after, I Came home and praied and then dined : after diner I talked of the sarmon, and reed of the bible with some Gentlewemen that were with me : after, I praied, walked, and went to the church againe, and after I walked a whill : and so I spent some time in writinge on my sarmon book and and prainge, and, after, I went to supper and, sonne after, I hard publeck praers and, lastly, when I had praied priuatly, I went to bed :

The :14: day

After praier I went about the house, and then went to my work and readinge : after, I took a lecture and praied : then dined : after, I went to my work and then went about the house, and, after, I wrett a litle and answered a letter from my Lady Ewrie, and then went to priuat examenation and praers : after, to supper and, when publeck praers was done, I went to bed:

The :15: day

After I was readie and had praied, I went about the house, and did eate : after, I hard newes of the Death of my Sister, Elzabeth Russill:[171] after, I praied, then dined ; and, after, I talked with a Cosine of mine, and, after, a Gold smith : then I hard Mr Rhodes read, and so I went to priuatt examenation and praier : after, I went to supper and, after, I went to the lecture : then I walked and praied priuatly, and so went to bed

The :16:

After I had praied priuatly I went to doe diuers thinges about the house : after that, I dined : I spent the after none in my Chamber and hard Mr

---

170 *purgatione*, purgation, a medicine to cleanse through and purify the body.
171 Elizabeth Russell, Sir Thomas Hoby's stepsister, died on 2 July 1600. A fortnight earlier, her sister Ann had married Henry, Lord Herbert, son of the Earl of Worcester.

Rhodes read a book that was mad, as it was saied, by my lord of Esex in defence of his owne Causes,[172] and, after, I went to priuat medetation and praier : then I went to supper : after, to publeck praers and so to bed.

The :17:
After praer I wrought and hard Mr. Rhodes read : after I praied, dined : after dinner I wrett a proportion for the Houshould diatt,[173] and then I went abroad with some freindes that Cam to me : after I had praied I went to supper : then I walked a whill and so Came in to publeck praers : after, I praied priuatly and so went to bed

The :18:
After priuatt praers I went about the house and deliuered some directions to Iurden : after, I talked with my Cosine Isons and about his goinge to yorke, and then I went to diner : after, I was busie pouidinge[174] some thinge to be carried to York: afte, I wrought and, lastly, I went to priuat examenation and praier : after, I went to supper, then I walked abroad : after, I Came in to publeck praers and, after, to priuat, wher I please the lord to touch my hart with such sorow, for some offence Cometted, that I hope the lord, for his sonne sake, hath pardoned it accordinge to his promise, which is ever Iust:[175] after, I reed apaper that wrought a farther humiliation in me, I thanke god

19: *of July* 1600:
After priuat praier I wrett an answer to a demand Mr Hoby had giuen me ouer night:[176] after, I went about and then wrett in my sarmon book :

---

[172]   Robert Devereux (1566–1600/1), second Earl of Essex, Lady Hoby's brother-in-law by her first marriage. Opposing Burghley's policy of peace with Spain (1598), his argument was printed but suppressed as he was in disgrace.

[173]   *a proportion for the Houshould diatt*, the amount of food, or portion, served to each person varied according to rank. Lady Hoby means that she has listed who will eat what, and when, and how much it is necessary to prepare. By contrast, in *To Penshurst* (1616) Ben Jonson celebrated the fact that 'the same beer and bread and self-same wine/ That is his lordship's shall be also mine'.

[174]   *pouidinge*, providing.

[175]   Lady Hoby is hard on herself, but places her trust in her Saviour.

[176]   We can only speculate as to why Lady Hoby feels the need to write to her husband rather than speak with him directly. Perhaps the paper she read last night has something to do with her husband's demand.

after that, I praied and then I dined : the after none I wrought tell all most 5 a clok, and then I went about the house : after, I returned vnto my Clossitt and altered that a litle which before I had wretten, and then I examened myselfe and praied : after, I went to supper, then to publeck praers and, lastly, after priuat, I went to bed

The 20 day the lordes day
After I had praied I reed of the Testement and did eate : after, I walked and did medetate of that I had reed : after, I went to the church, and, after the sarmon, I praied : then I dined : after, I talked with my neighbours of that we had hard, and Reed some thinge to them : after, I praied and went to the church againe : after, I talked with my Cosine Isons, and, when it was 5 a Clok, I went to priuat examenation and praier : after, I walked dawne and then went to supper : after, I hard the bubleck Exercise and then prainge, and, giuinge Mr Hoby that that I had wretten, I went to bed :

The :21: day
After priuat praier I went about and wrought tell dinner time : after, I went to work againe, and talked with Mr Gregorie and hard Mr Rhodes read of a sermon book : after, I walked about the house, praied priuatly, went to supper, and after, beinge not well, I went to bed:

The 22: day:
After I had praied I was busie with Roses, and, after, I did read of the bible, praied, and wrett in my sermon booke, and then went to dinner : after, I was busie workinge : after ward I talked with Mr Gregorie, hard Mr Rhodes read, and, after, I went to priuat medetation and praier : then I went about the house & so to supper : after, Mr listers Came and then I keept companie with them, and so, when I had praied priuatly, I went to bed

The:23: day
After priuat praier I talked with Mr Lister and satt with them at breakfast : after, I went about the house and wrought tell diner time : after, I wroug, and talked with Mr Hoby of the sall of linton,[177] and, when I had gone a whill about the house, I after went to priuat examenation and praier : then

---

[177] Lady Hoby's mother is selling her house to live in another of her properties at Newton near Wintringham. Cousin Robert Dakins will eventually buy Linton.

I reed of the testement, walked a whill, and went to supper : after, I hard the lecture and then returned to priuat praers and so went to bed

The 24 day
After priuat praers I wrett in my testement and reed : after, I went about and wrought, and, when I had Called vpon god, I went to diner : after, I went to work and then I went about the house, hard Mr Rhodes read, and, after I had walked a whill, I went to priautt medetation and praier : after, I went to supper, then to the lecture : after, I wrett to Mrs Carington,[178] and then I praied and went to bed

The :25: day
After priuat praier I brak my fast with Mr Hoby : after, I went to the church, then I came home and praied, dinner, and wrett in my testement : after, I was busie about diuers thinges, and, when I had walked abroad, I praied priuat and so went to supper : after supper I went to the lecture, and, when I had praied priuatly, I went to bed.

The :26: day
After priuat, I did musie my selfe a bout makinge of oile[179] and in my Clositt tell towardes diner time : then I praied : after, I dined : then I went afishinge, and so I Came home and praied priuatly : after, I went to supper, then to publeck praers, after to priuat, and lastly to bed

The lordes day : 27 :
After priuat praier I reed and then went to church : after, I praied and dined, then I kept Companie with some gentlewemen that was with me, and, when I had praied, I went to the church : after I Came home I walked and reed, and then I went to priuat praier and examenation : after, I went to supper, then walked a whill, and then hard the publeck exercise : after, I talked a whill and then went to priuat praier and so to bed

The 28 day
After priuat praier I was busie about the house tell allmost diner time : then I praied : after, I dined and took my leaue of my Cosine : then I

---

[178] Anne, wife of William Carrington, daughter of John Bonville. She brought her husband to the manor of Spaunton.
[179] *makinge of oil*, this oil was probably extracted as fat or grease from boiled down meat and fowl. It might also have been a lanolin extracted from wool.

wrett in my testement, and walked about, and, after, Came to priuat examenation and praier : after, I went to supper : after, I walked with Mr Hoby and, when I had praied, I went to bed

The 29:
After priuat praers I went about the house, and, when I had dispatched some busenes, I wrett in my testement : after, I praied and went to diner : after diner I was busie in my chamber and about takinge order for thinges all most all the after none, and then I wrought, walked about with Mr Hoby amonge workmen, and, after, I went to priuat praier and examenation : after, I supped : then I talked with Mr Hoby of sunderie thinges and so, when I had praied priuatly & reed a chapter of the testement, I went to bed

The :30: *day*
After priuat praier I went into the kitchine and did help to gett some of our meat readie vpon occasion : after, I dined, and then I was busie about the house a whill, and, after, I wrett in my testement : then I went to work, and, when I had ben a whill about the house, I reed of the testement and then I praied and examened my selfe : after, I went to supper : then I talked with John Douson a whill, & then I praied priuatly and went to bed/

The 31: *day*:
After priuat praier I went about the house, and sent my Cossine bouser some venison:[180] after, I wrett in my sermon book, then I brak my fast and went abroad to the haymakers, and, after I Came hom, I praied and went to dinner : after, I wrought and kept Companie with one that Came of purposse to me, and, after, I went to priuat examenation and praier : then I went to supper and, after I had talked a whill with one that was with me, I went to priuat praier and so to bed

August :1600. *The first day*
After priuat praier I went about the house, and then I measured some Corne to know what prouision we had : after, I dined with Mr Hoby and

---

[180] Presumably the meat she was making ready yesterday. Venison could not be bought or sold at this time, only given away to confer favour, or as a gift – in this case to Lady Hoby's cousin. It could be stewed with a boar's tail, or might have been served with frumenty, accompanied by pasties of doves and larks, vegetable and egg tarts, and peeled nuts.

so kept him Companie all the day, and then, towardes night, I wrett to my Cosine bouser, and reed of the Testement, and then went to priuat examenation and praier : after, I supped : then I walked with Mr Hoby, and, after, I went to priuat praier and so to bed

The :2: *day*

After priuat praier I went about, takinge order for diuers thinges, tell allmost diner time : after, I praied, then dined : after, I was busie in the house tell allmost supper time, at which time I talked a whill with Mr Rhodes, and after went to priuat examenation and praier : after, I went to supper, then to the lecture, after to publeck praers, and so to priuat and then to bed

The Lordes day :3:

After priuat praers I did read and went about the house, and, after I had broken my fast, I went to the church : when I Came home I praied : after, dined : and then I talked and reed to some good wiffes that was with me : after, I walked with Mr Hoby, and praied, and then I went againe to the church, and, after, I reed of the testement : and then I talked with Mr Rhodes and, after, went to priuatt examenation and praier, then to supper : after, to publeck praers, then to priuatt, and lastly to bed/

The :4: *day*

After priuat praier I went about the house, and, hauinge eaten som thinge, I went to work, and hard Mr Rhodes read : after, I praied, then I dined and, after, I did work, took accountes, and then I, towardes night, went to priaut examenation and praier, hauinge had the lord not only this day but long before Very gratious vnto me, in supportinge my weakness and in in ablinge me to be a litle Comfort to some of his seruants that was in greffe/[181] after, I walked with Mr Hoby : after I reed of the bible, and then went to priuatt praier and, after publeck, so to bed/

The :5: *day*

After priuat praers I went about and then was busie about a dressinge for my selfe : after, I praied & went to diner, and then I walked abroad with Mr Hoby and was allmost all the after none in the feld with him :

---

[181] In her counselling, Lady Hoby merely sees herself as an instrument in God's purpose.

after, I Came home and finished that wch be fore I was a bout, and, after, went to priuat examenation and praier : emediatly after I went to bed and, when Mr Rhodes had praied with vs, I rested, beinge before not well

The :6:
After priuat praers I went about the house and did many thinges tell diner time : after, I was busie about presaruinge sweetmeat, then I wrett to Mother Rhodes, walked with my husband, and after returned to priuat praier and readinge of the testement : sonne after I went to supper, then to the lecture, and after to bed/

The :7: day
After a priuat Cold praier, for what sinne that Judgment was, I know, in christ is pardoned, I went about tell allmost dinner time : after, I kept Companie with some neighbours and then went to Harwicke farme[182] with Mr Hoby : after, I Came home and praied, and so went to supper : after, I hard publeck praers, took some accounts and, when I had wretten to my Mother, I praied and went to bed

the :8: day
After priuat praers I went about the house, reed of the testement, wrett some medetation that I had the day before, praied, and then dined : after, I was busie with diuers thinges tell the afternone, and then I went to Hardwicke wth Mr Hoby, wher we reed aboute the growndes : and, after I Came home, I praied a litle and went to supper : after, I talked a whill and hard publeck praers and so went to bed

The 9 day
After priuat praers I went about my stilling,[183] and thene returned to priuat praier before diner : after, I was busie with sweet meat and went about with my Husband, and reed of the bible, and after returned to priuat medetation and praier : after, I went to supper, then to the lecture : after, to publeck praers and, when I had praied priuatly, I went to bed

---

[182] Hardwick Farm, mentioned earlier, in Harwood Dale. The Hobys go there by coach.
[183] *stilling*, Lady Hoby refers later to distilling aqua vitae, which in her case may have been a distilled ale, a kind of whisky based on fermented grain (see 20 July 1601).

The lordes day :10:
After praier I reed and went to the church : after I Came home I was not
well, wch Continewed allmost all the day, so that I nether Could hear,
praie, writt, or medetate as I ought which, as IIudgement, I praie the
lord to inable me to make right vse of it, that so it may be remoued

The :11: day :
After praier I went about a whill, and then talked with a freind of mine
tell diner time ; after dinner I walked a litle abroad, and then wrett of
my sarmon book a whill, and then, vpon a speciall disorder of my mind
arisinge, though, I thank god, not restinge, I went to priuatt praier : after
that I went about the house and, after, praied priautly, and so went to
supper : then I hard publeck praers, and after priaed priuatly and so
went to bed :

The :12: day
After priuat praers I went about the house and was busie tell all most
diner time : then I praied : after, I was busie in my Garden, and writinge
to Mr Hoby : after, I talked with a kinsman of mine, and so went to priuat
praier and examenation : after, I went about and wrought, and hard Mr
Rhodes read, and praied with him, and so went to supper : after, I hard
publeck praers and, when I had talked a whill and hard Mr Rhodes read
2 chapters of the Testement, I went to priuat praers and so to bed

The 13: day of the moneth :
After priuat praier I went about the house, and, after, I praied againe,
and then went to diner : then after none I spent in walkinge, presaruing,
and workinge, and then Came to priuat examenation and praier : after, I
went to supper : then I talked a whill, and when the lecture was done, I
went to priuat praier and so to bed :

August 1600 14 *day*
After priuat praier I was busie, according to my Custome, tell allmost
diner time, and then I praied : after I diner I made an end of writinge my
sarmon, then I walked, Red, and wrought : after, I returned into my
Clositt and wrett and praied : then, souna after, I went to supper, then to
publeck praers, after to priut, and lastly to bed.

The :15: day
After priuat praier I went about the house and then wrett in my
testement : after, I praied and then dined : after, I wrought, hard Mr

Rhodes read, and then walked abroad into the feeldes : after, I Came home and went to priuat examenation and praier : after, I went to supper, then to the lecture : after, I sung a psalme with some of the saruants and, lastly, reed a chapter, praied, and so went to bed/

The :16: day
After priuat praier I was busie in my chamber tell allmost dinner time : then I praied againe : after, dined and then talked a whill with some that dined with me : after, I kept Companie with some that Came to me, and then I buseed my selfe about some huswiffrie, and then, after I had imparted a think to my mother, I went to priuat examention and praier : and, after, I went to supper, then to publeck praers, after to priuat and lastly to bed

The lordes day :17:
After priuat praier I reed a whill to my mother, and then went to the church : after I Came home I praied and dined : then I talked and reed to some good wiues that dined wth me : after, I went to the church wher, after Catizising and sermon, I walked into the feeldes, and after Came home to priuat examenation and praier : then I went to supper, after to the exercise, and, when I had taken order for some busenes, I went to bed

The :18:
After priuat praier I reed to Hardwick with my Mother : then I Came home, and, when I had praied, I dined : after diner I went to linton with hir, and then I praied and went to supper : after, I I went to bed

The :19:
After I had praied I walked abroad with my Mother : then I Came home and praied : after, dined : in the after none I wrett a perticuler of some thinges touchinge linton, then I kept Companie with Mr Hoby tell praier time, at what time I went to examenation and priuat praier : after, I went to supper and lastly to bed

The :20:
After priaut praier I brak my fast and then took Horsse and Came Home to Hacknes, wher I praied and then dined : after, I went about the house and, at 8 a cloke, I went to priuat examenation and praier, after to supper, then to the lecture, and, after I had praied, I went to bed

August. 1600: *The* :21: *day*

After priuat praier I was busie about the house and wrough, and then, after praier, I went to diner : then I was busie tell a gentlewoman Came, with whome I kept Companie tell praier time, and then, after that, I went to supper : then I went to praiers, after to priuat praier, and lastly to bed

The :22: *day* :

After priuat praers I went about, and was busie about sweetmeat and wrett in my testement : after, I was Called to diner : then I talked wth Mrs ward, and after went downe amonge my Maides and, at the time of praier, I returned to priuat examenation, praier, and reading : after, I went to supper, then to the lecture and, when I had praied, I went to bed

The :23:

when I had praied I wrett notes in my testement, and, after, I went about the house, wrett :2: letters, praied, and then dined : after, I wrough, and talked with my maides of good thinges &, at praier time, I returned to priuat examenation and praier : after, I supped, then I went to publeck praers, and, when I had talked a whill, I went to priuat praers and so to bed

The lordes day :24:

After priuat praier I reed, did eate my breakfast, and then went to the church : after I Came home I praied and then dined : after, I talked of the sarmon, and reed to the good wiues that was with me, and then I praied and againe went to the church : after, I reed, wrett diuers notes, and, when I had talked a whill with Iurden of good thinges, I went to priuat praier and examenation : then I went to supper, after to the repeticion, and, lastly, to priuat prairs and so to bed.

The 25 day

After priuat praier I went to workinge some fringe:[184] then I went about the house, and, after I hard reed of the bible and praied, I went to diner :

---

[184] *fringe*, this may have been for Lady Hoby's dress or furnishings. In Elizabeth's reign fringed and embroidered petticoats were fashionable. Some were content with a single row of fringe at the bottom of a garment; others preferred as many as five or six rows. Fringe was also much used for the ornamentation of gloves. See Planche, *A Cyclopaedia of Costume* (1879). A 'green Pulpit cloth wth A Silk fringe' is listed amongst the 'Benefits In the Church' in the catalogue of Hackness church library (1702), f. 135.

after I went to work, and, when I had gone about diuers thinges, I returned to priuat examenation, hauinge good quiatt of Conscience and rest of the spiritt, the lord Continewe it to his glorie amen/ after I went to supper & then to bed, beinge verie heauie

The 26:
After priuat praier I did worke some thinge, and, after, praied and medetated often : some thinge I did eate, and then did reed, and made prouision for som strangers that Came:[185] after I went to priuat examenation and praier, then I went to priuat, supper, and after to bed

The 27:
After I was readie I spake with Mr Ewrie, who was so drunke that I sone made an end of that I had no reasen to stay for : and, after, praied, brake my fast, praied, and then dined : after, I was busie about the house and then I went to priaut examenation and praier : after, I went to supper, and, when I had praied, I went to bed

The :28:
After I had praied I went about the house and walked wth Mr Hoby : after, I praied, and so I dined and bestowed the after none in goinge about and takinge order for the entertaining strangers, and so went to priuat praier and examenation : after, I went to supper : then, hauinge talked with Mr Hoby about the abuse offered by Mr Ewere and his Companie,[186] I went to priuat praier and so to bed.

The :39:[187]
After priuat praers I went about some busenes, and after, when I had praied and reed of the bible, I dined : after, I was likewaise busie prouidinge for some strangers, and after I went to priuat examenation and praier : after, I went to supper, then to priuat praiers, and so to bed.

---

[185] The strangers are young William Eure and his rowdy hunting party. This is when the Eure affair begins, leading eventually to the lawsuit in the Star Chamber. See Introduction and Appendix 2.
[186] The Hobys have been much affected by the behaviour of the unwelcome hunting party.
[187] Lady Hoby had written 30, then changed it incorrectly to 39.

The :30: day

After priuat praers I went about the house, and, both before diner and after tell allmost night, I was busie prouidinge for such strangers as Came to me with Mr Rhodes and his wiffe, and then I went to priuat examenation and praier : after, I went to supper, then to publeck praers and then to priuat, and so to bed.

The 31: day The lordes day

After priuat praier I did eate and then went to the church : after I Came hom I praied, then I went to diner : after, I talked with my Cosine Bouser : after, I went to the church and then I walke abroad : after, I talked with Mrs Maude, and, after I had taken order for some thinges in the house, I went to priuat examenation and praier : after, to supper, then to publeck praers and then to priuat, and so to bed.

The 1

After priuat praers I went to my Cosine boschier, and, before diner, I praied : after, I kept Companie with the strangers tell all most night, and then I went to priuat examenation and praied, and after I reed and so went to supper : after, I hard the lecture and then, takinge my leaue of the gentlewemen, I went to priuat praier and so to bed.

The :2: day

After I had praied I went about and put some thinges in order which had benne vsed before : then I wrett in my sarmon booke : after, I praied and then went to diner : after, I tooke my Cotch and went abroad, and, soune after I Cam home, I went to priuat examenation and praier : after, to supper, then to the lecture and, after priuat praers, to bed.

The :3: day

After priuat praers I wrett in my sarmon book : then I did eate my breakfast, and wrought tell allmost diner time : then I praied and dined : after, I was busie in my chamber tell I tooke my leaue of som that Came to me, and, after, I hard a good booke reed by Mr Vrpeth, and sonne after I went to supper : after, to the lecture and then to priuat praers and so to bed/

September 1600: :4:

After priuat praers I tooke order for some thinges before my goinge to linton : after, I praied and dined : then I went to linton, and, when I had praied, I went to supper, after to publeck praers and so to bed

The 5:[188]

After priuat praers I reed of the bible, talked wth some of my freindes, praied, and then went to diner : after I walked into the feeldes with my Mother and others : after I Came home I hard Mr Ardington Read of Grenhame vnto me, and then I talked a whill with Mr Rhodes, and then went to priuat praier : after, to supper, then to publeck praers and lastly to bed

The 6:

After priuatt praers I went to break fast and then, hauinge talked wth my mother and diuerse freindes, I came to Hacknes, and there I talked with Mr Rhodes a whill: I went to examenation and praier : after, to supper, then to publecke praers and lastly to priuat, and so to bed

The lordes day the 7:

After priuat praier I reed of Mr Ardingtons booke, then did eate my breakfast : after, went to the church and from thence : I praied and so dined : after, I went to the Catizisinge, and, when the sarmon was don, I Came in and hard Mr Ardington Read a sarmon : after, I went to priuat examenation and praier : then I walked with him and Mr Rhodes tell supper time : after supper I hard the publeck exercise and then I wrett to my Mother, praied, and so went to bed :

The 8 *day*

After priuat praier I went about the house and then then reed and wrought tell diner time : after I had dined I talked with such companie as was with me, and then I hard Mr Ardington read a sarmon and talked with hime tell allmost night, and then I went to priuat examenation and praier : then I wrett some notes of the knowledg of the word of god : after, I went to supper, then to the publecke exercises : after, I went to priuat praier and so to bed/

The :9: *day*

After priuat praier I went about the house, then I wrett in my sermon book : after, I walked, then praied and dined : after diner I walke abroad and, when I Came home, I went about the house and then

---

[188] Sir Thomas is at Linton. It is today, 5 September, that he writes letters to Sir Robert Cecil and to the Privy Council about the disturbance on 26 August. See Appendix 2 (I).

praied : after, went to supper : then I hard publecke praers, and, after I had beden all my freindes good night, I went to priuat praers and so to bed/

The :10: day

After priuat praier I wrett out my sermon : then I wrett to my Husband:[189] then I talked, tell Diner time, with the Gentlemen and wemen that were with me, and, after Diner, I went about the house, wrett 2. Letters, hard Mr Rhodes read a sarmon, then walked with Mr Ardington, and after Came to priuat examenation and praier : after, I went to supper, then to publecke praiers, and, after, to priuatt and so to bed.

The :11: day

After priuatt praier I went about the house and then wrett notes in my bible : after, I praied, wrought, and went to diner : after, I walked a whill : then I went to worke and hard readinge, and, after, I went to priuatt praier, and examenation : after, to supper, then to the lecture, and, after a whill, I tooke my leaue of the Companie and went to priuat praier and to writinge some thinges I had hard : and so to bed

The :12: day

After priuatt praier I writt a whill notes in my testement, and then I walked : after, I praied and then dined : after diner I went abroad and, when I sawe Mr Hoby Come home, I talked with him and went about the house all the after none tell I went to priuatt praier and examenation : after, to supper : then I went to the publecke exercises and, after priuatt praers, to bed

The :13: day

After priuat praier I went about the house and then wrought : after, I reed and praied and so dined : after dinner I wrought a time, then walked abroad, and, after, I went to my busenes about the house, and so to priuat examenation and praier after, to supper, then to the lecture and after to bed

---

[189] Sir Thomas has gone to York in preparation for the hearing of the lawsuit before the Council of the North at the King's Manor. Lady Hoby joins him on 23 September.

The lordes day :14:
After priuat praier I went to the Church when I had reed and eaten somethinge : after I Came from thence I praied : then I dined, and then, tell church time a gaine, I talked wth Mr Genkines, and, after the sarmon, I wrett some notes in my Comune place book : and when I had reed a whill, I went to priuat examenation and praier : after, to supper, then to praers, and, when I had praied priuatly, I went to bed

The :15: *day*
After priuat praers, I wrett in my testement, and then I went about the house and wrought tell dinner time : after, I wrought and hard Mr Genking Read tell 4 a cloke : then I went about the house and, after, praied : then supped, and, after, I went to the lecture, and after I went to priuat praers and so to bed.

The :16: *day*
After priuat praers I walked abroad : after, I praied, wrett notes in my testement, then dined : after, I reed abroad, and, att night, after I had talked a whill with Mr Genkinge, I went to priuat praier : then to supper : after, I hard publecke praiers and so to bed

The :17: *day*
After priuat praier I went about the house and wrought tell all most diner time : then I praied : after I dined, I wrought, walked and reed tell allmost night, and then I went to priuat praier and so to supper : after, I talked awhill and then went to priuat praier and so to bed

The :18: *day*
After priuatt praier I wrett notes in my testement : after, I reed, praied, was busie about waxe lightes, and then I dined : after, I finished them and went about the house, and gaue a poore woman of Caton saulue[190] for hir arme : after, I walked and then went to priuat examenation & praier : after, to the lecture and lastly to bed

September 1600: *The* :19: *day*
After priuat praier I wrett my sarmon : then I went about the house : after, I praied and then I went to diner : after, I was busie about thinges

---

[190] *Saulue*, salve, or ointment.

that I Caried to Yorke, and, after I had reed a whill, I went to priuat examenation and praier : then to supper : after, to publeck praiers : after, I was busie a whill and then, when I had praied priuately, I went to bed

The lordes euen :20:
After priuat praers I went about the house, and talked with Mr Rhodes : then I was busie sortinge diuers thinges : after, I praied and then dined : then I was busie in the kitchine allmost all the after none, and then I reed of the bible, and so went to priuat examenation and praier : after, I went to supper, then to publecke praers and so to bed

The lordes day :21:
this day, and all the night allmost, I had greate paine of the tothache and was so ill that I Could not goe to the publecke exercises, but Mr Hoby reed in the morninge to me and praied with me, and, in the afternone, Mr Rhodes related vnto me what what[191] saied at the Church, and, after supper, praied with : and so, I thank god, I had good rest

The :22: *day*
this morninge, I beinge better, I praied and made me readie for my Iurnie : after breakfast I came to linton wher I went to bed, and, after, Mr Rhodes praied in my Chamber

The :23: *day*
Aft I was readie I praied and brake my fast, and so Came to York, when, after I had praied, I went to supper : and sonne after I hard publeck praers, and so went to bed

The 24. *day*
After I had praied I tooke some Gentle phesicke, which wrought verie well so that I kept my Chamber, and was vesited by S^{ir} Tho: farfax, my Cossine Stanope, and Mr Genkins

The 25: *day*
After I was readie I was glad to lye down againe, beinge weake, and was

---

[191]   *what*, was.

vesited by my lord of limbrecke[192] and his wiffe, Mr Gatt, Mr lister, and Mr Genkins

The .26: day
After I was readie and had praied, I went to dinner with Mr Genkins, his wife, and mother in law, that Came to se me, and kept Companie with them allmost all the after none : at which time, when they departed, I went to praier and after to supper, and then to bed

The :27: day
this day I Continewed my orderarie exercises of praier and readinge, and was veseted by Mr Frances Elzelie, and, at night, with Petter Corowe and his wiffe, with whom I had Good talke : and so, after supper, went to bed

The lordes day :28:
this day I went to the Church but Came from thence with litle frute, and, in the after none, I was veseted by Mrs Hilliard: and, after my priuat exercise, I went to supper and so to bed/

The :29: day:
After priuat praers I talked a whill with Mr lister, and walked abroad and did se his lodginges : after, praied, dined, and kept in with Mr Hoby, who took phesicke, and was Vesited by Mrs Thornborow, Mrs Blackcollor, and other: after, I praied and went to supper, hauinge Mr Lister and Mr Genkins, and after went to bed/

The :23: day[193]
After priuat praers I talked a whill with Mr Lister of some of my greues:[194] after, I praied and dined and wrought the after none, and

---

[192]   John Thornborough (1551–1641), Dean of York, Bishop of Limerick (1593) and later Bishop of Bristol. His duties elsewhere meant that he was not a particularly active Dean at York. Lady Hoby is a close friend of his second wife.

[193]   30 September.

[194]   *greues*, griefs. Lady Hoby may be referring to her humiliation occasioned by the hunting party, but she is here talking in confidence with her physician. This could, therefore, possibly concern the physical 'grief' of not bearing children. Spiritual matters would have been shared with her cleric. Gerard makes recommendations for the barren by suggesting the use of the 'balme apple' or 'apple of Jerusalem' – unfortunately, as he notes, a stranger to England and therefore grown with difficulty. Also see entry for 7 October 1603.

walked towardes night : and then I was, by my lord of limbreck, invited to his house wher we had a great supper : after which, I Came home and went to bed, hauing talked a whill with Mr lister

October 1600 *The* :1: *day*
After I was readie I praied with Mr Rhodes, then went to breakfast : and so took my Cotch and Came to linton, wher, after supper and publeck praers, I went to bed.

The :2: *day*
After priuat praers I veseted my Mother who, beinge better then she was, I went to breakfast : and so Came to Hacknes wher, after I had praied, I went to supper and then, after publeck praers, beinge not Verie well, I went to bed

The :3: *day*
After priuat praers I went to work and talked with Mrs Brutnell : after, I praied and then dined : the after none I walke and wrought, talkinge with Mr Hoby of our buesenes,[195] and gone a litle about the house : I went to priuat examenation and praier : after, to supper, then to publecke praers and so to bed, after some accountes were taken

The 4 *day*
After priuat praier I took accountes, did reead of the bible, praied, and walked, and so dined : after, I dippatched diuers thinges, and after talked with Mr Rhodes : then I took a note of such thinges as are in my Clositte, and then I went to priuat praier and examenation : after, I went to supper, then to the publecke exercise, and after I praied priuatly and so went to bed.

The lordes day :5:
After priuat praier and readinge a whill I went to the church : after the sarmon and sacrementes, I Came home and praied, then dined : after, I talked wth some of my neighbours and then reed againe, wrett some notes in my testement, and, after, I went againe to the church : then I reed a whill and walked a broad and, after, went to priuat examenation and praier : then to supper : after, to the publeck exercise and, after a litle talke and praier, to bed

---

[195]   Almost certainly the lawsuit.

The :6: day

After priuatt praers I took a medesone, and then I wrough, and praied : after diner I was busie receiuinge rentes,[196] and, at night, I went to priuat examenation and praier : I supper, then I went to publecke praers and so to bed, beinge not well

The 7 : day

After priuat praers I dispatched some busenes towardes my Journnie:[197] then I praied and so went to diner : after, I wrett a letter and then I walked abroad : after, I Came home and praied with Mr Rhodes, and medetated a whill, and then I praied and went to supper : after supper I hard the lecture, then sunge a psa : and, when I had praied, I went to bed.

The 8 day

All but the times of my orderarie exercises of praier and readinge I was busie takinge order for my going to london, and packinge of thinges[198]

The: :9: day

After praier and breakfast I Came to linton, wher, after I had praied and supped, I went to bed

The :10: day

After praied and a litle meat, I went to barton, wher I staied at Mr Smithes howse[199] tell the bote was made readie : all the speach ther was to so litle purpose that it is not worth remembringe : from thence to barton[200] wher I was so ill that, after I had praied, I went to bed

---

[196] Lady Hoby mentioned doing her accounts on Friday last, and today she is receiving the new month's rental payments from her tenants before her departure for London.

[197] The lawsuit is to go before the Privy Council of the Star Chamber. Her journey to London is indicated on a Road Roll, a form of diagram used in England for the first time in the road books of the period. See Road Roll (October 1600–March 1601) (see p. 117).

[198] The Elizabethans travelled with many of their necessities. Lady Hoby refers later to all the plate that is safely returned. She writes of possessions and purchases dispatched from London by water, coming in at Hull.

[199] Master Smith lives at Cottingham. He and Sir Thomas sit together on commissions for the Council of the North.

[200] Barton is on the Humber estuary which was crossed by ferry from Hull. The former discomforts of the Humber crossing were only recently alleviated by the construction of the great Humber Bridge.

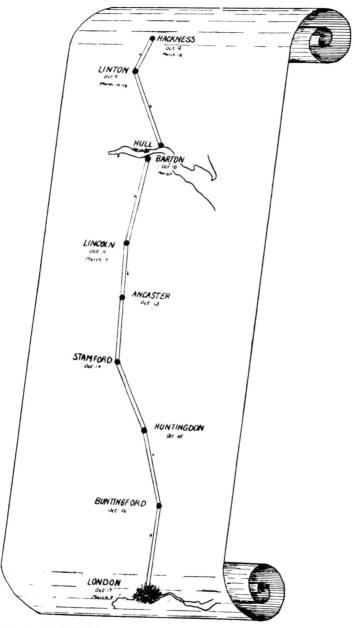

Road roll showing Lady Hoby's journey to London, October 1600–March 1601.

The Private Life of an Elizabethan Lady

The :11: *day*
After I had praied I brake my fast and Came to Mrs Girlingtons,[201] a litle from Lincon, wher I staied all the lordes day and hard 2 sarmons, beinge veri kindly entertained : after supper I wrett to Mr Rhodes and then, hauinge praied, I went to bed

The :13: *day*
After praier I brake my fast and, from thence, Came to Anchester, beinge brought on my way by yonge Mr Theckston and my Cosine Isones, and his wiffe : after I Came to my lodginge, I praied, went to supper and, when I had given god thankes, I went to bed

The :14: *day*
After I had praied and broke my fast, I went to Stamford wher I mett with my Cossine, Arthure Dakins : and, because I was not well hauinge my face swolen with a rume, I sone went to bed

The :15: *day*
From thence I Came to Huntingdon wher I was better, I thanke god

The :16: *day*
from thence I went to buntingeford, and their I was, in the morninge, verie ill so that I did eate no meat

The :17: *day*
from thence I tooke my Iurnie to London wher, in the way, I was tould that order was giuen to fetch all the stuffe from york, and and to giue ouer that house ther, vpon which and about we had laied forth 18^{li} , which newes did much touch me, so that I procured Contrarie directions forth with:[202] after I Came to london I praied, and was viseted with all my Cosine Cookes:[203] then I praied after supper and went to bed, wher I was more meanly lodged, with so great Cost, then to my remembrance I was euer in my Life :[204] and yet I was Glad of my brothers house[205]

---

[201]   The Girlington family were connected with Lady Hoby's cousins, the Isons.
[202]   Maybe this was the house the Hobys looked at in York in September 1599.
[203]   The Cookes, Sir Thomas' cousins, children of his late uncle, William Cooke. They lived in the parish of St Martin-in-the-Fields. Lady Hoby will see much of these cousins during her stay in London.
[204]   London is expensive for Lady Hoby.
[205]   The house of Sir Thomas's older brother, Sir Edward Hoby (1560–1617). His main home was at Bisham. Lady Hoby has before her a formidable programme of visiting and being visited.

The :18: day

After I was readie, I wrett by our men to Mr Rhodes then:[206] and then I praied, and talked with my Cosine Cooke that cam to me : after, I praied and dined : after diner I looked vpon accountes and wrought some worke : and then I, at night, I praied and so, after supper, hauinge provided for the next day, I praied and went to bed

The lordes day :19:

After prairs I went to Mr Egertons[207] sermon, and after Came to my lady Russils to Diner : after, I went againe to his exercise and thence home to my lodginge, wher I wrett some of his notes in my testement : and, after supper and praers, I went to bed

The :20: day

After priuat praier I reed of the bible, and then I wrought tell allmost diner time : after, I praied : then I dined : after diner I went to work againe tell my Cosine Cookes Came in : after them, I was vesited by my old aunte Cooke,[208] and, after she was departed I went to priuat praier and examenation

The :21: day

After priuat praers I brake my fast and then I wrought tell allmost diner time: then I praied, and went to diner : after diner I went abroad to vesitt my lady burley and my lady Russill, so that it was allmost night before my Cominge home : after, I praied and went to supper, and, after I had had talked a whill wth Mr Hoby of our beusnes,[209] I praied and so went to bed.

The :22: day

After priuatt praier I went to worke tell diner time : after, I wrought and reed, and was accompened with Mr Edward Gatt and after with

---

[206]   The servants who have brought Lady Hoby to London will now return to Hackness with messages and purchases. Jurden stays on to assist her.
[207]   Stephen Egerton (1550?–1622), Puritan divine; suspended for refusing to subscribe Whitgift's article (1584); imprisoned (1590); minister of St Anne's, Blackfriars (1598–*c.* 1621); introduced petition to the lower house of convocation for a reformed prayer book (1604); published sermons. Lady Hoby's mother-in-law, Lady Russell, lived in the Blackfriars and attended his church.
[208]   Frances Cooke, mother of the cousins mentioned earlier.
[209]   Probably the lawsuit.

Mistress Mari. Gatt : then I praied and then went to supper : after, I talked with Mr Hoby and when I had praied I went to bed.

The :23: *day*
After priuat praier I brake my fast and wroug, reed of the bible, and then praied and dined : after, I wrought, and then I was accompaned with my lady Graye and my Cosine Cooke that Came to vesitt me : after, I took som accounts and so went to priuatt praier and examenation : after, to supper : then I praied and so to bed

The 24: *day*
After priuat praier I talked with my Cosine baCon[210] that Came to se me : then I praied, reed of the bible, and went to diner : after, I wrought tell allmost night, and then I went about and sawe some prouision of wood laied in : and, after I had reed and praied, I went to supper, and then I talked a whill and praied, and so went to bed

The 25: *day*
After priuat praier I went to my booke, and after I dined : then I wrought, and was accompaned allmost all the after none wth Mr Smith and Mr Bell : after, I tooke order for supper and then I went to priuatt examenation and praier : after, I went to supper and then, hauinge praied, I went to bed

The 26: *day the lordes day*
After praier I went to wesminster Church and ther I hard Mr Graunt preach : after, I Came home and went to diner : after, I went by water to the blake friers and hard Mr Egerton : after, I saw my lady Russill and, when I was Come home, I praied, went to supper, and so went to bed/

The .27:
this day, after praier, I went to my lord Burles : and at night I praied and went to bed

---

[210] Lady Hoby refers to the family of the late Sir Nicholas Bacon (1509–79), Lord Keeper under Queen Elizabeth. His widow was Sir Thomas' aunt, Anne, one of the Cooke sisters. Their younger son was Francis Bacon, philosopher and statesman.

The :28: day : Simon & Jude

After priuat praers I went to the minster[211] and hard one Mr Smith preach, wher I hard, to my knowledge, nothinge worth the notinge, but that Aba father[212] was to note out that both Iewe and gentle should Call god father : after I Came home, I dined and was all the after none with in, and busied my selfe in my chamber, writinge some notes of sermons which I purposse to send Mr Rhodes : after, I talked with Mr Vrpith, and then praied and went to supper : after supper I was busie a whill, and then I praied and so went to bed/

The 29 day :

the lord Maire
is chosen att
London/

After priuat praers I went to my booke, and wrett a letter to Mr Rhodes : then I dined : and after I came home, allmost at 4 a cloke : then I went to priuat exaenation and praier, and after I went to my booke : then to supper : after, to priuat praier and so to bed

The :day:

After priuat praers I reed, and talked with Mr Vrpith : after, I dined and then buiseed my selfe/in my chamber tell supper time : and then, after priuat praier, I went to supper and lastly to bed

The :31: day

there dined with
vs Mr Beston and
Mr Vrpeth

After praier I wrought, and dined, and spent the after none in busenes in my Chamber : after, I praied and so went to bed

The first of Nouember

this day, the next day beinge the lordes day, the :3:4:5:6: daies, I was verie ill and weake with the toothache : the :7: day I was some thinge better, and so performed my exercises and dispatched Iurden fro hence with some letters: &, after I had praied and supper, I went to bed/

The 8: day

After priuat praiers I went to readinge : then I was busie tell diner time :

---

211 Westminster Abbey. Lady Hoby called it a church on 26 October. See p. 122.
212 This is unclear. Possibly 'a believer'?

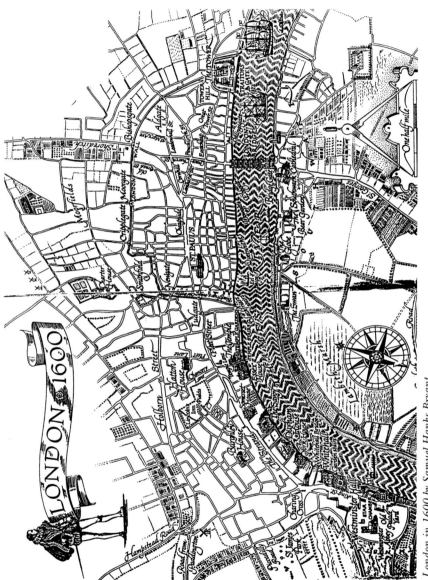

London in 1600 by Samuel Hanks Bryant.

after, I walked to wesminster hall : then I returned home, and reed, and after I was Veseted by my brother:[213] after, I went to priuat praier, and so to supper : then I praied and so to bed

The lordes day :9:
After I was readie I went to my Cosine william Cookes, and, from thence, we went to his parishe church : after I had hard the sarmon, I Came to his house, and their I praied priuatly : after I had Dined I went to my old aunte Cookes, and from thence by water home,[214] wher I praied, and then went to supper, and so to bed

The :10: day
After I had praied I was Veseted by Mr Vrpith, by whom I wrett into Yorkshere : Mr Coniers of Scarborow, Mistress Mary Gate, who went weth me to my olde Aunte Cookes house to Diner : from thence I Came home, and then I reed a sarmon, and so, hauinge praied, went to supper : and, after that & praier, to bed.

The :11: day
After priuat praier I went about and reed of the bible : after, I helped my mother to washe some fine linan, my Maide france beinge not able:[215] after, I strung som pearles, and then went to Cast vp som accountes that Concerned my beinge at Malton : and so, sonne after, tooke order for supper, and then went to priuat examenation and praier : after, to supper & then to bed

The :12: day
After I was readie I was busie to make some readie for Sir Edward Hoby, Mr Docter perkins, and Docter lister,[216] that came to vs to dinner : and so, hauinge praied I went to Dinner : after, I was busie about some linan, and at night I praied and so went to supper : then I went to Read a whill and, when I had praied, I went to bed

---

[213] Sir Edward Hoby, brother-in-law.
[214] The River Thames was a busy thoroughfare, used by many Londoners.
[215] Lady Hoby later writes for her maid Annie France to join her. Sir Thomas will dismiss Annie from service on 1 July 1605.
[216] Doctor Lister is the brother of Lady Hoby's physician (see 19 January 1600).

The :13: day
After praiers I went to diner : after, I went to a standinge to see the quene Come to London, were I Reed a serome:[217] after, I Came home : beinge not well, I went to supper and so to bed

The :14: day
After I had praied I went to Mr Deans Garden, with my Mother, to walke : and, at my Cominge home, I saluted my Cosine Robert Dakins, who Came about the buying of Linton:[218] then I helped to dress a litle meate that was made in my chamber, and after I had dined I reed of the bible, and so went to walke with my Mother in the house : after, I praied and supped, and then went to praier and so to bed

The :15: day
After I had praied I helped to prouide some thinge in my Chamber, and, after I had praied, I went to diner : and after I talked with Mr Godfrie Rhodes,[219] that dined with vs, of the Lawfullnes of huntinge in it selfe : after, I went to worke, and read, and so, when I had praied and supped, I went to bed

The :16: day the lordes day
After I had praied I went to the minstr, and, after the sermon, I Came home & praied and diner : after dinner I went, by water, to the friers to Mr. Egertons sarmon, and from thence to my Lady Russils : when I had seene hir I Came home to my brothers house, and their, after I had praied, I went to writ some notes collected in my testement : then I went to supper : after, I praied and so went to bed/

The :17: day
After I was readie I went to the blac friars and hard Mr Egerton preach : after, I dined with my lady Russell : then I Came home, and was busie in my chamber tell I went to examenation and praier : after, I went to supper and, sonne after, to bed

---

217 *serome*, sermon.
218 It is therefore confirmed that the Linton property will stay in the Dakins family.
219 Godfrey Rhodes lived at Great Houghton, Yorkshire, eldest son of the late Francis Rhodes, a Justice of the Common Pleas, knighted in 1615.

November, 1600 *The* 18 *day*

After priuat praier I helped my Mother with some linans : after, I dined :
then I was busie fouldinge and Airinge clothes tell all most night : then I
praied, and supped, and then, after A whill, went to bed

The : 19 *day*

After praiers I was busie in my chamber ; then I praied, accordinge to
Custome, and went to diner : after, I reed and wrought and was Vesited by
my brother, and, after I had praied and suped, I reed and so went to bed

The 20 : *day*

After priuat praier I went about some busenes, and then dined : after, I
wrette to Mr Rhodes, and reed of the bible : and then I went to priuat
praier and so to supper : after, to priuat praier and then to bed

The : 21 : *day*

After I was readie I went to the minster to the lecture, and then I Came
home and praied, and so went to diner : after I was busied in my
Chamber tell praier time, and then I praied, and so went to supper :
after, to praiers and so to bed

The : 22 : *day*

After praiers, I reed and dined : after, I bought a litle spininge whell, and
spanne of that tell prairs time : after, I went to supper and so to bed.

The lordes day : 23:

In the morninge I went to wesminster, and after Cam home and diner :
and so kept in all that day, it being so stormy I Could not goe by water
to the friers

The :24:

After I was readie I was veseted by Mr thickston : after he was gone I
praied, then dined, and my Cosine bouchier with vs : after, I pesused
some papers, and wrett to Mr Fenton for Annie france, and after, I wrett
alitle to Mr Rhodes, and so went to spininge ; after, I was veseted by my
brother, Sir Edward Hoby, and after his departure I went to priuat
examenation and praier : after, to supper and to bed

The :25.

when I had praied and repented for my slidinge, I talked with Mr
Ienkins, who brought me a letter from Mr lister: he staied dinner : the

talke we had was most of our bill,[220] and of his brothers matter with Mr beuerley : after diner Came Mr beuerley, with whom I talked a whill of itt : after they were gonn I buised my selfe in my chamber tell all most night, and then I went to priuat exemenation and praier

The 26: day
In the morninge Came my Cosine Dakins and offered his composition for linton : after I was readie I went to praier, and then talked with Mr Inkins, after, tell we went to diner : after, I begane to writt to Mr Rhodes, and then Mrs Thornborowe[221] Came, and with I had talke of litle purpose: after she was gone my Cossine bouser came, &, after he had tould me that the matter between Sir John Sauill and Mr Wortley was put over to the Comune Law, I went to priuat examenation and praier : after, I went to supper and, when I had praied, I went to bed

The :27: day:
this day and the next I went not forth, for I was not well, and was Vesited by Mr Genkins and my Cossine briges[222]

The :29: *day*
After I had praied I reed, and went to diner : In the afternone I was vesited by Mr Genkins, who tould me that young Goodericke, for his Drawinge of his Dager and strikinge one before the Readers, was fined /200^{li}/, expulsed the house, impresoned, bound to the Good behaviour, and inioyned to Confesse his fault and aske pardon in all the Courtes : and, furthermore, he tould vs orf the like punishment of an other that querled in the strett:[223] after he was gonn I went to priuat examenation and praier : after, to supper : and then I praied some after and so went to bed /

---

220 The lawsuit in the Star Chamber. Master Jenkins may be a lawyer.
221 Mistress Thornborough, wife of the Bishop of Limerick, is a regular companion during this London stay.
222 Elizabeth Bridges, daughter of Giles, third Lord Chandos. The Queen did not like the attention given to this lady by her favourite, the Earl of Essex.
223 In the light of William Eure's behaviour, Lady Hoby perhaps relishes hearing of the punishment of another young man for his unruly actions. Not unnaturally, legal matters are very much on her mind.

The lordes day :30:

After priuat praier I went to the minster, wher I hard a good sermon by one of the prebendes : after I was Come home and had dined, I went to the blake friers, from whence I returned home and sett downe in my testement the cheffe notes deliuered by Mr Egertone : and when I had praied I went to supper, and so, according to my Custome, I praied and went to bed.

December :1600: The : 1 day

After I was readie, and had praied and reed, I walked, sett my hand to a release to my Cossine Strangwaise of all the debtes and sutes that I might Clame any thinge from him, and so went to dinner : after Came yonge Mr Theckstone, and so I went to the minster to see the monementes: after, I walked and was veseted by my Cosine Cookes wiffe, and, after they were gone, I went to readinge and praier

The .2: day:

After priuat praier I reed, and walked to the Comune Garden : after dinner I was busie in my chamber, and was veseted by my Cosine bouchier : after, I performed my ordenarie exercises tell bed time

The :3:day

After praiers I reed, and wrett to Mr Rhodes, which I sent him by Mr Etheringtone: after, I dined and spent most of the after none wth Mr Genkins & Mr Hoby, walkinge abroad: and att night I went to priuat praier and exemanation

The :4: day

this day I obserued my ordenarie exercises and wrett to Mr lister : was veseted in the after none by Mr Iobe Throgmorton,[224] bought Mr Rodes plate, and so went to priuat praier

The :5: day

After praier I went about packinge of some stuff, and talked with my Cosine bouchier : after I had dined, I went to the Court to my sister Hoby:[225] and, after, I Came into the strand to my newe lodging : and, after, I went to super with my lord of linbrick

---

[224] Job Throckmorton (1545–1601), a Puritan controversialist; cousin of Francis Throckmorton, the conspirator, and related to Elizabeth, wife of Sir Walter Ralegh.
[225] Lady Hoby's sister-in-law.

The .6: day
this day I was veseted by Mr Iobe throgmorton, and at night my lord of limbrick and his wife supped with vs, she hauinge kept me Companie the after none at my lady bourles

The lordes day .7: day
In the morninge I went to Mr Docter websters lecture, and in the afternone to Mr Egertones, and, after I Came home, I wrete In my testementes notes of the sarmons

The :8: day
After praier I went to my lord bourleys, beinge invited thether : and, after I Came home, I paied Stephen Tewble 7^{li} that was owinge him, part of a greater som: and so, tell night, performed my orderarie exercises

The :9: day:
After praier I wrett to Mr Rhodes, and was, after dinner, visited with Mr Genkins, my cosine John Cooke, my Cosine bouchier, and Mr Gibsone the atturnie[226]

The :10: day
this morninge, after Mr Hoby had sent his letters by Mr Gibson, and I had praied, reed, wrought and dined, I was veseted in the afternone by Mrs Thornborowe, my Cosine william Cooke, Mr Roland whitt:[227] and, after they were gon, I went to priuat medetation and praier : after supper Came in Mr Genkins and, when I had praied, I went to bed

The :11: day
when I had praied I dined, and, sonne after, Went to my sistere Sidnes:[228] after, to my lady Russils: and when I Came home I went to priuat readinge and praier : after, Mr Genkins came to vs, and, after supper and he gome, I went to priuat praier and so to bed

---

[226] Master Gibson is perhaps the lawyer in charge of their case in the Star Chamber.
[227] Roland Witt is steward to Sir Robert Sidney, of Penshurst Place, Lady Hoby's brother-in-law by her second marriage. Master Witt is probably arranging tomorrow's visit.
[228] Barbara Gamage wife to Sir Robert Sidney, mother to the writer, Lady Mary Wroth, Lady Hoby's sister-in-law.

The :12 day

After praier I talked with Mr smith and /dimed : afterward I was vesited by my Cosine Sthnope, and, when he was gone I went to priuat praier and then to supper wth my lord of linbrick who Came to vs

The .13: day

After priuat praier I went to worke, and, after I had dined, I was vesited by my Cosine John Cooke : after, I busied myself in my Chamber and then went to priuatt readings and praier, and after went to the Busshoppe of limbrickes to supper, from whence, when I Came, I went to praier and so to bed

The lordes day :14:

After priuat praier I went to the church ; after, I Came hom and sett downe some notes : then dined : after, I went to Mr Egertons sermon and so, within litle time, I went to priuat readinge and praier, and setting down some notes I had Colected

The :15: day

After priuat praier I went to worke, and after to diner : in the afternone I was vesited by my Cosine Iohn Cooke, and, when he was gome, I went to priuat praier and readinge : after, Mr Mansfeld Came, and Mr Genkins, who suped with vs : and after supper Came in Mrs Thornboro, and, when they were all gone, I went to priuat praier

The :16: day

After priuat praier I went to worke and sonne after to diner : when I had dined, Mrs Thornborowe, my Mother, and my selfe, went in a Cotch in to the feeldes[229] and there walked : after I Came hom I rested me a whill, and then went to priuat examenation and praier : after supper I went againe to priuat praier and reading, and so to bed

The :17: day

After my praier and readinge I went in to the feeldes with Mistress Thornborow : after, I Came home and went to dinner : then I wrought tell it was allmost darke, and then Mrs Thornborowe came in, and, after

---

[229] Lady Hoby may refer to Lincoln's Inn Fields, or to the fields of Hampstead beyond. See map of the city of London. South of the river were houses backed by countryside, but most people crossed by ferry. London Bridge was barely wide enough for two carts.

she was gone, I went to priuat praier and readinge, and so to supper, hauinge Mr Genkins and Mr Iauson : and, after they were gone, I went to praier and so to bed

The 18: *day*
After praier I went a walkinge and my Mother : after I Came home and had praied and dined, I was vesited by Mistress Thornborow and Mistress Cotton : after, I wrought, and was visited by my brother Hoby : after, I was busie about the house, and receiuinge asute of blake satan[230] for Mr Hoby, and after went to priuat examenation and praier

The :19: *day*
After priuat praier and readinge I went to walke : after, I Came home and praied : then I dined and with vs my lord of limbrick and his wiffe : after, I went wth hir to hir howse, wher she made me a medeson : after, went to my lady Russils, and then I Came home and praied, and so went to supper and then to bed

The :20: *day*
After priuat praier and readinge I went to worke, and then to praier and so to diner : after, I talked wth Mr Betnam who dined wth vs, & then I went wth Mrs Thornborow to the exchang:[231] after I Came home and praied

The lordes day :21:
After praers I went to Mr websters sarmon : from thence to my lady Russils to diner: from thence, to the black friers and so home, wher I was vesited by my Cosine Iohn Cooke and Mrs Thornborow, who I left a whill, and went to priuat praier and examenation

---

[230] Black satin for the Puritan Sir Thomas would have been to wear at special functions. The use of satin, made from silken cloth, in the dress of the gentry led to its application as a generic term to persons of fashion. Its high price in the Middle Ages had led to its being worn only by noble and wealthy persons. Under Henry VIII the wearing of satin had been prohibited to all persons whose income was less than a certain amount.
[231] *exchang*, exchange, the commercial centre of London (see p. 131). Built (1566) by Sir Thomas Gresham (1519–79), it was originally called the Burse, until restyled the Royal Exchange by Queen Elizabeth I who opened it in 1572. Luxury goods were brought for sale, and there was money changing and the negotiation of loans. It was destroyed by the Great Fire in 1666, but later rebuilt.

The Inner Court of the first Royal Exchange.

The :22: day

The most of this day I was not well : we were accompaned at diner wth Mr Smith, and, in the after none, wth Mrs Thornborow : and after hir departinge I receiued letters from Hacknes by Tho: wray : and so, after, I went to priuat praier and reading. The 23.24:25 et 26 : daies I was not well of a great Colde, so that I kept my chamber and went not in to my clositt, and was visited by Mrs Thornborowe euerie day

The :27: day

I was somthinge better, but had so great a Cough that I Could not goe abroad, nor the next day goe to the church, but excercised my selfe at home in writinge, readinge and prainge, as well as I Could

The 29 day

After praier I reed ouer certaine papers of instruction wch I had receiued from Mr Rhodes : after, I dined, and, in the after none, I went abroad to walke : after I came home Mrs Thornborowe kept me Companie, and when she was gone I went to priuat praier : after I went to the busshope of limbrickes to supper

The :30: day

After priuat praiers I kept all this day with Mr Hoby, who was very far out of temper with a lousnes, fearing auguy:[232] at night I went to priuat praier and readinge : we were visited by Mrs Thornborowe, who dined with vs, and, in the after none, wth Mr Smith and Mr Dene

The .31: day

After priuat praier I was busie about Mr Hoby, and then went to dinner : after diner I went to the exchange to buy a new years guifte:[233] after I Came home, Mr Gatts Came visitt vs, and, when I had done some busines in my chamber, I went to priuat praier and examenation.

---

[232] *auguy*, ague was a stomach upset, followed by a violent fever, particularly marked by successive fits. Gerard recommends 'angelica roots': 'The decoction of the roote made in wine, is good against the colde shiverings of agues'. Thomas Tusser's 'good houswifelie Physicke', in *Five hundred pointes of good Husbandrie* (1580), offered the following:
> Good aqua composita, vinegar tart
> Rose water and treakle to comfort the hart,
> Cold herbs in hir garden for agues that burne
> That ouer strong heat to good temper may turne.

[233] It was customary to present the sovereign with a New Year's gift on 1 January.

1601

Ianuarie :1600: *The* :1: *day*

After prairs I kept Companie with Mr Smith that dined wth Vs, and, in the after none, Mr Hoby & I went to westminster : after, we Came home and then I, not beinge well, did sonne after supper goe to bed

The :2: *day*:

After priuatt praiers I went about, and did help to make readie diner : after, I was Vesited by Mr fuller and Mrs Thornborowe : after, I went to priuat examenation and praier, and so to supper

The :3: *day*

After priuat praier, wherein I praised god for the safe receite of some letters, I went about som busenes for Mr Hoby tell dinner tim : after, I spent it with him at my booke and at my work, he being not well, tell 5 a cloke, and then I went to priuat examenation and praier

The lordes day :4:

After priuat praier I went to the church : then to dinner : after, to Mr Egerton lecture, and from thence to my lady Russils : after I had talked priuatly with hir a whill, I Came home and, sonne after, went to priuatt prairs and medetation

The 5: *day*

this day I performed my ordenairie exercisede, and was vesited by my Lord Clinton, and suped with the busshope of limbricke at his lodginge

The 6: *day*

this day Mrs Thornborowe and hir Cosine dined with vs, and, in the after none, Mr Hoby, my Mother, and my selfe went to visitt some freindes who, beinge not at home, we retourned : & at my accustomed time I went to priuat praier and readinge

The 7: *day*:

After priuatt praers I went about, and, when I had dined, I went to my lady Russils, and there I hard of the solemnetie at Courte : after I went with my mother to se the glase house,[234] and from thence to vesitte my

---

[234] *glase house*, glass-works. Glass manufacture in London had been encouraged since the time of Henry VIII. The Venetian, Jacob Verzellini, had a glass-works in Broad Street, taken over by Jerome Bowes in 1592.

lady shurley : and I Came home and found Mr Gatts, and, when I had talked a whill with Mr Hoby, I went to priautt praier and examenation

The 8: *day*
in this time I was accompaned wth Mr Fuller

After priuatt praier I dined, and, sonne after, I went to walsingams house, wher I saw my lady Rich, my lady a Ruttland, and my lady walsingame:[235] after I Cam home I was pained in the toothach which Continewed with me 4 days after, in which time I exercised prainge & readinge as I was able, and tooke phisike of Doctor Lister, who, coming to se me the 4 day after my paine, beinge the .12: day of this moneth, tould me of my lady of Bedfords death[236] the night before, which was the Lordes day, who was well at the sarmon in the after none, and dead that night

The 13 *day*
After prairs And readinge I went to diner : after dinner I wrought, and was accompaned with Mrs Thornborow : after, I went to priuat praier and examenation

The :14: *day*
After priuat praier and readinge I went to worke, and brake my fast, and wrought tell diner time : after diner I went to work againe, and was accompaned with Mrs Thornborow, and, after, walked a whill, and then went to priuatt praier and examenation

The :15: *day*
After priuatt praier I went to readinge and worke tell diner, and after, tell some Companie Came in, Mrs Thornborowe and Mr Theckston : after, I walked a whill and then went to priuat examenation and praier

---

[235] Lady Walsingham, wife to the late Sir Francis Walsingham (c. 1530–90), Secretary of State to Queen Elizabeth I. Their daughter Frances, when married to Sir Philip Sidney, had a daughter, Elizabeth, the future Countess of Rutland. In 1590, Frances secretly married Robert, Earl of Essex, brother to Penelope Devereux, Lady Rich. Lady Hoby was therefore related, by her first two marriages, to all of these ladies. John Florio dedicated his translation of Montaigne's *Essays* (1603) to Lady Rich and the Countess of Rutland.
[236] Bridget, wife to the late Francis, Earl of Bedford.

The :16 day

this day I was vesited in the afternone wth fuller, wth whom I had good christian Conference, how[237] Expounded apsa:[238] vnto me, and tould me his praier was to god that, in the actions of god which he was to perform, none of his owne affections might be mingled

The :17: day

After priuat praier I went to my worke, and of that wrought tell I had made an ende after diner, beinge accompaned wth my brother and Mrs Thornborow : after, I went to priuatt praier and medetation

The Lordes day :18:

After priuatt praers I went to the Church, and then I came home and went to diner : after, I went to Mr Egertons sermons, and then went to se my Lady Russill, and so Came home : and, after a whill, went to priuat praier with Comfort, I thanke god, hauing preualed against mine enimie

The 19 day

After I had praier I went to keepe my Mother Companie, who was not well : then I wrought tell diner time : after I had dined I went againe to worke, and so Mr Doc: Lister Came in to me, who gaue me a letter from his brother, signifiyinge the death of Mistress Rhodes:[239] I wrett presently to Mr Rhodes and him, and, sone after, Mr Smith and Mistress Thornborowe Cam in, and tould vs of the execution, and when they were gonne I went to priuett praier and medetation/

Iaunarie .20: 1600:

After priuatt praier I went to worke : after, I praied and dined : after, I wrought againe tell all most night, and then I talked with my mother of good thinges, and so went to priuatt examenation and praier

The 21: day

After priuat praier I went to work, and at diner time Came in Mr Smith who, of his owne kindnes, brought vs /10[li]/: after dinner Came

---

237 *how*, who.

238 *apsa*, a psalm.

239 According to the Hackness Parish Register, Rebecca Rhodes, wife of Richard Rhodes, was buried at Hackness on 8 January 1601.

in my Cosine Iohn Cooke and Mistress Thornborow, and she gaue me a fann : and so, after they were all gone, I went to priuatt praier and medetation

The :22: day
After I had praied and wrought, and wrought a whill before diner, I after I went with Mr Hoby to my Lady a wossters,[240] with whom we sawe my Lady harbert : after, we went to Mr Anslowes, and thence to my lady Russils and so home, wher we found a letter from Mr Lister : after I had rested awhill, I went to priuat praier and medetation

The :23: day
After praiers I wrought tell diner : after, I wrought tell my Cosine Cooke Cane[241] and Mistress Thornborow : then I went with them and my Mother to my lord Burley : after I was Come home I receiued a measag from my Lady Russils, by the busshope of Limbricke, touchinge a house that she had Gotten for Vs : and, after, I was busie in my Chamber, and so went to priuat examenation and praier

The 24 day
this was a day of vesetation, in which I dined with my lady Russill, after went to the Courte to my Sister Hoby, then went to my Aunte Cooks : from thence to my lady Burley and so home, wher, after praier, I went to supper

The Lordes day 25
this day I hard Mr fuller preach at my lord Burleys, wher I dined, and, after diner, Came in Mr Ewry, so that we Came a way, rather giuinge place to him then our affections whic might haue bin prouoked :[242] after I Came home Mr Hoby rede to me a sarmon of Vdale,[243] and After I lay downe, being not well, when, after a litle sleepe, Mr fuller Came in, and he repeated to vs the substance of Mr Egerton Sarmon/

---

[240] *wossters*, the Countess of Worcester, mother-in-law to Ann, Lady Herbert, Sir Thomas's half-sister.
[241] *Cane*, came.
[242] The lawsuit is still in progress, so this would have been a potentially embarassing encounter.
[243] John Udall (1560?–92), a Puritan divine who published many sermons in his time (see 14 April 1602).

The 26 *day*

this day I, beinge not well, praied and reed in mine owne chamber, and had Mr Bettnam to diner : after I had talke with Mr Bettnam touchinge my Mothers assurance, and then, beinge agreed that he should drawe the bookes, Mistress Thornborowe Came in, and, after she was gonne, My Aunte Cooke wth hir sons and Daughters : after, I went to praiers and so to supper

from the :26: of Iaunarie vnto the :8: of feb: I remained weake, and so ill that I Could not goe out of my chamber : And, vupon the Lordes day in the morninge, begann the treason of the Earles of Esix, Suthhamton, and Rutland, with their assotiates, to appeare to the vewe of all that were not ouer partially blind :[244] from that day I remained sickly, but

this 19 day Came our Horsses to London from Shepie

not so ill, tell the :16: day, vpon which day was Captain Lea Arained, and, the day following, Executed for his intention to Murther the Quens Maiestie : the :19: day was the Earle of Suthhamtom and Esixe arained and Condemned : this day, I thank god, I was better then before, so that I Continewed my orderarie exercises in my Cchamber

The 20: day was 3 Arained and Condemned S^ir Edward Mr Iohn Litelton and Orill[245] whih was of the Consperisie

[244]   Having failed in his post as lieutenant and governor-general of Ireland (1599) Essex had provoked the queen's anger. He attempted to raise citizens of London in an abortive coup (8 Sept. 1600) and was proclaimed traitor (Feb. 1600/1). He was tried in Westminster Hall, sentenced to death (19 Feb.), and executed (25 Feb.). Lady Hoby was in London throughout the time of Essex's rebellion, but her references are guarded. As his sister-in-law by her first marriage, she may well have been much troubled in her heart and mind, and consequently in poor health. But she may also have believed that he was morally wrong. The whole sequence of events is barely referred to here, so maybe his conduct and bad judgement were too much even for this kind-hearted relative. There is also the possibility that his self-destructive act cleared the way for Sir Thomas Hoby's cousin, Sir Robert Cecil, to strengthen his position. He had taken over from his father, Lord Burghley, many affairs of state and was not only in good favour with Elizabeth but also in communication with James in Scotland. With Essex out of the way his future was assured.
[245]   Lady Hoby added the names later.

The 21: *day*

I was well recouered and kept Mr Betnam Companie, who dined with vs, and Mr Stillington : at night I praied and so went to bed

The Lordes day :22: day

this day was rainie so that I Could nor durst goe abroad but exersised in the house, with prainge and reading and singing psa:, and Conferinge : in the after none Came Mr fuller from Mr Egertons sarmon, and he deliuered vnto vs the some of what he had deliuered : after, I praied and supped, and so went to bed

The :23: day

After priuatt prairs I went to my worke, after I had reed of the bible : sonne after, to Dinner : then we went to packinge some thinges for the Contrie : after Came in Mr Iohn Mansfeeld, who treated with Mr Hoby and my selfe touching a priuatt agrement wth his Cosine Ewrie:[246] Mr Robert Stillington like wise Came to visitt vs : after all was gone I went to priuat praier, and, after, I went to supper, and after to bed

The :24: day

After prairs I went to work, and, hauinge reed a Litle, I talked with some that Came to Dine with vs, as Mr Betname, Mr Stillington, and Mr Smith : after diner I talked with Mr Betname, and after a whill, Cam in Mr Etherington, Mr Ienkins, and Mr Briges : after, I Concluded with Mr Betnam touchinge a recognesance, and so I went to priuat prairs : after, I bought a whell:[247] then Mr Yeardly Came in and after that Mr Smith, who staied supper

The :25: day

After priuat praiers I brake my fast and reed and sonne after Came in Mr Stillington and tould vs of the Death of the Late Earle of Esixe at the Tower : after, we went to diner, and, after, I wrett a letter to Mr Rhodes

The :26: day

After priuatt praers I reed of the bible, and then went to worke : after, I dined : after diner I wrought a whill, and after I talked with those that

---

[246] Pressure is put on the Hobys to settle their lawsuit out of court. They resist (also see 4 October 1601).
[247] This is the second spinning wheel to be bought in London (see 22 November 1600).

Came with my Cosine Dakins, and others Came in to se me : after, I went to priuat readinge and medetation

The 28: *day*
I went to the Court to se my Lady warwick, and the next day I went againe to se the Quene : and the Day followinge I trussed vpe our stuffe to be sent into the Cuntrie : the next day, beinge the 2 day of March, I tooke my Iournie towardes Yorkshire, and, the Lordes euen followinge, I Came to Mrs Terlingtons house, wher I staied the Lordes day : the day after I Came the water side, and the next morninge I, hauinge a faire tide, to Hull : I Came that night to Linton wher I, beinge sicke, staied there from the 10 to the :18: of March : and then I Came home to Hacknes[248] wher I remained very well vntell the 25, which night I was Verie sicke of a fitt, as I think of the stone,[249] and Collike, for one hower and an halfe : after which time, I praise god, I, hauinge ease, tooke good rest all the night after

March 1601: *The* 26: *day*:
this day I kept my chamber, and, as I was able, I wrought and reede and had Mr Ardington to read to me and Mr Rhodes : some time we sung psa: and, att my accustomed times, I went to priuat praier and medetation

The 27: *day*
After my accustomed prairs I did eate and read : after, I was busie tell dinner tim : then, after diner, I paied /10^li/ to Mr Lacie of Seamer, and Continewed to exercis my selfe in some beusenes tell praier, hauing Mr Rhodes and Mr Ardington to read to me : after, I went to supper and so to the Lecture : after, I went to bed well, I thank god

The Lordes euen 28: *day*
After prairs I was busie tell diner time : after, I talked with Mistress Bell who Came to offer me the saruice of one of hir Daughters : after, I hard Mr Ardington Read, and reed my selfe Catzisimie of the Lord supper,

---

[248] Lady Hoby left Hackness on 9 October 1600. She has been away over six months.
[249] *the stone*, the kidney or gall stone. Lady Hoby may have suffered from it, but her condition of temporary sickness and colic also sounds akin to stress or something disagreeable that she has eaten. Nevertheless, she suffers again in July 1601, for a couple of days at a time. See entries for 13 July ff.

and, preparinge my selfe by priaer and medetation, I sonne after went to supper

The 29: the lordes day

After priuat prairs I tooke leaue of Mr Ardington and Mr Netelton, and then, tell diner time, was busie packinge stuffe to send to Yorke : after I had dined I was busie in the kicthine, and, at my accustomed time, went to priuatt prairs and so to supper

The 30:

After priuatt praier I went downe and wrought with my maides : before diner I praied and read of the bible : after Diner I went downe againe, and was busie tell 4 a clock : then I wrought and hard Mr Rhodes read, and, after, I went to priuat medetation and praier

The 31:

After prairs I went about the house and wrought tell allmost Diner time : then I praied and reed, dined, and was busie tell all most night in the house : and then I went to priuat medetation and praier

The :1: day:

this day, for prainge, readinge, and workinge, I Continewed my ordenarie exercises, with much Comfort and peace of Conscience, I thanke god, hauinge Learned some thing from Mr Rhodes his readinge vnto me, as, first, that no Callinge is lawfull with out a growne[250] for itt in godes word : 2°, that the title of Lord Archbusshopes are Vnlawfull :3°, that no minister should be made without a minestrie and charge, vnto which he should be ordained

The 2: day

Hauinge my health, I thanke god, I Continewed my accustomed exercises

The 3 day

this day we were accompaned with Mr Crakeroffe att diner, and Iohn Dowson : Mr Hoby wrett Concerninge Mr Bankes, his dealinge by him, vnto the Counsill att Yorke, and, att night, I went to priuat praier and examenation/

---

[250]   *growne,* ground.

Aprill :4:
this day I performed my accustomed exercises, I praise god, and was allmost all the after none in the Garden Sowinge seed, whether Mr Busshill came to se vs : after, I returned in to my Chamber, and there reed and praied tell all most I went to supper

The lordes day :5:
Hauinge praied I brake my fast and then went to the church, wher, hauinge hard the sermon and receiued the Lordes supper, I returned home, and priuatly gaue thankes : the rest of the day, after the afternone sermon, I spent in readinge, singing, praing, and hearinge repeticions :

The 2 day of the week .6:
I, hauinge praied according to my Vse, I wrought in the house with my maides all the afternone, tell I went to priuatt medetation and praier

The 7: day
After prairs and readinge I kept Mr Gatt Companie : after Diner, I wrought and hard Mr Rhodes read, sent away besse Stafford : after, walked about with Hoby, and then returned to priuatt reading and praier

The 8: day:
After I had praied and that Mr Hoby was gone towardes Yorke I went about the howse, and then reed and wrought a whill before diner : after, I went wth my Maides in to the Garden, and, towardes night, I kept Mr Maude Compenie a whill : then I went to priuatt prairs and medetation and readinge/

The :9: day
thes day I Continewed my ordenarie exercises, I praise god, without sicknes or trouble : and so, like wise, the 10 and :11: day

The lordes euen 11: *day*
After priuat praiers I was busie in the Kitchine and garden tell diner time, and, after, tell Mr Hoby Came home : and after I had walked a litle abroad, I went to priuatt prairs and examenation

The Lordes day :12: *day*
This day, I praise god, I hard the exersices and receiued the sacramentes with much Comfort, and in health Continewed my Custom

The 2 *day of the weeke* 13: *day*

As, through corruption, we vse not the blessinge of peace as we ought, so are we to expecte new temptations to humble vs for our former necclegence, and so I haue benne, this day, boffeted for better heed[251]

The 3 *day of the weeke* :14:

After I had reed and praied I went about the house, made a saule for a sore beast, then I Came to worke into my chamber, and so went to diner : after, I walked a whill & spake to Iohn Dowson for Mault,[252] and so went to worke tell praier time

The 15 *day The* 16 *day*

These 2 daie I Continewed my accustomed exercises, and wrought most of a token I sent to London

The 17 *day*

This day blakeborn Cutt his foot with a hatchett[253]

The :18: *day*

this day I finished my worke, wrott Letters to London, talked with Mr Stillington, praied at my accustomed times, and dressed Tho Blakbornes foott : and, after, went to readinge and preparation for the next day

The Lordes day :19:

this day it pleased god to blesse my reading and medetation, and, in the afternone my heringe of Mr Vrpith : after, I Came home and Caused Mr Stillington to Read of Grenhame, and, after, I went to priuatt readinge and praier

---

[251] Such an entry where no mention is made of the day's activities is unusual.

[252] *Mault*, malt. To be prepared for brewing, the grain was dried on a malt-floor, steeped in water and fermented, then dried in a kiln. 'Soft fire makes sweet malt' was a contemporary admonition to be gentle or merciful.

[253] Lady Hoby tends this wound for more than a week. It obviously improves, for Thomas Blackbourn is dealing with the sale of sheep in a month's time (see 21 May). Gerard recommends clowns-all-heal for such a cut, and in *Damon The Mower* (1681) Marvell wrote:

> With shepherd's-purse, and clowns-all-heal,
> The blood I staunch, and wound I seal.

The 2 *day, of the weeke, the* 20:
this day my Mother Came to Hacknes, and staied the next day, which
was it when Mr Hoby tooke his iournie to London : att which time, I
thank god,

21: *day*
I Continewed my exercises in good health, and at night hard Iohn
Corrow praie :

The 22
my Mother went in the morninge betimes, and after she was gonne I
dressed vp my Closett, and was buseed about that all the day tell night,
at which time Iohn Corrow praied and reed publeckly : and, after I had
performed some priuat dutie, I tooke order for peters going to the
markett, and went to bed

The 23 *day*
Mistress Brutnell accompaned me at diner, and in the after none Mr
Rhodes Cam home, and his brother Edward, who brought me a booke
from his wiffe : after, I talked with Mr Coniers of Scarborow, who went
to London : and, after he was gone, I praied, and dressed Tho
Blackbourns Legg, and after went to readinge and medetation

Aprill The 24:
This day I performed my ordenarie exercises, and wrett to Mr Hoby by
Mr Coniers

The :25: *day*:
After praers and breakfast I went to church : when the sarmen was done
I praied, and dressed blackbourns Legge : after diner I went Diuerse
busenes about the house, and hard Mr Rhodes read, and after went to
priuatt examenation and praier

The Lordes day :26:
After I was readie I went to the church, and, after praers and sermon,
I Came home and dressed Blackbourns foote : after, I dined, and after
I talked and reed to some good wiffes : after, I praied and reed, and
wrett notes in my bible of the morninge exercise : after, I went to
the church, and, after sarmon, I dressed a poore mans hand : and
after that I walked a broad, and so Came to priuat examenation and
praier

The 27 day

After priuat praier I was busie about the house, and dressed my saruants foot and another poore mans hand, and talked with others that Came to aske my Counsill : after, I went into the Garden, and gaue some hearbes vnto a good wiffe of Erley for his[254] garden : after, I Came to diner, praied, and went to diner : after, I talked a whill wth Mr Rhodes and his brother, and, after that, went to worke, and hard Mr Rhodes read of Mr perkins new booke : and, after, went to walke, and about the house, and then went into my Clositt, and then examened my selfe and praied

The 28 day

After priuat praier I went to worke, and, before diner time, came my Cosine Iohn Bouser, with whom I kept Companie vntell diner : after, we walked forth, and, when he was gone, I dressed packeringes hand : after, I hard Mr Rhodes read of perkin, and after I went to priuat examenation and praier

The :29: day

After prairs I wrett to Mr Hoby and my Cossine Bouchier : after, I dined and wroughte tell allmost night : then I praied, and, after supper, I hard Mr Aston[255] praie and reade, and so went to bed

The :30: day

After praers I went downe, and, before diner, Came Mr Hunter, wth whom I kept Companie tell his goinge away. After, I went and wrought with my Maides tell allmost night, and then I went to priuat examenation and praier

May :1: day

After I had hard the sarmon at the church, I praied and dined ; and, after diner, wrett to Mr Hoby by Mr Etherington : after He was gone I went to priuat examenation and praier

The 2 day the Lordes euen

After I had praied I wound yearne tell dinner time : then I praied, and dined : in the afternone I receuied letters by Mr Vrpith from Mr Hoby, and, after he was gon, I went to priuat praier and examenation/

---

[254] *Erley*, Everley, a small hamlet very near Hackness; *his*, her.
[255] The parish priest of Hackness.

The Lordes day :3:
After I had ben at the church I praied : and, after diner, talked of good thinges to some of my neighbours, and, when they were at Catizisinge, I wrett notes in my bible of the chapter : after, I dressed the sores I had in hand, and, when I had wreten a letter to my Mother, I went to priuat examenation and praier

The 4 day
After a few drowsie praiers I went about the house, omittinge, thorowe necclegence, some exercise I practised : after diner I walked abroad, god notwithstanding giuinge me comfort, in some thinges, beyond hope : after, I praied, and, after supper, hard the lecture

The :5: day of May 1601:
After praers I went to the church, wher I hard a sarmon : after, I Came home and hard Mr Rhodes read : after diner I went abroad, and when I was come home I dresed some sores : after, I hard Mr Rhodes read, and wrought with in a while : after, I went to see a calfe at Munckmans, which had :2: great heades, 4 eares, and to ether head a throte pipe besides : the heades had longe heares like brissels about the mouths, such as n'other Cow hath : the hinder legges had no partinge from the rumpe, but grewe backward, and were no longer but from the first Ioynte : also, the backe bone was parted about the midest bicke, and a rowne howle was in the midest into the bodie of the Calfe : but one would haue thought that to haue comed of some strocke it might gett in the Cowes bely:[256] after this I Came in to priuat medetation and praier

The :6: day
After I had praied, buesed my selfe about dyinge some cloth : and, after I had dined, I went to the dales[257] wher I was, all the after none, seeing som work : and, after I Came home, I kept Mr ward Companie tell praier time

---

[256]   The unusual length and detail of the entry mark Lady Hoby's surprise at this unexpected freak of nature.
[257]   This is a walk of nearly 2 miles (about 3 km) alongside a stream known as Lowdales Beck. There are several small dales around Hackness with springs running into becks and thence into the River Derwent.

May 1601: *The .7: et 8 day*
these :2: daies I Continewed my accustomed exercises of praier and
medetation, and was at the Dales all most all the after none/

The :9:: day
this day I kept my chamber and tooke phisicke, being, all the night
before, pained in my teeth so that I nether slept nor tooke rest

The :10: day
I was for paine Eased, but my fase was swolen, and so I kept my
chamber, saue that I went to the Church, both fornonne and after, to the
sarmons : and so, I thanke god, had good Comfort

The :11: day
I kept my chamber, and hard Iohn Corrow and Mr Rhodes read to
me : and, in the afternone, some of my neighbours Came and sate w^{th}
me

The :12: day
I hard this day, after I had praied, Mr Rhodes read the booke of my lord
of Esixe treason, and I wrought : and so like wise in the after none Iohn
Corowe and he did read by Course vnto me tell a litle before I went to
priuat praier and medetation.

The 13: day

I Receiued 41:	After praier I wrough, and hard Mr Rhodes and younge
sheppe from	Coroow read: after diner I dispatched all buseneses in
my Mother	my chamber, because I was not well, and at night I went
	to priuat praier, and after supper to the Lecture

The :14: day
In the morning I praied, hard Mr Rhodes read, and wrought : after diner
I went about the house, and kept with my Maides tell all most night :
then I went in to my Chamber and did some busenis : and, this after
none, tooke a Lecture of Rhetorike : and after, at my time, went to priuat
medetation and praier

from the 14th	Only the Lordes day, in the Morninge, I hard the sarmon,
tell the 20: I	but was so ill that I Cold not goe the afternone,
was both in	and was accompanied with my Cosine Isons wiffe
paine and weake	tell allmost night, when I went to bed

The :21: day
After prairs I went about the house, and sonne after to the church : after diner I went about and wrought, and, before supper, tooke Blackbours accountes for shepe he had sould : and after praied and so went to supper

The 22:
In the morninge I receiued letters from Mr Hoby : after, I praied and dined : then I wrougt : and, after, I walked to the Dales, and at night I returned to priuat examenation and praier

The :23:
In the Morninge I wrett to Mr warde of Skarborowe : after, I praied and went about the house : after dinner I was busie in the Kitchine and in my chamber, and after I went to priuat examenation and praier

The Lordes day the :24:
After praier I went to the church, and after I Came from thence, I praied and reed : after, I dined : then I talked a whill, and after wrett notes in my bible, and reed, tell church time, to a sicke maid in my house : after, I went to the church, and at my accustomed times went to priuatt praier and medetation

May. The :25: day
In the morninge, after priuat praiers, I sente vp for Mr procter, and Gaue him 20^{li}, in parte of paiment of a greater some : after diner I wrought, and Continewed my accustomed exercises

The .26: day
I praied, wrought, and dined : tooke a lecture of Rhe:[258] in the After none, and then went to priuat praier at my accustomed hower

The 27: day
After priuatt praier I wrett to Mr Stillingt, and dispacthed a messhinger to him : after, I reed, and wrought tell :2: a cloke : then I praied and,

---

[258]   *Rhe,* rhetoric. The Elizabethans were indebted to compilations of quotations, metaphors and similes, classical references and proverbs. Extracts may well have been copied out into personal commonplace-books. Such works as Sir Thomas Wilson's *Art of Rhetorique* (1553, with eight editions by 1585) were prized for their concentrated wisdom and utility as instruments of instruction.

after, eate a litli : then I went about the house and was busie in the Kitchine, and after I praied.

The .28: d:
After praier I wrought, reed, went about the house, and praied againe before diner : after, I talked with Mr Bell and one Halles, that brought his daughter heather : and after I kept Companie with my Mother, that Came from Linton : and after I went to priuat examenation and praier

The :29: day:
this day I Continewed my accustomed exercises, and was vesited by my Cosine, Mr Arthur Dakins, and others

The :30: day :
This day, beinge the lordes euen, I went to the church in the afternone and hard the Exercise against the recepte of the lordes suppe

The lordes day :31: day
this day I was at the church and hard both the sarmons, forenone and after : yet I had some paine of the toothach, but did not much nor long trouble me, I thanke god

The first day : June :
this day I went againe to the church, hard the sarmons before diner and after, and was vesited by Mrs Harision and Mrs Bell/

The :2: day:
this day I was vesited, in the forenone, by the Balifes of Scarborow and the preacher there : and, in the after none, after they, my Cossine Dakins, Mr ward and his wiffe had taken their leaues, and that I had dispatched letters by Mr Stillingtons messhinger to himselfe and Mr Hoby, I went to Mr Rhodes house wth my Mother and diuers other good wiffes, wher we supped : and, after we had all praied togeather, we Cam home

The :3: day :
After priuat praier I talked with Mr Hunter, and after wth my Cosine Bouchier and his wiffe, who like wise Came to vesitte me : in the afternone Came Mrs Elwick about hir husband and, towardes night, when they were all gone, I went to priuatt praier and examenation :

after, I hard some of our men, and Mr Rhodes, were serued to be examened for the lord Ewrie[259]

June : 1601 : 4: day :
After priuat prairs I went to worke, and then I went to the church because there was a child baptised, and asermon : after I had dined, I wrett to Scarborowe by Mr Ballife Coniers, and then talked with some of my me[260] touchinge directions, sent from London, touchinge their examenations at Malton : and at my accustomed time went to priuat praier

The :5: day
After praier I went to work, and hard Mr Rhodes read of a good booke : after, I had newes from my Mother that the lord Ewrys man had serued hir to be examened:[261] after I had don about that matter I went to work, and then to priuat examenation and praier/

The :6: day
I hauinge performed all my accustomed exercises, I went, after diner, to Hacknes dales : and when I Came home Mr Nettelton and his wiffe Came to see me, and, when I had saluted them, I went to priuatt praier

The lordes day. 7: day
After praiers I went to Church, and, hauinge health, performed my exercises, as I might, for Strangers

The :8: day
this day I went to vesitt my Mother and my Cosine, Mai Isons : and, after I Came home, I went to priuatt praier

The 9 day:
In the Morninge after prairs I walked abroad, and after diner I went to TrutesDall:[262] and when I was Come hone I went to praier, and, after supper, to the lecture

---

[259] They are to give evidence for the lawsuit at a special hearing in Malton.
[260] *my me*, my men (see 13 June).
[261] So even Lady Hoby's mother has to give evidence in the lawsuit.
[262] There are superb views over Troutsdale looking north from the moors above Snainton.

The :10: day

After prairs I went about, and so to worke : after I had dined I spake with Cockerill and Glouer : after, I went to visitt Mothe pate,[263] and so I Came home and went to examenation and priuat praier

The :11: day

After priuat prairs I went about the house and wrought amonge my Maides, and hard one read of the Booke of Marters : after, I walked with my Cosine Isons who Came to Vesitt me : after, I dined and, in the after non, walked againe with hir, and after we had talked a whill I went to priuat praier

The :12: day

I praied, walked about the house, wrett to my mother, and continewed my accustomed exercise with much Comfort, I thank god

The :13: day

I wrett this day to my Lady Russill, and went about the house, and praied at my accustomed times, hauinge talked wth Hilarie and Bratwhath that Came from malton/

The lordes :day the :14:

this day, after I was Comed from the church, Came Mr Genkins and his brother, by whose meanes I Could not performe those exercises which I was wont to doe

June 1601: the :15: day:

After I was readie, and had disptached Hilari with letters to london, I talked with Mr Genkins tell he went away : after, I praied and dined : after diner my Cosine Robert Dakins Came, by whom I receiued letters from London : and so I wrett againe to mr Hoby, and kept him Companie tell his departure : and after I went about the house, and so went to priuatt praier and medetation/

The :16: day:

this day Mr Theckstone and my Cosine, Ned Isons, Came and kept me all the after-none : and, after they were gone, I went about, and then to my accustomed exercises

---

[263] *Mothe pate*, Mother Pat? An example perhaps of Yorkshire dialect where the consonant is pronounced more emphatically by the addition of a brief vowel (Pat/Pat**er**).

The :17: day
After I had gone about the house I Came to priuatt praier, and after I went about : then, hauinge dined, I walked abroad, and was busie tell praier time wth my Maides : after I receiued a letter from Mr Hoby, & so went to priuatt praier

The :18: day
In the Morninge I went about my accustomed exercises, which I Continewed all the day tell night, at which my olde Cosine, Arthur Dakine, Came to Hacknes to me : and, after supper, I hard the Lecture wth Comfort and proffitt, I praise god/

June 1601: *the* 19 *day*
this day I performed all my exercises, and in the after-none walked abroad, but Came not well home, and, sonne after supper, went to bed

The : Lordes euen :20: day:
After prairs I went about the house : after, I talked with my Cosine Dakins about his sonne, and, after dinner, wee walked abroade : and then at night I went to priuatt medetation and praier/

The Lordes day 21: *day:*
After priuat praier I reed of the bible, and so went to the church : after, I Came home, and after diner I reed a Litle to som good wiffes, and after talked with my Cosine Dakins tell church time againe : after, I praied and went to church : then we walk abroad, and, after I Cam in, I went to priuatt praier and medetation

The :22: day
After priuatt prairs I reed abroad wth my Cosine Dakine : after I Came home and that I had dined, I talked of good matters wth him, and he reed to me, and after we went forthe and sawe some sheppe which he was to buy : after, I returned and went to priuatt praier and medetation

The 23 *day*
this day, in the afternone, Cam my younge Cosine, Arthur Dakine, and so his father and he were reconsiled

The :24: day
This day Came my Cosine Isons wiffe, and Mr Bell and his wiffe, and Lay att my house, to goe the next Morning to se my Mother and to hear a sarmon

Iune 25:

In the morninge I and the rest of the Companie went to winteringam and hard Mr willsone preach : after, we dined wth my Mother, and then went to weatheropp[264] and hard Mr Rhodes preach, which was desired thether, and so Came home to Hacknes

The :26: day

This day I went on the way with my Mother as farr as eberston, and saw Mrs Etherington and so Came home, wher I found H Netelton Come from London, and Blackbourn from Yorke/

The :27: day:

After priuat prairs I went about the house, and, after diner, I hard Mr Rhodes read, and wrought : and, after I had gonn about, went to priuatt praier and medetation

The :28: day

After prairs I went about the house, and after talked with Mr Lacy of Seamer : then dined, and in the after none was busie in my Chamber, and talked a whill wth Mr Lister who Came from York : and, sonne after, went to priuatt prairs and readinge

The :29: day:

this day, after prairs, I tooke my leaue of Mr Lister, and after praied : then I wrought, and dined, and after walked to the dalls.

The 30 day

After priuatt praier I went about, and then wrought, dined, reed of the bible, walked abroad : and, after I had taken order for some thinges, I went to priuatt praier

July : 1601: The 1: day

this day I Continewed my accustomed exercises, and was veseted by Mr Hunter of the Mawis[265]

---

[264]   Weaverthorpe, in the Wolds near Hunmanby. The church stands looking down on the village.
[265]   *Mawis*, moors. In Yorkshire there is 'white moor', containing coarse grasses, and 'black moor', consisting of heather, turf and peat. Within the manor of Hackness there were

The :2: *day*

As I was accustomed, I vsed my exercises, and was veseted by my Cosine Boucher, and Mr Gatt of Seamer:

The :3: *day*

After praiers I went about and wrough, and then I praied, dined, and was busie painge saruantes wages, and seeinge som dispatched to the Markitt : and, at my accustomed hower, I went to priuatt praier and medetation

The :4: *day*

After I had praied I went downe, and was busie in the pasterie:[266] hard Kate read a chapter : after, I went to worke and praied tell diner : after, I wrought tell church time, and then I went to haear the sarmon which was in regard of the Comunione the next day : and after I went a litle about, and at 5 returned into my Clositt

July the :5: *The lordes day*:

After priuat prairs I reed of Mr perkins, and after went to the church and hard the sarmon, and receiued the Comunionn : after, I praied, dined, and reed, and Conferred of good thinges to such wemen as dined with me : after, I went againe to the church, and after went a walkinge : then I came home and went to priuatt praier and medetation

The :6: *day*

After priuat prairs I went to Seamer, wher I dined, and staied tell all most 5 for the heat : and after Came hom and went to priuat prairs

---

open commons, moors and wastes where turf and ling were collected. Names included Low Mouth Moors, Silpho Moor and Harwood Dale Moor. Tenants were not to burn the moors ('swizzen') after March, and to take no more turf than they needed for their grates. A border of 20 foot if possible had to be kept on each side of the road and round the moor for pasture, and the footpath was never to be 'grated'. (NYCRO MIC 951 Survey 1608 of the Hackness estate). Mr Hunter becomes father-in-law to Mr Rhodes, who marries his daughter Mercy.

[266] *pasterie*, the bakehouse, a room beyond the kitchen, normally with one or two large brick ovens. Other service rooms included the buttery, the pantry, 'wet' and 'dry' larders, the laundry and preserving room.

The 7: day

I praied and writt notes this day as I was accustomed, and in the after none walked to the dals

The : 8 day

After priuatt prairs I walked a bout, and dined, and was busie all the afternone about necessarie busenes, and at my time went to priuatt prairs

The 9 day

After prairs I receiued a letter from Mr Hoby, and Continewed my exercises

July :1601: The :10: day

After prairs I went about, and was busie as I was accustomed nether doinge nor receiuinge any great matter of note : and at my accustomed time went to priuat prairs, and sonne after supper to bed : and, after I was aslepe, Mr Hoby Came home

The 11: day

this day I Continewed my accustomed exercises

The Lordes day :12:

After I had praied I went to the Church, and, after Comunion and all was done, I Came home : in the after none I went Llikewise, and that day Continewed well, I thanke god

The 13 day

I had a sore fitt of the Colicke from 7 in the Morning tell 2 in the after none, and all that day Continewed both sick and weake

The 14::

this day Likewise I was verie weak, and therfore Could hardly performe any spirituall exercise

The 15 day

I was somthinge better this day, and praied a litle in the morninge, and in the after none went about : and, at my time, went to priuat prairs and examenation

July 1601. 16: day

this day Mr Varnie and my Cosine Bouser Came, and, after diner, I was a whill busie, but at my time I went and praied

The 17 *day*
After priuatt prairs I went about, and after diner I walked to the dals,[267] whether Mr Hoby Came to me : after, I Came home and went to priuatt examenation and praier

The 18 *day*
I was so weake with a fitt of the stone that my Mother Came to me, and I kept my Chamber

The 19: *day*
I was weake, yet so well that I went to the church, and was accompaned wth my Cosine Isons and his wiffe, Mr Hunter, and Mr Robert Limen /

The :20: *day*
I was reasonable well, and Continewed my ordenarie exercises, and stilld Aqua : Vita :

The 21: *day*
Mr Hoby went to yorke, my Mother to Newton, and I was vesited with my Cosine Isons wiffe, who Came for hir brother in law, Heslerton /

The 22: *day*
this day I praied, and went about the house as at other times /

The 23 *day*
this day I gott dinner for the house, and went about my accustomed exercises as I was wont

The :24: *day*
this day I Continewed my accustomed exercises, and in the afternone walked to pickringe Close /

The :25: *day*
After priuat praier I went Newton to my Mother, wher I dined : and, after diner, Mr Hoby, with Mr Measse, Mr Smith of Cottingame, Came home to Hacknes with Bese Beuerle and he that was to Marie hir : and so I went to priuatt prairs and medetations.

---

[267] Lady Hoby is going to visit the farm that her mother makes over to Sir Thomas (1 August 1604).

The Lordes day :26: day:
After priuatt prairs I went to the church, and, after, I praied, dined, and in the afternone Mr Hoby shewed Mr Smith the house : and, after we had againe beene at the church, we walked abroad, and after I returned to priuatt praier & medetation.

The :27: day
After I was readie and had praied, I wente downe and wrought tell diner time : afte I walked abroad to some hay, and, at my accustomed Hower, I returned to priuatt readinge and praier.

The 28: day
After priuatt praier I went went a bout, and was busie tell dinner time, and after I wrought, and went to the dalles : and, when I Came home, Mr Hunter and his brother was gonne, and had bought 40 sheepe for 11^{li} to be paied att Bartlmew tide:[268] and att my time I went to priuat praier.

July :1601 The .29: day:
After priuat praier I walked into the Garden : after diner I wrought tell all most night,[269] and then I went abroad with my Maides that were busie pullinge hempe:[270] and after I Cam in to priuatt examenation and praier.

Thursday the :30:
I vsed my acustomed exercises, and hard Mr Rhodes read of the true diCeplen of christes church[271]

---

268   *Bartlmew tide*, 'Bartle' is Yorkshire dialect for Bartholomew. Lady Hoby refers to St Bartholomew's Day, 24 August.

269   The long summer evenings would have been important for the extra daylight.

270   *pullenge hempe*, hemp was easier to grow than flax, being less exhausting to the soil and requiring less attention while growing. It was steeped in water (retting) to begin the separation of the fibres from the rest of the stem. Because of the danger of pollution and the poisoning of cattle this could not be done in springs or running streams. Drying hemp in ovens or by the fireside was generally forbidden, presumably because of the offensive odour associated with retting. Once it had become 'harden yarn' it was woven into a course workaday fabric or used for rope. It was possible to weave harden, linen and woollen cloth on the same loom with different, adaptable gears. 'The Season of Gathering of it is first about *Lammas*' (1 August), in *The mystery of Husbandry Discovered by J.W. Gent* (n.d.), Hackness church library.

271   Probably a 'Book of Discipline' which set forth Puritan views on church government and teaching. Stephen Egerton had been involved in drawing up such a treatise.

The 31 *day*
this day I praied, and at dinner time Came Mr ward and his wiffe from Scarborow, who staied all the day with me : and, before supper, I went to priuatt praier and medetation/

The first day of Auguste
this day I went about, Continewinge my accustomed exercises, and was Vesitted by Mr Ardington.

The Lordes day :2: day
After all the exercises were done, fore none and after, I slept a whill, being not well, and was vesited by my Cosine Isons and his wiffe

The 3 *day*
I Continewed my accustomed exercises, and was busie in the house all the day[272]

The 4 *day*
this day I was busie in the house, hauinge manie strangers, because of the Courte[273] that was kept after Mr Hoby and my self, by godes goodnes, had gotten thestate of Hacknes: and when they were busie I went to vesitte Ingram procter who Lay sicke/

The 5 *day*
this day I Continewed my accustomed exercises, and wrough, hard Mr Ardingto read, and singe psa : tell I went to priuatt praier

The :6: day
After prairs I went about awhill, and then went to the church to the sarmon, which was made att Mr Procters buriall, who died this morning about 4 a Clock : after Diner I was vesited, and, after, I walked abroad, and so Cam in to priuatt praier and medetation

---

[272]   This is one of Lady Hoby's simplest entries. She has regularly informed her diary that she has been busy, but her entries are becoming steadily shorter and more concerned with ordinary daily happenings.
[273]   This was a court of special sessions held for the inhabitants of the manor of Hackness by the owner of the manor, and attended by JPs from the immediate district.

The 7: day

After praiers I wrett to my Mother, then I walked abroad : after, I dined : after, I was busie in my Clositt and then walked againe : and then I busied my selfe about the house, and hard some readinge, and after I went to priuatt praier

The 8 day

this day I praied, walked : and Mr Hoby agreed with our Millner,[274] and in the afternone Mr Ardington Reed to me, and Mr Netelton Came to the howse : &, at my time, I went to priuatt praier and medetation/

The Lordes day :9:

After prairs I did eate, and went to the church, and againe in the afternone : and at : 6 : went to priuatt examenation and praier

The :10: day

After I had praied I was busie seeinge some roomes mad hansome for Corne : after, I praied, and dined : in the after none I made waxe lightes, and wrought : after, I went to my clositt, and there reed and praied/

The :11: day.

After prairs I wrought, and hard Mr Ardington Read : after, I praied, and dined, and then I went about busie tell allmost night, when I went to priuatt praier/

The :12: day.

After prairs, I wrought, as I was accustomed, with my maides, and hard Mr Ardington read : and, after I dined and had slept a Litle, I went to my worke againe, and hard Mr Ardington againe : after, I walked about with Mr Hoby, and so went to priuatt praier

The :13: day

this day I was not verie well, yet I praied with Mr Ardington, priuatly, in the Morninge and before supper.

---

[274] *Milner*, miller. The harvest will soon begin (see 10 August). When it is safely gathered in, the traditional Yorkshire cry is 'We've getten t'mell!' and then the mell-supper follows.

The :14: day
After priuatt prairs I wrett a letter to my lady Bowes:[275] after, I wrought and went about tell dinner time : after dinner I walked to some haymakers, and after went aboute tell prairs time, and then read and praied priuatly, beinge vesited wth my Cosine Robert Dake

The :15: day:
After priuatt praier I wrought, and talked with my Cosine Robert Dakins : and after diner I went about, and walked abroad, and hard Mr Ardington read : after, I Cam home and went to priuatt praier, I praise god, hauinge obtained to ouer Come in some measure disordered affection

The Lordes day :16: day:
After priuat praier I went to the church, and after I Came home I praied, dined, and went againe to the Church : after, I walked with my Mther abroad, and went at my time to priuat praier and writinge, after we had sunge a psa:

The :17 day
this day I praied as before, and in the after none I went with my Mother to Mr Proctres house, his sonne beinge gonn that day : after, I wrett to my lady Bowes, and a after I went to priuatt praier.

August 1601: the 18 day:
After prairs I tooke my leaue of my Mother : and after dinner I wrought a whill, and went to the dalls : after, I went about the house and so to priuatt praier.

The 19: day:
After priuat praier I went about the house, and after wrought and walked tell diner time : and so Like wise, after dinner, I walked into the feeldes, and at my time went to priuatt quiatt praier

The 20: day
this day I went, after priuatt prairs, to se workmen stubb furrs:[276] after, I

---

[275] Isabel, wife of Sir William Bowes of Barnard Castle.
[276] *stubb furrs*, cutting trees to the stump. Timber was an important part of the economy and it would have been taken to the coast some 4 miles away to be shipped out. The Hackness countryside still has large wooded areas and there are named woods, such as Intake Wood, Hawthorn Wood and Broxa Forest. In Lady Hoby's time the great Forest of Pickering was not far away.

dined, and all the afternone was busie in the house, and then went to priuatt praier

The 21: *day*
After prairs I walked to some workemen : after dinner I Walked againe into our pastur, and so, after I had talked a whill with Mr Hoby, I went to priuatt praier/

:22: *day*
After priuatt prairs I went to the Church : and in the after none I walked (after the sarmon) and thence Came in, and talked with my Maides of the sarme : and, after I had wretten, I went to priuatt praier

Lordes day The :23: *day*:
After priuatt prairs I went about to gett some thinges readie against my Lord presedent[277] Cominge : in the after none Came Mrs Gerlington, who staied not Long, and then, at my accustomed time, I went to priuatt praier

The :24: *day*:
After priuatt praiers I busied my selfe all the day in the house, and sent for my Mother, and after, at 5, I went to priuatt prairs

The 25 *day*
After priuatt prairs I was busie all the day in expectation of my Lord Burleys Cominge : and att Night I went to priuatt praier :

The 26: *day*
this day, in the afternone, I had had a child brought to se that was borne at Silpho, one Talliour sonne, who had no fundement, and had no passage for excrementes but att the Mouth : I was earnestly intreated to Cutt the place to se if any passhage Could be made, but, although I Cutt deepe and seearched, there was none to be found.[278]

The 27 *day*
the Lord Burley Came to Scarborowe and so to Seamer : and at Night Mr Strickland Lodged with vs.

---

277   Thomas Cecil, Lord Burghley, President of the Council of the North.
278   A sad call on Lady Hoby's expertise as a physician.

August 1601 *the* 28: *day*:
After priuatt prairs I tooke my Leaue of my Mother : and after dinner Came Mr Etherington, after whose departure I went to priuatt praier.

The 29 *day*:
After priuatt praier I went about the house : and after dinner Came Mr Stricklande, with whom I walked : and after I went to priuatt praier.

The 30: *day*:
After priuatt praiers I reed, and kept Companie with Mrs Girlington and diuers that Came in the after none I went to the church, wher I hard Mr ward preach : and after I had Considered of the sarmon, and taken my leaue of the strangers, I went to priuatt praier.

The :31: *day*:
After a few prairs I went about, and in the afternone walked to the dalls : and when I Came home I went to priuatt examenation and praier/

The first day of September:
After prairs I went about the house, and in the afternone I talked with Hilaree Beuerley : after, I walked abroad with Mr Hoby, and, with a litle after, I went to priuatt examenation and prair

The .2: *day*:
After priuatt praier I went about the house, and all the day Continewed att home : and att night, I had read a letter that Came from Mr Rhodes, I went to priuatt praier.

The :3: *day*:
After priuatt praier I went about : and after dinner I Mistress farlay Came and Mr Rhodes Mother : & after I had gonn a whill about the house I went to priuatt praier

The :4: *day*:
After priuatt praiers I walked to take order for the alteringe of my Mothers house : after, Mr Hoby and I talked of some Complaintes made to him : then I dined, and after diner I Copied out a letter which Mr Hoby had wretten to the Busshopp of Limbricke, touchinge his agrement to peace : and after I went, at mine hower, to praier

Septb: .1601: The Lordes eue:

After priuatt praiers I had occasione to returne to praier againe by a domestecall iniurie : and after diner I vsed my accustomed exercises about the house : and, after I had perused Iohn wass his accussinge Letter,[279] I went to priuatt praier.

The Lordes day :6: day:

before I went to	After priuatt prairs I went to the church : and after
church wasse	dinner I walked a whill with Mr Hoby : and, after
asked me	I had againe binne att the church, I dressed Hilares
forgiuenes	finger, taked wth Anne Mathew bout some abuse,[280]
	and at my time went to priuatt praier

This :7: day:

I writt, after priuatt praers, in my bible : after diner I walked to the dalls : and at Night after the Lecture went, I thank god, well to bed.

The .8: day

After priuatt praier I went about the hous, and after I kept Mrs Etherington Companie vntell dinner time : after diner I walked a bout wth hir, and some[281] after hir departure I went to priuatt praier

The :9: day

After prairs I walked to see some wheat : and after dinner I went to vesitt Mother Rhodes : after I Came home I talked with some of the house touchinges busenes and so went to priuatt praier.

The :10: day:

After priuatt praier I went about the house, and hard Mr Rhodes read : after, I praied and dined : then dispatched a letter to my Mother, and after walked abroad, and then Came in to priuatt praier

The :11: day:

after priuatt prairs I Continewed all the day, tell night, as I was accustomed

---

[279] John Wasse seeks forgiveness tomorrow. Every so often, there are these hints of disharmony in the Hackness household. It would not have been easy keeping such a community at peace. See next entry.

[280] Lady Hoby occasionally mentions such intervention in the lives of her servants and tenants. She would have regarded her role as intermediary an important one.

[281] *some,* soon.

The :12: day
After prairs, I was busie all most all the day about Houshould matters tell 4, and then I had some paine in my teeth, about which time I went to priuatt prairs

The Lordes day 13:
In the Morninge I praied and went to the church, but in the afternone I was so ill that I Could not goe, but went to bed : and, beinge weake, I kept my chamber all the week followinge, tell the Lordes euen, after which was the :19: of Sept:b:, vpon wch day a miller Came and offered his seruice, of whom we accepted for a triall a time[282]

The Lordes day :20:
this day I, beinge well, went to the church both forenone and after, and was accompaned with Mr Netelton who Came ouer night to visitt vs

The 21: day
After priuatt praier I went about the house : and in the after none I walked abroad, and, sonne after my home Cominge, I went to priuatt praier and medetation.

Septb. 1601. .22: day:
After priuat praier I went about the house : and after diner Came Charle Tuctuile to se Mr Hoby only, as he saied : and att night I went to priuatt praier.

The 23: day:
After a few prairs I went about the house : and after dinner I presarued som damsons Mrs Etherington sent me : after, Sara spake to Me, and then I went to priuatt praier and praisinge god, who had binne more kind to me then I had desarued

The :24: day
After priuatt prairs I was busie in my Chamber tell dinner time : and after I walkd about with Mother Rhodes, and, when she was gonn, I Scealed a Lease of the Intake to Stpthen Tubley : and, sonne after, went to priuatt praier.

---

[282]   Another miller. He starts work on 28 September.

The :25: day:
After priuatt prairs I kept with Mr Vrpith : and all the after none I was busie, some time at the plowers,[283] and after in the house tell praier time : and then I went into my Clositt.

The Lordes euen :26:
this day I exercised my selfe as I was accustomed, and had sowen of Rye :5: pecks[284]

The Lordes the 27:
this day I went, both Morninge and after none, to Church, and walked in to the feeldes with Mr Hoby :

The 28: day
the Miller came
After prairs I wrought : and, after dinner, I spente my time with my Maides : at 5 I walked and spake to the newe Miller that then Came : and so went to priuatt praier.

The :29: day
After priuatt prairs I went to the sarmon : after, I saluted Mr farley, and, after diner, staied a whill and talked with Mr Dowling, who Came ouer night to keepe our Court : and buseed my selfe tell towardes night, and then went to priuatt praier.

The :30: day:
The Court was kept
After prairs I walked about to workmen, and writt the doc':[285] of the former daies Sarmon in my booke : after dinner I was buseed about settinge some wheat : and then I went, at Night, to priuatt prair

The : 1 : day
After priuatt prairs I was busie allmost all the day settinge Corne and towardes night I went to priuatt praier as I was accustomed This day

---

[283] Lady Hoby is busy this week and next supervising the autumn ploughing and sowing.
[284] A peck is a unit of dry measure equal to 8 quarts, or 1 quarter of a bushel. Gerard notes that rye grew very well in the north of England.
[285] *doc'*, doctrine.

went Robert Nettelton and Iohn wase to be examened before the Counsill[286]

The :2: day:
After priuatt praier I went about the house : and in the afternone Mr Hoby receiued a Letter from my Cossine Stanope to Come to York : and after I went to priuatt praier

Octob: 1601: *The :3: day:*
This Day I went, after priuatt prairs, to Yorke wth Mr Hoby, and dined at Newton with my Mother, wher I was much greued touchinge hir weaknes in receiung faulse reportes : after, we Came to York and was invited to supper to my Lord of Limbrickes, wher, after supper, I had much talke, Litle to my Comfort : and, sonme after I Came home, with teares and praires I went to bed.[287]

The Lordes day 4:
This day I, beinge not well, kept att home and was vesited by Mrs Thornborowe and others. The 5 day, 6, 7, 8, 9, and 10, both Mr Hoby and my selfe was solicited, by my lord presedent and my lord of Limbricke and others, to take vp our sute wth my lord Eure in the Star Chamber, which, in regard of christian peace, we were inclined vnto : but, perceauinge our selves to be wrongd, in regard that an end was sought which would haue tended much to our discredets, and that the truth of our Iniures Cwould not be Considered, we Came away Abruptly one Saterday, the 10 of this Mumth[288]

The :11: day the Lordes day
This day we Came to Hacknes, before the Sarmon in the afternone, and in good health, I thanke god/

The 12: day
This day and the next I went about the house, after I had hard Kate

---

[286] Lady Hoby probably alludes here to the Council of the North at York. In a couple of days the Hobys themselves will visit York for a hearing of their lawsuit.
[287] A particularly unhappy day for Lady Hoby. What false reports has her mother received and apparently believed? They may have something to do with the lawsuit.
[288] Again, the Hobys are pressed to give up the lawsuit. They continue to resist, having a real sense of personal grievance over the matter.

Rear[289] a chapter : and about my accustomed time went to priuatt praier : and, after supper, to the Lecture and sonne after to bed

The 13:14:15: *and* :16: *day:*
I Continewed my accustomed exercises, I thank god, wth my health : and on the :16: day Mr Hoby tooke his Iournie towardes London.

The Lordes euen :17:
After priuatt prairs I walked abroad : then I was busie wi^t my Maides: after, I praied and dined, and then went about the house: and at night paied the saruantes their wages, and workmens bills

The Lordes day :18:
After briuatt prairs I went the church, and, after the sarmon and dinner, I reed to the wiues and talked of the sarmon : then I want to the afternone sarmon, and after I walked abroad w^t my Mother : and when I Came home I went to priuat praier, hauinge receiued a Letter from Mr Hoby

The 19 *day*
After priuatt prairs I tooke my breakfast, and then went w^t my Mother to Troutsdal : and when I Came home I went to priuatt praier

Octob: :02:[290] 1601:
After priuat praier I tooke my leaue of my Mother, and after was busie in the house tell dinner time : after, I wrought amonge my Maides tell all most night, and then I went to priautt praier.

The :21: *day*
After priuatt praier I went about the house, and, before diner, Mr Stillington Came, w^t whom after diner I walked : wret to Mr Hoby, and Lent a poore man of Scarborowe 20^s: [291] after I went to priuat praier.

The 22: *day the* :23:
these daies I performed my accustomed exercises, and was vesited by a

---

[289] *Rear,* read.
[290] 20 October.
[291] 20 shillings, i.e. 1 pound sterling.

kinswoman : which was some trouble at the first, but, Consideringe all Crosses ought thankfully to be bourne, I was well guiated[292]

The Lordes euen 24: *day*:
this day, I praise god, I had my helth very well, and performed my accustomed exercises

The Lordes day :25:
this day I performed my accustomed exercises, and reed to the good wiffes, as I had wont, after dinner

The 26 *day*
this, after priuat prairs and taking order for the house, I went to the dalls : and, after a Lecture there, I dined w^t diuerse others wiffes : and at night Came hom, and praied as I was wont

The 27: *day*:
After priuat prairs I went about, and had occasion giuen to chide, which I euer take to be a buffitt of satans Malice : after, I went to the workman, and at my time to praier.

The 28: *day*:
After priuatt praier I went to walke : and after dinner I walked to the Dalls : after I went to priuat praier.

The :29: *day*:
After priuat praier I went to our workman : and all the afternone was busie about the house : and at night I went to priut praier /

The 30: *day*:
this day and the next I Continewed my ordenary exercises and sett some trees which Mr Stillington sent me

The Lordes day the :1: *of Novemb*:
This day, after priuat praire, I went to the Church : and after dinner I reed to some good neighbours : after, I went to Church, whether Came Mrs Gerlington to me, and his sonne[293] and Daughter : after, I had some

---

[292] *guiated*, quieted.
[293] *his sonne*, her son.

neighbours at Supper, and wrett to Mr Hoby : and so, after the repeticion, I went to bed

The :2: day
This day I vsed my accustomed exercises : and was veseted by Mr Smiths sonne, that should marie my Cosine Elzabeth Beuerly:

Nouember 1601: The :3: day:
After priuatt prairs I bed young smith farwell, who was to be maried the Munday following : after, I wrett a litle, and praied, dined : and after dinner wrought tell towardes night, and then went to praie.

The 4 and 5 daies
thise daies, I thank god, I had my health, and practised my accustomed exercises

The 6: day
this day I tooke order for the finishinge of my Mothers house, and performed my exercises

The :7: day
After priuatt prairs I went abroad : and the afternone I was Veseted by Mr Ardington, who Came to winter w^t us

The Lordes day the 8:
After priuatt prairs I went to the sarmone : and so likewise in the after none

The 9: day:
This day, after priuatt prairs, I went being desired by letters w^t w^r ward and his wiffe, Mr Bell and his wiffe, Mr Ardington and others, to Dinner to Mrs Rhodes : and, after, they Came and staied w^t me that night/

Nouember: The 10 and :11: dayes
I Continewed well, I thanke god, these daies : and reed some medetations of the Lady Bowes hir Makinge, as I hard

12 day
sicke/

The 13 day
After I had praied I went to seamer, being sent for to my Cossine

A wood-cut engraving of Elizabeth I.

Bouchiers wiffe who was that Morninge, brought to bed of A boye : and after I was retourned home againe I receiued a Letter from Mr Hoby

The :14 day
I was well : and in the after none went to the Church, wher I hard a sarmon in preperation before the Comunion : after, I was busie about the house and then went to priuat prairs, which,

The Lordes day 15 day
the next day, I exercised att the church as before.

The 16: day
My Mother Came to Hacknes w^t Mrs Netleton : and the Quens day[294] we all were at the Church, receiued the Comunione, and hard sarmons

The :18: day
this day I had my health, I thanke god, and held my accustomed exercises

The 19: day
this day I went about, accordinge to my Custome, and kept my Mother Companie

The 20 day
I paied my Mother /18^li/ and was, By hir, forgeuen 20 for thinges I had Laied forth

1601: Nouemb:
Thes day after prairs I was invited to my Cosine Bouchiers childs Babptisinge : and in the afternone dispatched some houshoulde busenes

The Lordes day 22:
After priuatt prairs I went to Church, and vesited my Mother who was not well : and at night performed my accustomed exercises

The 23 24 et 25 daies
I vsed my accustomed exercises, and had my health Continewed vnto me, I thank god.

---

[294]   *Quens day,* Queen Elizabeth I ascended the throne, 17 November 1558. See pp. 170, 172 for contemporary wood-cut engravings.

A wood-cut engraving of a fashionable lady.

The 28 *day*
Came Mr Hoby home frome London

The Lordes day 29:
This day I went to the church and hard both the Lecturs : and at Night went to priuatt praier, after Mr Hoby had reed vnto me some notes of Mr Egertons Lecturs

The 5 *of December:*[295]
All this week ffollowinge I was well, I praise god, beinge vesited by diuers that Came to see Mr Hoby : by whome we hard som newes, as by Mr polard, that the wednesday forthnight, before which was the 4 of Nouember, died of Drunkenesse one S^{ir} Hunter adame, Minister of the Bethelme of Yorke : we hard also of Mr Busshup Mariag to Mr Cholmeles Daughter, beinge about 14 years olde and himselfe fiftie:[296] besides, we hard of woodruffs hurt by younge Gorge Dakins, w^t some other thinges of less moment

The 11 *of De*
I had, I thanke god, my health all this time, hauinge no change of alteration fallinge out : only I must note[297] that my tronke, which I expected from hull, was by Contrarie windes brought in at Skarbrowe, so that all Mr Hoby his prouision Came vnto vs before we expected itt : from friday the :11: vnto the Lordes day the :20: I remained, I thanke god, well in helth, and Continewede my accustomed exercises, and hard no thinge worth notinge, but only of Mr Bell : the :19: day, in ridinge, his horse fell and brake his Legge : which thinge, although the world account but a mischance, yet godes Iudgmentes is to be obsarued, for the humblinge and admonition of all that heare of it & such like thinges.

The 26: *day*:
was young farley slane by his fathers man, one that the younge man had before thretened to kill and, for that end, prosecutinge him : the man,

---

[295] Lady Hoby departs from her customary brief entries to record much more news, but the time gap is wider between them. There are only four entries this December. January is very thin.
[296] Such an age gap was not unusual in the arranged marriages of the Elizabethan period.
[297] This formulation is unusual. Lady Hoby appears to be bursting with the news and writes as if this is a letter to a friend.

hauinge a pike staff in his hand, rune him into the eie and so into the brane : he neuer spoke after : this Iudgment is worth notinge, this young man being extreordenarie prophane, as once Causinge a horsse to be brought into the church of god, and ther christininge him w^t a name, which horable blasphimie the Lord did not leaue vnreuenged, euen in this world, for example t'others[298]

The Lordes day 27:
this day I Continewed to heare, and read, and pray, I praise god, w^t much Comfort as before.

---

[298] Another young man whose unruly behaviour Lady Hoby deplores.

1602

Ianuarie :1:[299]
Hetherto, I praise god, I Continewed in helthe and my accustomed exercises : hearinge no greate matter of note, but only, as Mr Hoby Came from the church, 2 men Cam to tell him of that they had hard touchinge Dentes Guiltenes to Harisons Death, wch was Comitted 5 years before, and, tell that time, smothered : and what will beCome of it more herafter will appeare

The :11: *day*:
vnto this day, I praise god, I continewe in extreordenarie health : and hard of no newe or strange thinge worthy notinge

The Lordes day :16:[300]
This day, as before, I went to Church, and hard the Sarmone w^t good proffitt

The :17:
This day Mr Hoby tooke his Iournie towardes London

The :19:
I receiued a letter from him that he was in helth

The 22:
this day I was busie in the house : and att night I praied as I vsed, and laboured to prepare my selfe for the next day :

The Lordes day :23:
This day, I praise god, I was well, and harde the lectures fornone and after, w^t the Catazising.

The Lordes day :31:
likewise this day, I praise god, I was likewise at Church, and hard the exercises and hadd my accustomed exercises

Feb: :2:
this day I made a dinner for some of our neighbours : and my Mother, w^t Mr Mills and his wiffe, was there Likewise, who Came the night before to my Mother.

---

[299]   There are large gaps from now to the end of that part of the diary that has survived.
[300]   16 January was Saturday, not Sunday.

The :4: day

this day I had a
fatherly warninge
of god.

I was sent for to Trutsdall to the trauill of my Cossine Isons wiffe, who that Morninge was brought to bed of a daughter : the same day, at night, I hard of a fish that was taken vp att Yarmoth, 53 foott Long and 23 broade

The Lordes day :7:

I was a wittnes for my Cossine Edward Isons Child

The 17 day

Mr Hoby Came from London hauinge ended all his busenes there, I praise god:[301] from which time, vntell the lordes day senight after, I was not well but kept my Chamber, and was Vesited by Mrs Carington on the Thursday, the 25 day, and by my Cossine Bouschier the 26: day

28.

The Lordes d[302] I, beinge indefferently well, I went to the Church before dinner and after, Receiuinge much comfort and quickning, I praise god, by the exercises then Vsed

March the Lordes day 8:[303]

This day I, hauinge my health, went to the church and hard the exercises of the wholl day, I praise god.

The :14: day

this day, although ill at ease of the new sicknes, I went towardes York, and that night lay at Newton w^t my Mother

The :15: day

I receiued a recouerie
Hacknes

This day I went to York, and that night dispatched my for busenes before Iudge Sauil : [304] and the next day returned to Newton to my mother.

---

[301]   After nineteen months the lawsuit is finally settled in the Hoby's favour. See entry for 29 May 1602. Release from the associated tension leaves Lady Hoby feeling unwell and confined to her chamber.

[302]   *d*, day.

[303]   8 March 1602 was a Monday.

[304]   Lady Hoby has not yet signed over all her property to her husband, so there must be legal matters for which she alone is responsible.

The :17: day 21: *day*
I Came home safe, I praise god : and the Lordes day followinge I received the Comunion at Hacknes, and in the after none kept my Mother Companie, who was not well and went not abroad : ther I hard that Robert Dent was Condenned, at York, for the plottinge of Harisons Murder and his wiffe

The 22: day
Mr Hoby Came from Yorke

The :25: day
in the afternone Mr Gerlington and my Younge Cosine Isons Came to Vesitt Vs

The Lordes day following
I receiued the Comunion wᵗ Mʳ Hoby and my Mother

The 29: day:[305]
Mr Hoby went to Beuerly,[306] and the 31: day satt on the subsedie[307] at Snanton

The :8: day
Andrew Harison Died, beinge a Young man

The Lordes day :11:
I exercised my selfe at Church, for none and after.

The :12: day
from the 12 to the .15, I praise god, I Continewed my health and exercises all that time as before

[305] Quarter Day.
[306] Beverley is the county town of the East Riding of Yorkshire and in former times it was of greater importance than Hull. The Minster (dating from 1220) is a magnificent church, standing on the site of one of the most ancient religious establishments in England.
[307] *subsedie*, subsidy. This was the general term for a tax granted to the sovereign by parliament to meet special needs. In Tudor times it was applied pre-eminently to a tax of 4s in the pound on lands and 2s 8d in the pound on movables. Sir Thomas is therefore involved with the collection of local taxes and levies, on such as wool, leather and cloth. He would have had before him the Subsidy Book, which contained a record of names of those liable to pay subsidy.

1602

1602 *Aprill* 4:
The Lordes day we all receiued againe the Comunion:[308] and at the after none exercises Came Mrs Gerlington and hir sonne.

The :6: day
In the Morninge, hauinge slept well, I promised to my selfe health & quiatt, according to the nature of man who thinkes the estate present will neuer alter, but god, who seeth the thoughtes Longe before, doth vsially shewe his Children the vanitie of their Cogetation by sendinge some gentle Crosse that may pull them from driminge of earthly quiatt : wch I found, I praise god : This day Mr Dobman kept the Corte at Hacknes

The Lordes day
This day I hard the exercises, and therby was somthinge eased

The 12 day
Came Robert Coltas, at euen, to be a gardener

The 13 day:
I wrett Letters to London

The 14 day
Hilarie Beuerley tooke his iournie towardes London : and this day, in parte, I found the truth of that Deceatfullnes of mans hart, which Ierimie speaketh of, that it is wicked about all thinges, and who Can Know itt[309]

The 23 day:
vntell this time, I blesse god, I have found more and more Comfort: and on the :19: day Came Mr Nalton to visitt Mr Hoby, and exercised one

---

[308]   Easter Day. Lady Hoby's interest in the meaning of the Eucharist is to be found in her annotated copy of Philip of Mornai, *Doctrine of the Holy Sacrament* (1600), in which he has 'intreated of the auncient doctrine of the holy Supper, comparing it with that of the Romish Masse'. A tradition throughout Yorkshire at Easter-tide was for people to walk to a high point to 'see the sun dance' at dawn: an ancient custom deriving from the belief that the sun dances as it rises in honour of the Resurrection.

[309]   Lady Hoby's reading may be prompted by some immediate experience or even a sense of her own insufficiency, or by a contemporary line-by-line exposition of the meaning, with application, in John Udall, *A Commentarie Vpon The Lamentations of Ieremy* (1593). See Jeremiah V: 23–8.

hower verie profitable : I haue Continewed my duties of praier and readinge, both findinge my corruption and receiuinge stringth

The 27: *day*
my Mother Came from the weould:[310] I had conferrence w^t hir of sundrie thinges

The 28:

May: 1602: *The Lordes day* 2:
this day, I prase god, I, hauinge my health, I hard all the exercises w^t good proffitt, yet had I some Conflict w^t one of my kinsman, for a freind I Cannot Call him : and godes mercie and truth is euer w^t me, god make me thankfull, amen/

The :6: *day*
I praise god I had health of body : how so euer Iustly god hath suffered satan to afflicte my mind, yet my hope is that my redemer will bringe my soule out of troubles, that it may praise his name : and so I will waite w^t patience for deliuerence :
from the 6: vnto the 20, I praise god, I continewed well, and found godes mercie in vouchsaffinge me comfort euerie way : and now I beseech the, o Lord, giue me power to render vnto thee the Calnes[311] of my Lipes, and w^t my wholl hart to follow righteousnes.

The 25: *day*:
After my Morninge exercise I wrought tell dinner : and after diner I walked w^t my Mother and Husband to sundrie places about the house : Riceiued Henrie Dickinsons account : and after went to my Clossitt

The 29 *day*
This day Came the Lord Ewry his men to Hacknes to pay 100^li : wch was appointed them and others to pay, by the Lordes of the priue Counsill in the starr Chamber, for their riott Comitted and vnsiuill behauour att Hackenes : and so it fell out that, as it was done in the sight of our

---

[310] *weould*, wold. This is open, rolling countryside. The Yorkshire Wolds are renowned for their patchwork of ploughed fields, panorama of undulating chalk hills, and spectacular views.
[311] *Calnes*, calms. Lady Hoby perhaps seeks tranquillity in her prayers.

tenantes, so many of the tenants were bye when the mony was brought :
wch I note, as seeinge the Istuice and mercie of god to his seruants in
manifestinge to the world, who litle regardes them, that he will bringe
downe their enemes vnto them.[312]

The Lordes day :30:
This day Came Mr Busshill and his wiffe, and the Younger brothers wiffe,
Mrs Gerlington, to the sarmon in the after none, and others : god make me
truly thankfule for all his godnes, spirituall and temporall, a men.

1602 *June* 13
vntell this day, I praise god, I haue had my health, haue binn able to
attend my busenes, and hard the exercises w^t proffitt and quieet and
peace from god

The 20:
After priuatt praier I went to the church, and hard the exercises and
receiued the Comunnion : after, I Came home and praied : and hard
from my Cossine Arthur dakine : and so, in the afternone likewise, hard
some readinge of a book he sent me : and then went to my Clossitt : god
of his infinitt mercie, in his sonne, in able me to walke worthy of my
Callinge, amen, ame

The Lordes day :27:
vntill this day I haue continewed in bodely health, notwithstandinge
satan hath not ceased to Cast his mallice vpon : but temptations hath
exercisede me, and it hath pleased my god to deliuer me from all : Mrs
Girlington, w^t hir Daughter and sonne in lawe, Came, but after the
sarmon : & so, when the Communion was ended and after diner, we all
hard the afternone exercises togeather

July 4 :1602: *The Lordes day*:
This day, I praise god, I had great Comfort, both in prainge, hearinge,
and ouerCominge : but all is the Lords, to him be ascribed all praise and

---

[312]   This is an important day for the Hobys for it marks the real end of the lawsuit. Lady
Hoby takes pleasure in the public humiliation of the Eure family in front of her tenants.
For the Hackness estate, as well as for the Hobys, it was a very satisfactory resolution,
because £100 per anum had to be paid in perpetuity as a charge on the Eure land. Not
surprisingly, it has been contested by the descendants, though unsuccessfully.

thankesgiueng : we were accompaned wᵗ Mistress Girlington and hir sonne and Daughter, My Cossine Robert Dakins and his wiffe, Mistress Busshill, Mistress Brutnes, Mr Netelton, and others

The Lordes day :11: *day*:
This day, I praise god, although I was provoked to haue binne disquiated, yet god, that is nere all that Call vpon him, gaue me abilitie that I hard the exercises wᵗ Comfort and profitt : we were accompaned wᵗ Mistress Busshill and 4 other good wiues

The Lordes day :18:
This day I hard the exercises and now, as though Satan would returne, I felte his buffets : but I know my god will make them, in the end, profetable to me : we were accompaned wᵗ Mr Stillington, Mr Measse, Arthur Beuerley and his wiffe, good wiues, and, in the afternone, Mrs Girlington and his[313] sonne Theckston.

the Lordes day 25:
I praise god I hard all the exercises, although I was not verie well

August 1602: *The Lordes day* : *the* :1:
this morning it pleased the Lord Iustly, but yet mercifully, to suffer satan buffetts so that I hard not the morninge exercise so frutfully as I ought, but after ward, I praise god, I was refresshed : we were accumpaned wᵗ M Nic': Busshill and his wiffe, Mr Nettlton, and others

The :2: *day*:
Euerill Aske went from Hacknes to Mʳ Robert Stillingtons, wᵗ whom Mr Hoby sent 30ˡⁱ (besides hir wages) wᶜʰ was all the monie he had receiued before, in 4 yeares, that was dwe to hir, Lefte hir by hir father, wᶜʰ Mr Bethell had, by his will, for the bringing hir vp:[314]

The Lordes day the :8: *day*
This day, I praise god, I hard all the exercises wᵗ good health

---

[313] *his sonne*, her son.
[314] Everill's small inheritance has therefore not been used up in the Hackness household, where she has instead paid her way through her own labour.

The lordes day the :15: day
we were accompaned this day w^t Mrs Girlington, my Cossine Isones and his wiffe, Mr Hunter and his wiffe

The :16: day
Mr Thornborowe and his wiffe Came to vesitt vs, my Cossine Bourchier and his wiffe, Mr Gatt, w^t diuers others : the day following, Mr Hunter

August:1602: The :17: day
Mr Hunter Lefte his daughter Mercie[315] w^t vs, to attend my selfe

Septb:
The first of this muneth S^{ir} Tho: Hoby, my mother, and my selfe, went to Snape[316] to my Lord Burley, wher we were verie Honorably vsed by both my Lord and Lady : we lodged in our goinge thether at one Mr Vauans house, at byland Abie:[317] and in our returne we Lay at Mr Natcleffe house, at Nunington,[318] and Came home the 4 of this munth

The Lordes day :5:
The Lordes day followinge, I praise god, I hard all the exercises and was not, in all this iournie, ether sick or wearie

The :6: day
this day Mr Rhodes tooke his iournie towardes Cambrige : I was buseed about sortinge Houshould stoffe that Came from Yorke, and keept my accustomed exercises

---

[315] Mercy will do well, for she marries Master Rhodes next February.
[316] The Hobys make a journey across North Yorkshire to Snape, north-east of Masham. The castle, or hall, inherited by Lady Burghley, had been substantially restored in about 1587.
[317] Byland Abbey, near Coxwold, was founded by a small band of monks from Furness Abbey in 1171 and once boasted the biggest Cistercian church in England. So soon after the Reformation, it would not have been quite the majestic ruin we now can find.
[318] Nunnington Hall, a manor house on the banks of the River Rye near Helmsley, partly sixteenth but mainly seventeenth century, now owned by the National Trust. There is a magnificent panelled hall with a fine carved chimney-piece that Lady Hoby must have seen and known.

The 19 the Lordes day
Came Mr Rhodes home from Cambrige : and so we spent that day as be-fore

The 26: day the Lordes day
This day Likewise, I praise god, I harde all the exercises w^t profitt : and haue had my health a Long time extreordenary

October the Lordes day the :3:
This day Mr Hoby was not well, and therfore nether of vs went to the church

The Lordes day :10:
This day ve were both well, and hard all the exercises

The Lordes day :17:
this haue we peaceable the holy exercises of religion.

The Lordes day :24:
This day we were accompaned w^t our neighbours

The 27: day:
Came Mrs Girlington and my Cossine Isons to Visitt Vs

The 28: day:
Robert Coltas and his sonne was discharged our seruice

The Lordes day :31:
thIs day I hard the exercises, not so affected as I ought, and at night went to priuatt praier : some new quickeninge.

Nouemb:
all this moneth, I praied god, I haue had my health, and inioyed much Quiatt.

Decemb:
The 4 day Cam Mr Hunter from Beuerley, to Conclude a mariage betwene Mr Rhodes and his daughter:

the 28:
william Heslerton was quitt for Coininge of monie, and his fellow that taught him hanged.

1603

Ianuarie 1603:

the 25 day it was tould Mr Hoby that a shipp was wreced vp at Burnestone vppon his Land : and thus, at all times, god bestowed benefittes vpon us : god make vs thankfull[319]

ffebruary :10:

Thursday : Came Mr Robert Hunter the younger, with his Sister Elzabeth Hunter, to serue me in hir sisters place

23:[320]

This day was Mr Rhodes maried to Mercie Hunter by Mr Langdall preacher : Mr winter preached in the forenone : Mr ward should haue done the Like in the afternone but the raine hindered vs

March :8:

Elzabeth Hunter went home to hir father

The :18: *day*

this day I had some paine in my splene and faintnes in body, but god, that in rich in mercie, hath bestowed both outward and inward peace vpon me

The 23 *of March*: *which day the Quene departed this Life* /[321]

Mr Hoby receiued Letters w[ch] Came from the preuie Counsill to the Lord presedent and all the Iustesis of peace, that our Quene was sicke, w[ch] wrought great sorow and dread in all good subiectes hartes : these Letters were dated the :16: of March

---

[319]   It is recorded that the owner of Hackness is 'to have and to convert to their own proper use a wreck of the sea, flotsam, jetsam and lagan and fish royal, treasure found, lost or cast away in the sea, goods of pirates, goods of suicides, deodands and other casualties of the sea whatsoever' (Title Deeds, Whitby Confirmation Charter. NYCRO. ZF 2/1–3). Lady Hoby finds her own financial gain a more important consideration than the loss to the families of the sailors on board the wreck.

[320]   23 February, although the Parish Register for Hackness gives the date as 15 February 1603.

[321]   Queen Elizabeth I died at Richmond on 24 March 1603, having declined to go to bed until she collapsed. The accession created considerable anxiety for those in positions of power, including Sir Thomas Hoby. The entry for 27 March below records a concerned trip by the Hobys into York to check out the situation.

March :1603: The :26:
this day, beinge the Lordes day, was the death of the Quene published,
and our now kinge Iames of Scotland proclaimd kinge to sucseede hir :
god semd him a long and Hapie Raing, amen.

The :27:
went Mr Hoby and myselfe towardes Yorke, thinkinge to Continewe
there vntill all thinges were established : but he receiued letters from the
Counsill att Yorke : we both returned from Linten the 29 day to Hacknes
where we found all quiatt, god be praised

The :27: day
the sam day my Cossine Gates brought his daughter Iane, beinge of the
age of 13 yeares auld, to me, who, as he saied, he freely gaue me[322]

Aprill :1603: The 4 day
Came Letteres from the Kinge that euerie Counsiller and other offecer
should Continew in their places vntill his further pleasur were knowne,
bearing date the 30 of March

Aprill :11:
This day Mr Hoby and my selfe tooke our Iournie from Hacknes,[323] and
that night lay at Linton, wher I entertained my Cossine Dakins wiues
daughter to serue me : the day followinge we all went to Yorke

The :12:
the :13: day Mr Hoby and I, wth our owne Companie, went to Dankester
: the :14: day to Newarke : the :15: to stilton : the 16: to ware : ;and the 17:
to london, w[ch] was the Lordes day, and gott thether in time to Mr
Egertons exercises

The :18: day
all our men and Horsses rested, and the next day we sent them downe
into the Contrie

---

[322]   Young Jane will now be educated and trained in the Hoby household in return for her services.
[323]   See Road Roll (April–June 1603) (see p. 188). The Hobys are going to London for the funeral of the Queen.

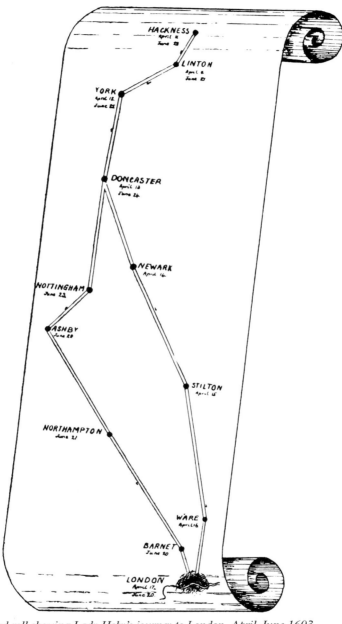

Road roll showing Lady Hoby's journey to London, April–June 1603.

The 28: *day*:

Was our Late gracious Quene buried at wesminster,[324] in that sort as became so great a prince

The 31: *day*

I dined w^t my Lady Russill, who after required the names of such as I would trust to passe some Liuinge, after hirr death, vnto me[325]

May 1603:

The 7 day our kinge to London from Tebales[326]

The 19 *day*

the Court remoued from the Charterhouse to the Tower

The 13:[327]

his Maiestie remoued from the Tower to Grennige[328]

June 7:

this day Mr Hoby and my selfe remoued from London into kent,[329] to Mr Bettnames house, wher, I praise god, I had my health very well

---

[324] Lady Anne Clifford records in her diary: 'When the Corps of Q. E. had continued at Whitehall as the Council thought fit, it was carried with great solemnity to Westminster, the Lords and Ladies going on foot to attend it'. See Clifford, *Diaries* (1990), 22. Her mother, Lady Margaret Russell, Countess of Cumberland, was sister-in-law to Sir Thomas Hoby's mother.

[325] Lady Russell was known for her interest in death and the life hereafter. She also took a delight in the ordering of pompous funerals and is obviously now thinking of her own demise.

[326] *Tebales*, Theobalds, in Hertfordshire, home to the late William Cecil, 1st Baron Burghley. It was so much frequented by Queen Elizabeth I that he had to enlarge the original house to accommodate her entourage. Her thirteen visits made it almost an auxiliary royal palace. At this date, it is the home of Robert Cecil, Lord Burghley, later 1st Earl of Salisbury (1605). King James here met Elizabeth's household officers and held conference on his way down from Scotland. He so liked Theobalds he forced an exchange for Hatfield.

[327] 23 May.

[328] *Grennige*, Greenwich. King and court are on the move to avoid an epidemic of plague which began in March and devastated both London and the provinces during the summer of 1603. In London alone, where it was said the plague lasted for eight years, 38,000 were killed. As with most illnesses, it was regarded as a sign of divine displeasure.

[329] The Hobys move out of London after the King's order on 29 May that all should leave on account of the plague and not return until the coronation. James was crowned on 25 July at Westminster.

the 20: *day*
this day we remoued from thence towardes Yorkshere, and the fist night ley at Barnett

The 21: *day*
this day we lay at Noth hamton

The 22::
at Ashbye, wher I kissed the Quenes hand[330]

The 23
we lay at Notingame/

The 24
we lay at Dankester

The 25
at Yorke, wher we staied all the Lordes day.

June 27:
we lay at Lindton wᵗ my Cosine Dakins

The 28:
we Came safe, I praise god, to Hacknis[331]

July the :5:
this day I Continewed my ordenarie exercises, and had my health very well : Mr Bouth sent Mr Hoby 6: Gulls[332]

The :6: *day*
this day Came Hilarie from London, and brought our plate wᵗ him : god be praised who hath deliuered vs from all opprission and vsrie[333]

---

[330] Anne of Denmark, married to James (1589). The Queen travelled south in a progress separate from the King, but accompanied by many court ladies jostling for favour. The home of the Countess of Huntingdon, where Lady Hoby had been educated and trained, was at Ashby-de-la-Zouche.
[331] The Hobys have been away from Hackness for two-and-a-half months.
[332] Gulls' eggs were boiled and traditionally served in a nest lined with moss.
[333] *vsrie*, usury.

The :11: *day*
Some trouble and sonme Victorie, I praise god

August :5:
this day I went to the Church before diner and after, because the day was kept Holy day in remembrance of the Kinges deliuerance for the Conspericie of the Goweres in skotland[334]

The 10 *day*
Mr Hoby ride to Yorke to the Assises from Hacknes : S[ir] Edward Stanape died the 12 day

The 13
I went to vesitt my Cossine Isons wiffe, who I had not seene since hir deluerie[335]

24 *day*
Came Robert Netelton from York, and tould vs that the number of those that died of the plauge at London :124: ; that Newcastill was greously veseted w[t] a sore plaug, likewise Hull:[336] the Kinge tooke, About this time, his iournie into walls[337] w[t] the Quene and the younge prince

Septemb 16.
The :2: day my Lord Ssheffeld Came vnto York, beinge our presedent

The 4: *day*
we hard that the plauge was spred in whitbye,[338] and that ther died at London :3200: a week

---

[334] *Conspericies of the Goweres,* James declared 5 August a public holiday in commemoration of his deliverance from a supposed conspiracy of would-be kidnappers, led by John Ruthven, the Earl of Gowrie, in Scotland (1600). A special prayer was issued for use on this day.
[335] *deluerie,* delivery.
[336] All seaports were vulnerable to plague carried by dogs and rats' fleas in ships.
[337] *walls,* Wales.
[338] This is serious for the surrounding countryside. Lady Hoby mentions the plague on and off in this part of Yorkshire throughout the period between September 1603 and May 1605. Whitby is a picturesque ancient fishing village. It has been a port since the twelfth century and was the home of the explorer, Captain James Cook. It is now much frequented by tourists. Lying on both sides of the River Esk, the old town is on the East Cliff. Famous

The :8: day
Mr Hoby and my selfe went to Newton to my Mother, and on Saterday the :10: day Came backe from thence to Hacknes, wher we hard that one in the towne, hauinge binne in Harwoodall at Mr Busshills house whouse childrine were Come from whitbie was fallen sicke w^t :3: of his childrin more : vpon which, fearing the worst, we Returned the same night to Newton againe, wher we remaine vntill god shall please, in mercie, to deall w^t vs[339]

The Lordes day the :18:
Mr Hoby, my mother, and my selfe, w^t our saruants, went to Thorpbasitt wher we hard Mr phileps preache : in the after none we hard him at winteringame,[340] wher he Continewede his exercise vntill 5 a cloke att night

Sept :21: 1603
This day, beinge the Remembrance of St Mathew, Mr philipes Came and preached at winteringame : we were accompaned w^t him and his wiffe, Mr Stricland and his wiffe, my Cossine Dakins and his wiffe, w^t diuers others : we hard of Mr BeuerCotes death, an Honest Religious Counsiler at Yorke

The 22: day
Mr Crakeerste Came and dined w^t vs

The 23
Mr Hunter Came and kept vs Companie at diner, who tould vs of the exercise that should be held for this great mortalitie,[341] which was not only at London but all most disparced throw all the Realme of England : god of his mercie pardon our sinmens, for his Christes sake, aAem.

---

for its jet and former whaling industry, it is full of tradition and history, and possesses a fine ruined abbey whose lands once included Hackness. Yorkshire's earliest poet, Caedmon of Whitby, was an old cowherd working at the abbey. The abbess was so impressed with his song about the Creation that she admitted him as a monk.

[339] Fear of the plague has driven the Hobys from their own home.

[340] Thorpbassett and Winteringham are near Linton where Lady Hoby was born.

[341] In remembrance of the dead and dying, the King ordered that a public holiday and fast should be held on 4 October. Special prayers were offered, sermons of repentance preached. Lady Hoby notes, on 25 October, that a special collection was made by local people for those afflicted in Whitby.

The Lordes day :25:

This Morninge Mr Hoby, w^t our Houshould, went to Thorpbasitt, wher we hard Mr phileps : and in the after none we hard Mr Clarke at winteringam

The 26: day

Mr Hoby Ridd to sitt w^t S^ir Henrie Griffeth of the subsedie at Garton : I was accompaned w^t Iohn Dawson and his wiffe at dinner, and and my Cossine Gatt

The 27 day

thes day we hard from Hacknes that all there was well, But that the sicknes was freared to be at Roben Hood bay,[342] not farr off : I Continewe my accostomed exercises but my increasinges in goodes waies is not as I thirst for.

The 28: day

this day Mr Hoby went to snanton[343] to sitt vpon the subsedie, vhir Mr Coniers of Scarborow and he had some vnkindnes

October :2:

This day Mr Langdall Came to winteringe,[344] and preached in the forenone verie profetable : we were accompaned at dinner w^t Mr Langdall, Mr Crakcrofte, Mr Dobson, Mr farfaxe, my Cossine Robert Dakine and his wiffe, and my Cossine Robert Lakine

The .3: day

we Came to Hacknes safe home, I praise god : Mr Hoby this morninge discharged Henrie Brathwath

---

[342] Robin Hood's Bay is an old fishing village in a picturesque district popular with tourists. The old part, with its steep, narrow little streets, lies in a stream-cut ravine at a point where the cliffs drop to the sea. The outlook seaward is superb and the National Trust protects much of the fine surrounding countryside. In spite of the name there is no historical evidence to connect the village with Robin Hood, but there may be truth in the tradition that he took refuge here. The old church of Fyling Hall nearby was probably erected by the Abbot of Whitby and would have been visited by the Hobys.

[343] Snainton is now a rather straggling village westward of Scarborough. The Victorian church has a lych-gate with a striking Norman arch that Lady Hoby must have known.

[344] *winteringam*, Lady Hoby attends services at the church at Winteringham quite often.

The :4: day

Mr Rhodes exercised in the church from 9 in the morninge vntill 4 : in the afternone, when we had a generall Comunione : which fast was appointed by the Kinge to be heald thorow out the wholl Realme in regard of the generall mortalite

The :5: day

Mr Hoby, my Mother, and my selfe, went to the dalls this day : we had in our Gardens a second sommer, for Hartechokes bare twisse, whitt Rosses, Read Rosses : and we, hauinge sett a musk Rose the winter before, it bare flowers now. I thinke the Like hath seldom binnseene : it is a great frute yeare all ouer[345]

The :6: day

After praier I buesied my selfe w^t presaruing, and other thinges wch was to be done in the House : in the morninge my Mother went to Newton

The .7: day

this day I fasted untill Eueninge, eatinge nor drinkinge any thinge, begging of the Lord that blissne wch yet I want:[346] the Lord Heare me for his Christs sack, amen

The Lordes day :9:

This morninge I did eate a litle bread before I went to the church, wher, the exercises being done, and after dinner, Immedieatly, we went to the church, for Mr Rhodes Reed to Skarborowe to exercise there : at Night, Mr Rhodes, his wiffe, and Mr Netelton his wiffe, and Mr ferfaxe, supped w^t vs and staied the repeticion

---

[345]   October brings an 'Indian' summer. See also the entry for 1 November. The artichoke is one of the world's oldest plants. The Elizabethans grew it both as a vegetable and for ornament, and it was believed to be ruled by Venus, 'to provoke lust'. Gerard, however, states in his *Herball*: 'which way soever they be drest and eaten, they are a meat more fit for swine, than men'. Lady Hoby may well have had white Yorkshire roses in her garden. Samuel Johnson's *Dictionary* notes that 'In May and June come roses of all kinds, except the *musk*, which comes later'. She is clearly pleased that it is blooming. It is known that in their gardens Yorkshire folk are fortunate in that their roses last longer and have enhanced colourings in the northern climate. The distilled water of roses was considered good for strengthening the heart, refreshing the spirits, and easing pain in the eyes. Gerard gives a recipe for Rose Conserve, in which roses are boiled for three to four hours; four parts sugar are added to one part roses; then boiled gently and stirred till cool.

[346]   *blissne*, blessing. This is one of those haunting entries that might hint at Lady Hoby's desire to conceive.

The :11:
Mr Hunter Came to vs to dinner : and in the afternone he, w^t Mr Hoby, Mrs Netelton, and my selfe, went to the dalls : this day Cam Jane Grange

The 12: *day*
the most of this day was spent in the church : and at night I, after supper, I praied publickly and priuatly, and went to bed

The :13: *day*:
After praier I did eate, went about my beuse, & after diner I talked w^t Mr Rhodes : then went to praier and, sonne after, to supper

The :14: *day*
this day Came Mr Hicksone from Scarbor and dined w^t vs : and in the afternone Mr Hoby and I went to the dalls.

The Lordes day
MrVrpith was buried[347]

The 19 *day*
this day the exercise was kept by Mr ward, Mr Staneford, and Mr Rhodes

The 22: *day*
this day Mr Hoby made Mr Staneford (who was w^{t}out a place) an offer to Come and winter w^t vs, wher he shoul haue all things needful touching his diat and Lodginge, w^{t}out monie:[348] I was necessarily buisie all this day, & at eueinge I praied according to my Vse.

The 23 *day*
this day I hard the plauge was so great at whitbie that those wch were cleare shutt themselues vp, and the infected that escaped did goe abroad : Likewise it was reported that, at London, the number was taken of the Liuinge and not of the deed : Lord graunt that these Iudgmentes may Cause England w^t speed to tourne to the Lord[349]

---

[347] This means the loss of an old friend. Master Urpith, possibly a cleric, has been mentioned several times.
[348] Another charitable gesture on the part of the Hobys.
[349] This gives an indication of how the plague was regarded as a punishment from God.

The :24 day
This day my Mother Came from Newton and Lay wᵗ vs at Hacknes : Mr Hunter and his wiffe Came, and lay at Mr Rhodes his House.

The 25: day

there was a Colection for those at whitbie and was gotten 50s volentarie

This day the exercise of fastinge and preaching was Continewed by Mr ward and Mr Rhodes Vntill 2 : or 3 A Clocke at night : Mr Hunter and his wiffe supped wᵗ vs: Mr Rhodes and his wiffe, Mr Netelton and his wiffe, and Mr Constable

The :26: day
After priuatt praier I went forth and dined wᵗ Mr Hoby at Mrs Rhodes House : and after diner went to the dall's to see my mother

The 27: day
This day Mr Hunter and his wiffe dined wᵗ vs, and others : we hard the sicknis was still great at whitbie

The Lordes day 30:
This day the exercises were Continewed at Church, forenone and after, although great defecte was amongst Vs in the morninge.

Nouember :1: day
at this time we had in our gardens Rasberes³⁵⁰ faire sett againe, and allmost euerie Hearbe and flower bare twiss : Mʳ ToutVill dined vᵗ vs :

The 2: day:
This day the exercise was kept by Mr Rhodes at the church alone : Mrs Darley Came to see Vs, and, after we had supped, went to Mrs Gatt to Eaton, wher she lay at Routhes

The 4 day:
Mr pollard, the Head Constable, dined wt vs : stronge is the force of vanitie but the Lord is greater than all:³⁵¹ readinge, praier, and the word, be exelent Helpes to a godly and peacable life Ease slaethe the foollishe

---

³⁵⁰ Traditionally, raspberries are made into a strong sweet Yorkshire vinegar often served with meat but also used as a remedy for colds and sore throats.
³⁵¹ Master Pollard was sometime High Constable of Pickering Lythe. Is Lady Hoby here making a veiled comment on his pride?

15: *day*

This day we had Mr farfaxe and his wiffe, Mr Skatey, Mrs Netelton, at dinner wᵗ vs : we sawe the printed pater³⁵² of those that died at and about London this sommer, wᶜʰ were :31967: from July to october

The 16: *day*

The exercise was kept by Mr warde, Mr Smith, and Mr Rhodes

The :17: *day*

Elzabeth Penock Came. Mr Netelton brought vs the Kinges proclimation for the restraninge som Combustious persones that sought reformation.

The Lordes day :20:

this day I hard Mr Rhodes at the church Before dinner : and, after, My Mother and my Cossine Isons dined wᵗ vs and others: it pleased god to exercise my Cossine Edward Isons, about this time, wᵗ A fealinge of his sinned and sorow for them.

The 24 *day*

Came waddi:

The :26: *day*:

Vntill this day, I praise god, I had my health, and hard nothinge much worthy recordinge : but this day I receiued a letter wᶜʰ much troubled me, vntill I went to God by praier, who hard me and, in mercie, taught me to make a good vse of itt : I harde Likewise, by Mr Lacie of Seamer, of the misirie wᶜʰ Mrs Gatt was in

The 30: *day: December /*

This day the exercise was Continewed at church : and after all was done there, Mrs Girlinton and hir sonne, wᵗ my Cossine Edward Isons, Came in wᵗ vs, about whom there was some speach touchinge his estate

December : :12: *day*:

This day Mr Hoby tooke his Iournie from Hacknes to Linton, and so the next day to York

---

³⁵² *pater*, paper.

The :15: *day*:
this day, towardes night, Came to Hacknes my yong Cossine Brigges : at wch time I hard that Sir Robert Swift had slane Ryes sonne of dankester :

The 20:
Came Mr Hoby home from Yorke.

1604

Januarie the 5: :1604:[353]
This day Came to Hacknes my Cossine Robert Dakins and his wiffe

The 4 *day*
beinge the Lordes day we receiued at the church

The :10: *day*
Mr Hoby, myselfe, and both my Cossines, w^t Mr Rhodes and diuerse others, dined w^t my mother at the dalls

The :11: *day*
My Cossine and his wiffe went home

The 19: *day*
Mr Hoby went this day to kellame[354] about a Comitione for Mrs Goringe.

The 20: *day*
this day, towardes euen, I went to vesitt Munkmans wiffe who was sore aflicted in minde, but for what she hath not Yet vttered : after I Came home, my Cossine Arthur Dakins Came to Vesitte vs.

This 21: *day*
we dined at Mr Rhodes house, and Mr Hoby Came home

The 24:
Mr Hunter and mr william Stricklande Cam

The 25 *day*
we all dined at the dalls w^t my Mother :

The 26: *day*
Mr Hoby sent Iames to Yorke

The Lordes day 28:
This day I hard the exercises at Church

---

[353] Here Lady Hoby dates the New Year from January.
[354] *kellame*, Kilham, in the East Riding of Yorkshire.

The 29 *day*
Mr Hoby sent Iames towardes London, and my Cossine Robert Dakins went hom

The :31: *day*
Came Mr ward W^t his wiffe, Mr Teuble w^t his wiffe, from Skarborow to vesitt Mr Hoby and my selfe

ffeburie 1605[355] *The* 1: *day*
This day my cossine Dakins departed and the Rest of our Gess after dinner

The 29 *day*
this afternone Came Mr. Teublie from Scarborow and brought Mr Hoby That he was Chossine Burgisse for the Town and Mr ffrances Ewrie[356]

March :1604:
This day, after prairs, I tooke my Leaue of Mr Ward of Skarborow : sent for Mrs Netelton to dinner : in the after none, when she was Gon, I reed a Little of Mr Rogers book to Anne france : and, Leauinge Mr Hunter w^t Mr Hoby, I went to priuatt praier and medetation.

The 12 *day*
The baleffs of Skarborow ffeasted Mr Hoby

The 13: *day*
This day Mr Hoby went towardes London : Mr Rhodes and Mr Netelton accompaned him to the watter side : my mother Came the same day and Lay w^t me

The :23: *day*
I sent Netelton to Yorke w^t a letter to Mr Hoby, and Lockes to watters.

The 25:
This eueninge Came waddie from London and brough me word of Mr Hobis health : but althinges may not Concurr, for in this Life we must

---

[355] February 1604.
[356] The date of the return of the writ stating that Sir Thomas Posthumous Hoby, Knight, and Francis Eure, esq., were elected to represent Scarborough is 6 March 1604. Sir Thomas had previously represented Appleby, Westmorland, with Ralph Bowes.

haue Gaul as well as Hunie : but blessed be god that tourneth althinges Vnto good to his Childrine

March 1604: *The* 27: *day*
This day I kept my Chamber, and was not well able to performe good dutes : in the After none I took Iames accountes

The :28: *day*
I was better in health and

Aprill 1604: *the* :4
This day Mr Ward sent me letters from Mr Hoby, wherby I vnderstood that he was in health, I praise god

The :5 6 et 7
day verie stormie and snowie wether.[357]

Easter day : 8 :
A great snowe and did snowe allmost all the day

The :9: *day*
All the morninge till none, sleet and extreme Could:

The :15: *day which was the Lordes day*
This morninge Came Mr Hoby Home from London, I praise god, very well, and in a good time for diuerse respectes for vs both.

The :16: *day*
Came Mr Ward and his wiffe, and Mrs Tewblie to vesitt me

The :17:
Mr Baileffe Battie, Hearinge Mr Hoby was Come Home, Came to vesitt vs from Skarborow.

The 23:
This morninge Mr Hoby tooke his Iournie Towardes London, and Lefte me not well

---

[357] A traditional word in Yorkshire for such weather is 'floudby'.

May :1604: *The* :18:
This afternone Came my Younge Cossine Arthur Dakins

The :19:
day Came my Cossine Arthur Dakin Came, and The Lords day

The :21: *day*
This morninge I went w^t diuerse freindes To Skarborow, wher we tooke a boote and went to sea : supped at Mr Teubles, and after Came home

The 22 *et* 23 *day*
I Continewed sickly and weake, hauinge inward and outward weaknes

The 28: *day*:
I went w^t my mother and other freindes to the woold to Newton

The :29:
Mr Ward exercised the forenone at wintringame Church, and Mr Rhodes in the afternone

The 30:
my mother, and my Cossine Isons and his wiffe, went w^t me to Vesitt my Cossin Boucher that Lay in child bed :

The :31:
I Came home to Hacknes, I praise god, in saftie and peace

Iune 1604: *The* :13:
This day I sent Randoll Carlill towardes London With Horsses for his Master to Com downe

The 16 *day*:
Came Mrs Stricklande and his[358] sister Katrime to Vesitte me

The 18:
Came Mr Gatt of Seamer, his sonne, and Mr Lacie, Mr ward and his wiffe, and Mrs Teuble

---

[358] *his sister*, her sister, Katrine or Katherine.

The 19: *day*
these strangers went away in the after none

The :30:
This day Came Mr Hoby home from London to Hacknes very well, I praise god.

Iuly The Lordes day 1:
This day at Night Mr Hoby discharg Anne france his seruice

The :12: *day*
This day Came Mrs farley, Mrs Girlington, my Cossin Isons and his wiffe, and Mr ward.

July : 1604: *The 8 the Lordes day*:
This day Came Mr Saxtone to dinner to vs, who preached in the after none

August :1:
The first of this month my Mother Turned ouer the farme at the dalls vnto Mr Hoby, beinge werie of itt[359]

The 3 day
Cam Sir Rash :

September The 8: *day*
This day Mr Hoby and my selfe went to Newton to vesitt my Mother : he escaped a daungerous fall from his horsse at his first getting vp :

The Lordes day :9:
we rested this day at Newton, wher we were accompaned w^t Mr Strickland and his wiffe that Came to see vs : in the afternone Mr Rhodes preached.

The .10: *day*
I Came home to Hacknes, and Mr Hoby went to Cottingame to sett vpon a Comittion betwene Mr Smith and Mr Maltby

---

[359] This is the farm that Lady Hoby visits when she writes of walking to the dales, possibly Lowdales or Highdales Farm.

1604: *September The* 19 *day*:
This day there was a fast in our church : the exercise was Continewed from 8 vntill :3 in the afternone by Mr ward and Mr Rhodes

The Lordes day the 23:
Cam Rafe.

October :
This morning went Mr Hoby to snanton to sett vpon the subsidie : and after went to portintane[360] to the sessions

The 1 *day of Nouember*:
I tooke Elzabeth wood.[361]

The :12: day we Came from Linton to Hull[362]

The :13: day we Came from Hull to Linkon

The :14: day we Came Linkon to Ankester

Nouember:
The :15: day we Came from Ankester to Stilton.

The 15: day we Came from Stilton to Roiston, wher the kinge Lay that Night.

The :17: day we Came from Roiston to London, and alighted at my Cossine Strangwaies his house, wher we supped : and after supper we went to my Lady Russills house were we lay

Nouember 1604: *The Lordes day* :18:
The :18: day I went to Mr Egerton Sarmon before denner, and in the afternone

The 19: *day*
we sent our men and Horsses backe againe towardes Yorkshere

---

[360] *portintane*, Portington, near Howden in the East Riding.
[361] Lady Hoby means that she has taken on Elizabeth as one of her servants.
[362] See Road Roll (November 1604–February 1605) (see p. 206).

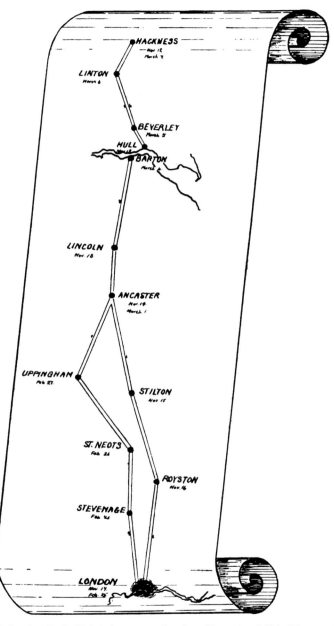

Road roll showing Lady Hoby's journey to London, November 1604–February 1605.

The :21: day
I waited on my Lady Russill to Mr Egertons Lecture

The :23: day
I Likewise went to the Church

The Lordes day :25:
I went in the Morninge and in the afternone to hear Mr Egerton : and after my Lady was Come home, Mistress Cartwright Came to se my Lady, to whom I deliuered Sir Arthure Dakins message.

December 1604 :3:
This morninge did william Harison serue a supena vpon Mr Hoby and my selfe to Answer to I know not what.[363]

Saint Iohns Day:
This morninge Sir Antonie Cooke[364] was Cutt, and died, hauinge an Artrie Cutt wher of he was tould before

December the 29: *The Lordes day*
This eueninge after supper, Sir Edward Hoby, wt a fall of his Horsse as he was Ridinge to his Lodginge, brake his Arme in 2 places

[363]   Yet more litigation for the Hobys.
[364]   This is Sir Thomas Hoby's cousin. In September 1591 Lady Russell had proposed enlisting his help to steal the young widow Margaret Devereux away from Thomas Sidney. At this time 'artery' was the name given to the trachea or windpipe so his fatal operation may have been an attempt to ease his breathing. Long before, Galen had discovered that arteries were not merely air pipes but contained blood as well as vital air or spirit, but it was not until 1616 that the English physician, William Harvey, began his lectures to reveal his discoveries about the circulation of the blood.

1605

Ianuarie 23: 28 *day*
This day Mr Hoby entertained Christopher Geninges

feb: 1604:
The 5 day in the Morninge S^{ir} Edward Staffor died[365]

The :8: *day*
This day was Mr Egerton, w^t diuers others, silenced by the Busshoppe of London.[366]

The :11: *day*
Sir Tho: Vauesores child was Christened : wittensses were The Lord Effingame and his Lady, w^t my Lady Elzabeth Suthell : wher I was

The :14 *day*
was my Lord Delawares Child Christened : wetnesses were the Lady Anne Gleman, my Lady Tracie, and my Lord Suche : wher I was.

The 25:
This Morninge Mr Hoby and all our Companie Came forthe of London : and the same night Lay att Stpheniage[367]

The 26: *day*
we Came from thence to Saint Needes[368]

The 27 *day*
The 27 we traueled to Vpingame

ffeb 28: *day*
This day S^{ir} william Bolstred brough vs to his House, wher we staied all the day

---

[365] Sir Edward Stafford (1552?–1605), diplomat, ambassador to France (1583–90).
[366] This may have had something to do with Egerton's introduction of a petition to the lower house of Convocation for a reformed Prayer Book (1604), signed by no less than 1,000 discontented Puritan ministers. Certain alterations were agreed at the Hampton Court Conference, but they went in the direction of catholicizing rather than of puritanizing the Prayer Book.
[367] *Stpheniage*, Stevenage.
[368] *Saint Needes*, St Neots.

The 1 *of March*
Theis day we went from thence to Ankester

2 *of March & the* :3:
The 2 of March we Came to Sir william wrayes house house, wher we staied the Lordes day

The 4 *day*
we gott verie well vnto the water side, and Came to Barton to bed.

The 5 *day*
we Came to Beuerley, wher we Lay with Mr Iohnson

The 6 *day*
we Came all safe, I praise god, to Linton, wher I saw my Mother, and Lodged w^t S^ir Arthur Dakins.

The 7: *day*
I thanke god we gott verie well Home to Hacknes.

The 11: *day*
Mr ward, the preacher of Skarborowe, and his wiffe w^t hime, Came to sse Vs, and staied that Night

The 31: *day Ester day : the Lordes day*
This day was verie Cold, and diuers shoures of snowe & hall:[369] we had a Comunone at the Church : my Cosin Isons was here

Aprill 1605:
The first day Mr Rhodes preached in the Morninge : Mr Hunter, his father in Law, and he, after the Sarmon, took possision of Vnderill his house to Mr Hobys Vse and mine : at Night I thought to writt my daies Iournee as before, becaus, in the readinge over some of my former spent time, I funde some profitt might be made of that Course from which, thorow two much neccligence, I had a Longe time dissisted:[370] but they

---

[369]   *hall*, hail.
[370]   Lady Hoby decides to be more disciplined over her diary. For the remaining months she does make an almost daily entry, but it is often just a brief list of her activities and encounters. The original intention to record her religious exercise has been superseded by the busy life of the Hackness household.

are vnworthye of godes benefittes and especiall fauours that Can finde no time to make a thankfull recorde of them

The 2: day:

This day, after priuatt prairs, I went about vntil dinner time : and in the afternone Came Mrs Bell wᵗ hir daughter, good wiffe Langdall, and hir sister warde : after, I walked about a litle, and then went to priuatt praier

The :3: day

This day we were accompaned with Mr palphereman & his wiffe, Mr Netelton & his wiffe, And Younge Mr Gatt : I hard Newes of my Mothers health.

Aprill :4:

This Morninge, after priuatt prairs, I went about the House : in the Afternone Came goodwiffe Darfeeld to me, to intreat of hir Daughters Cominge to me who was disirious to serue me : and towarde Night I went to my accostomed exercises of Readinge and praier.

The 5 day

I must giue   This day I entertained Elzabeth Darfeld : all the day I was busie
hir 8s: at   in the Gardin, and after I went to priuatt praier & readinge.
Mar:

The :6: day

This day I bestoed to much time in the Garden, and therby was worse able to performe sperituall dutes

The Lordes day :7:

This morninge, after priuatt preperation, I went to Church : & so likewise in the afternone : and after the exercises I went to readinge and priuatt praier

The 8 day

After priuatt prairs I went about vntill praier time : and after dinner went into the Garden, vntill I retourned to priaut praier and readinge.

Aprill :1605 The :9:

This morninge, after priuat priars, I was busie in the Garden : and after dinner Likewise vntill euenige I ws ther, at which time I returned to priuat prairs

The 12
this day Came vnto Mr Hoby The wardons of the Ospetall

The :13:
from the 9 to the 13, I praise god, I had my health, and was buseed in my garden the most of the day

The 14 *the Lordes day*
This day was the first day that the Commune praier Booke was read in our Church[371]

The :15: *day*
This day Came Mr Hunter and his wiffe, wᵗ his sonne Johnsone, who supped with vs

The :16: *day*

Bese Bell Came.   This Morninge went Gorge ward towardes London : Mr Bell and his wiffe brought his daughter to serue Mr Hoby, who wᵗ my selfe and others, dined at Mr Rhodes : Sⁱʳ Richard Cholmley Came to Conferr wᵗ Mr Hoby : and at night I went to priuatt readinge and praier

17: *d*
This day, after I was readie, Came Mr Hunter and his wife to take their leaues : I was busie vntill night : and then Came Leters, touchinge Recusants,[372] from the Counsill vnto Mr Hoby, and after I went to priuatt praiers

The 18 :
This day, I praise god, I was euerie way prouided for : Mr Stillington sent for his monie we ought hime : I had occasion of Anger : at my vsiall time I went to priuatt praier and medetation.

The 19 :
This Morninge I sent to Trutsdall, to Vesitt my Cossine Isons wiffe who Lay in childbedd : I sent, Likewise, to Iosuas wiffe who was brought to bed : after I went about, and in the afternone I went to priuatt prairs and readinge

---

[371]   In 1605 Master Richard Rhodes signed the parish register as priest.
[372]   This is the first time the word 'Recusants' is used.

The 21: *day The Lordes day*

This morninge Came my Cossine Isons to invite vs to the Christeninge of his Childe : after all the exercises was don I walked w^t Mr Hoby, and after Came to priuatt priaer

1605 *Aprill* : *The* 22 *day*

This day, after priuatt prairs, I was bused w^t many thinges about the house : and at night returned to priuat readinge and praier.

The 24:

This day Came my Cossine Robert Dakins to Hacknes from Trutsdall, wher he, w^t my Lady Cholmley and my Lady Dakines, were wetenses[373]

The 25 *day*

This day my Cossine and Mistress Rhodes dined w^t vs : and towardes night I went to priuatt readinge and praier

The 26: *day*:

This day, I praise god, I was better in health then before : I deliuered the linan, that was in Anne Mathews keepinge, to Elzabeth Bell : and After went to priuat praier.

The 28: *day*:

This Morninge Came Mr Gat and Mr Lacy from Seamer, and after they were gone I retourned to Readinge and priuat praier

Aprill 1605 29 *The Lordes day*

This day, after both the Exercises were done at the church, and had walked a whill, I retourned to priuatt praier

The 31:

This day Came Mr Hicksone and his sonne, Mr ffranke of fallie,[374] to see Mr Hoby

---

[373] *wetenses*, witnesses.

[374] *fallie*, Filey, on the coast, now a popular tourist area because of its magnificent and safe sands. The old fishing quarter still has some cottages with secret hiding places, and sliding panels, originally for the use of recusant clergy.

May :1:
This day I was accompaned w^t Mistress Netelton untill night : and after I went to my priuatt exercises

The :3 *day*
This day Mr Hoby satt at Snanton vpon a Commition : Mr ward and his wiffe were w^t vs, and mr fishe of Skarborowe.

The :4: *day*
After Mr fishe, Mr ward and his wiffe, were gone, I went about and tooke some order in the house : and after went to priuatt praier and readinge

The :5: *day*
This day Mr warde exercised, for Mr Rhodes was absent : we weare accompaned w^t Mr fish of Skarborow and others

May 1605: *The* :6: *day*
This Afternone I went to Trutsdall to vesit my freindes there w^t my Mother, Mr ward and his wiffe, Mr fishe, Mistress Netelton and Mistress Rhodes : and at my retourne I went to priuatt prair

The :7: *day*
This after none we all went abroad to take the Aire and to fishe : and after I Came Home I went to priuatt praier.

The 11: *day*
This day was waddie accused to haue gotten a Child, but he denied the facte:[375] Mr ward of Skarborow sent me Botles and Blue starch, and Gorge warde Came Home from London.

The Lordes day :12:
This day I went to the Church, but, hauinge an Indisposition of Bodie, I profitted not as I ought

The :13:
This day I tooke somthinge for my Shoulder, which had a paine in it by reason of Could, w^ch, I praise god, did me good : afflictions drawe one nerer to god.

[375] Waddie admits to this, however, on 17 May.

The :14: d
This day Mr Hoby reed filinge church, there to take order for recusants[376]

May 1605: The :15:
This day, I praise god, I had health and [torn][377] and at night I went to my accustom [torn] exercises

The :16: day :
This day, after prairs, I went about n [torn] able to ouercome all that exalted itself : but god, that is riche vnto all, be mercifull to me : I was busie about necesarie affars, and at my time I retourned to my ordenarie exercises

The 17 day
This morninge Mr Hoby went to Snanton, and Mr ward w^t him, to sitt vpon a Comition for recusantes : wher waddie, beinge examened, Confessed himselfe to haue binne Lewde w^t Elzabeth Penocke, Snanton, Brumton, and Eberston, were restraned for feare of the plauge.[378]

The 18: day
This day I was busie about the House, but withall full of wandering distractions : at Night I went to priuatt praier

The Lordes day 19
This day our ordenarie gess[379] and our accostom [torn] exercises were performed.

The 20 day
This morninge we went to the Church and Hard a sarmon : after dinner Mr Hoby, and our Neighbours of Skarborow that dined w^t vs, [torn] went into the fairs : and towardes night, when all was gonn, I retourned to priuatt praier

---

[376] Sir Thomas probably rode to Fyling Hall church near Robin Hood's Bay.
[377] The next three lines of the diary are affected by the torn page.
[378] Residents were forbidden to leave their villages for fear of carrying the plague with them.
[379] *gess*, gests: actions, things that routinely had to be done.

1605 *The* 21: *day*
This day we were accompaned w^t Mistress Rhodes : and towardes eueinge Mr Hoby and I walked abroade : and after I went priuatt praier.

The 23: *day*
This morninge Came Mr Gatt from Seamer, and shewed Mr Hoby the bill wch was put into the Chancerie against hime by the tenantes of Seamer : at night I went to priuatt priaer.

The :24: *day*
This day Mr Hoby sent to Trutsdall erley : Mr Robert Hunter Came to see vs : we hard of the Creation of Erles and Barons at London, and of the Christeninge of the Kinges Daughter by the Ducke of Brunswicke, the Quens Brother, and by the Lady Orbela,[380] and the Lady NorththumberLande : towardes Night I went to priuatt praier and readinge

The 25 *day*
This day, after prairs, I was busie about the House: in the after none S^{ir} Arthur Dakins Sent his man to see vs : and after I had praied I went to readinge.

May 26: *The Lordes day*
This I Continewed my accustomed [*torn*] at Church, and in the afternone went to [*torn*] wherby I was reueued beter able to performe good dutis

The 27 *day*
This day Came Mr ward from Skarborow : and towardes eueninge we walked forth : Mr Hoby discharged Henrie Turner.

The 28: *day*
This day Mr Hoby hard, Certainly, that Hunenbye was infected.[381]

The 29 *day*
This day I Continewed in health and Comfort, I praise god.

---

[380] Lady Arabella Stuart (1575–1615), first cousin of James I.
[381] The plague is in Hunmanby, a village at the foot of the Wolds.

Iune 1605: *The* :5: *day*

This day Mr ward went to Trutsdall to vesitt my Cosine Isons wiffe, who was sicke : and, towardes night, went away

The :6: *day*:

This day we were busie about clipping : Mr ward went to Trutsdall w^t Mr Rhodes : and towardes Night I went to my accostomed exercises :

June :1605: *The* :7: *day*

This day I went to vesitte my Cossine Isons wiffe who was sicke : I was accompaned w^t Mr ward, Mr Rhodes, and Mistress Netelton / at Night my Cossine Robert Dakins Came, desiringe Mr Hoby to be a Godfather to his grandchilde.

The :8: *day*

This day, after I had binne abroad, I had some talke w^t Mr ward touchinge Mr Rhodes : after dinner Mr ward departed : and towardes night I went to priuatt examenation and praier.

The Lordes day :9: *day*

This day, hauinge care to rise in time, I went to church, and so likewise in the after none, but not so profetablye as I ought, beinge not well

The :10: *day*

This day I had my health better, I praise god, as also the peace of my mind, w^ch, throwe vaine affections before, was vnquiatt : at Night I went to priuatt readinge and praier, the best helpes in such Cases.

The :11: *day*

This day S^ir Henrie Cholmley was sarued w^t a Kinges Letter for fisshinge

This I went to church, beinge a mariage and a sarmon : in the afternone I was busie about the house, and towardes night I went to my accostomed exercises this a[382]

June 1605: *The* :12: *day*

This day Mr Rhodes went to the would [*torn*] at the Babtisinge my Cossine Robert Dak [*torn*] Childe : I Continewed exercises, and, towardes night, went to priuatt praier.

---

[382] An incomplete entry.

The :13: day
This day, I praise god, I Continewed in health [*torn*] hard from my mother : and towardes night went to priautt readinge and praier.

The :15 day
This day, towardes night, Cam S^{ir} A [*torn*] Dakins : wch day I went to my Mother [*torn*]

The Lordes day The :16: day
This day Mr Rhodes Continewed his exer [*torn*] w^t much profitt : we were accompaned [*torn*] Mr Busshill at dinner, and my Cossin [*torn*] Robert Lakine extreordenarie.

The 17
This day in the after none I went to [*torn*] Mother, and Mr ward Came from [*torn*] borowe

The 18: day
This morninge I went to Newton to s [*torn*] my Mother

The :19: day
This day I retourned very safe, I praise god.

[*Torn*] 1605: [*Torn*] 20: *day*
This morninge Came Mr Belbye and his wiffe, w^t Mr Lacye of Seamer, to vesitt Mr Hoby and me

[*Torn*] *the* :21:
This day I was busie about the House : and towardes Night I went to my priuatt exercises

The :23: day:
This day I went to church and hard the exercises : Mr Busshill Cam hom and dined w^t vs

The 24
This day I went to church wher there was a sarmon, by reason ther was a Mariadge:

The :25:
This day Mr Hoby Reed to Meett Mr^{is} Henrie Greffeth at Northburton.

The :26: day
I was busie about the house : and in the Afternone had some Conference
wᵗ Mr Rhodes.

[Torn] he 27:
This day I went about the house : had temporall prosperitie but found inward
Corruption, to my great greffe : and towardes night I went to priuatt praier.

The 30 day The Lordes day
This day I hard the exercises and receiued the Comunione : my Cossin
Isons Came in the afternone.

July :1: day
This day, after praier, I was busie [torn] after, diuers accedence Came
worthy of [torn] and towardes Night I went to priua [torn] inge and praier.

The :2: day
This day I was accompaned in the a [torn] wᵗ Mistress Peternel Farley,
who offered me hir seru [torn] The pettie ssescesions were kept here
[torn] towardes night I went to my priua [torn]

The :3: day:
This day Mr Hoby kept his chambe [torn] Edward Gatt Came, and
brought him a L [torn] his father

The 4 day
This afternone Henrie Dickonson brou [torn] me a fanne from Sᵢᵣ Henrie
Const [torn] and towardes night I went to priuatt [torn]

[torn]
s day there was a Comuniom and I [torn]t to the church : it hath binne
now [torn]t time of Raine.

[torn]
Mr Hoby hard from London of [torn] also of the Holanders ve [torn]
Spaniards by sea I Likewise [torn]s Health [torn] I praise god and
towardes [torn] it to priuat Readinge and [torn]

[torn] 11:
This day my Cossine Edward Isons Came and dined wᵗ vs : in the
afternone came Mr Rhodes : and-towardes Night I went to priuatt praier

[*torn*] 12. *day*
This day, as it pleased god, was faire, and so Mr Hoby and I walked abroad : in the after none Mr Hunter Came : and towardes night I went to my ordenaire exercises.

[*torn*] *day*
Mr Hunter, Mr Pollard, and frances Merie dined w^t vs : in the after none Mr Hoby and I walked to our Hay makers : it was a Faire day, god be praised

[*torn*] 16: *day*:
This morninge Mr Hoby reed towardes Yorke to the sittinge.

[*torn*] *the* :20: *day*
This day, after I was readi [*torn*] Rhodes and after Came Mrs [*torn*] after came younge Mr [*torn*] and when I had seene [*torn*] Night before was pr [*torn*] priuatt medetat [*torn*]

The Lordes day :21:
This day we were [*torn*] tenantes and at su [*torn*]

Epilogue

Although written for religious reasons, Lady Hoby's diary relates increasingly to her external world rather than to her spiritual and inner life. Our perusal of her daily record gives us but a small insight into her character and can render us only partly conversant with the workings of her mind. There is a charm, however, in speculating as to how she employed her time, and this enables us to identify ourselves to some extent with her secret thoughts as well as with her everyday proceedings. We begin reading the diary through its careful keeping of records, its daily accounting, its keeping up to the mark; but it falters, and ends with fragmentation and breaking up, even with torn folios, cryptic, broken, accentuated by missing words. In a sense, though, it does not matter, for by this stage, with the unfolding of her life over this short period, we have already discovered enough to interest, enough about a very private woman finding a secret way of expressing herself, enough to make us feel that we know her so well. This is a record of bygone days and there is pleasure in our reading, prompted as we are by hints, by suggestion, and by the underlying dramatic account.

Nothing is known of Lady Hoby after this time, but she is spoken of as 'the best Lady that ever any knight in the world inioyed'[383] and Francis Bacon writing about his own marriage to Sir Thomas says, 'Your loving congratulations for my doubled life, as you call it, I thank you for. No man may better conceive the joys of a good wife than yourself with whom I dare not compare'.[384] We can imagine her days at Hackness continued in much the same way and that Sir Thomas remained active in his various affairs. With the loss of her mother in 1613, and no children of her own, she was the last in her direct family line yet never devoid of youthful company. She continued to receive into her household the children of others, including some of her husband's relations, John and George Sydenham, and possibly their sister, as their

---

[383] MS Sloane 4276, f. 93, quoted in Fox, *Diary* (1908), 159.
[384] Bacon, *Works*, ed. Spedding (1868), X, 298–9.

221

Epilogue

'Mother was an ill woman to her children';[385] and she looked after a young cousin of her own, Jane Lutton, who felt she had gained 'much spirituall profit'. Lady Hoby also took under her wing her kinsman, John Chapman, intending that her property would eventually fall to him. With this in mind, a deed of settlement was drawn up in July 1632 passing the Hackness lands over to her husband – but on the understanding that certain of her own relatives would benefit on his death.

At the age of sixty-three, on 6 September 1633, her body was finally laid to rest in the chancel of Hackness church. A fine monument, still in place, was set on the south wall inside the altar rail. It is in the form of a black marble tablet, surrounded by a white marble border, bearing an inscription, coat-of-arms, and various sculpted symbols (see p. 223). On it her husband pays tribute to the virtuous and devout woman who gave so much of herself in God's service to the needs of others:

The Lady Margaret Hoby, late wife of Sr Thomas Posthvmvs Hoby Knight, and sole Davghter and heire of Arthvre Dakins Esqr by Thomasin his wife, after she had lived seven and thirty yeares and one moneth wth her said hvsband in mvtvall entire affection to both their extraordinary comfortes, and had finished the woork that God had sent her into this world to performe, and after she had attained vnto the begining of the sixty third year of her age, on the fovrth day of the seventh moneth of that yeare, it was the will of Almighty God to call her fovrth of this vale of miserie; and her body was bvryed in this chancell, on the sixt day of the same moneth (beinge September An^o 1633) soe neer vnto the bodies of her sayde father and of her sayde mother (wch was interred by her sayde fathers bodie on the thirteenth day of November An^o 1613) as that all three will become but one heape of dvste. ties reqvired of every faithfvl Child of God, both in their pvblike and private callings : not only by propagatinge his holy word in all places where she had power, but alsoe by exercisinge her selfe dayly in all other particvler christien dvties, and endevoures to performe the whole will of God through her faithe in Christ; the frvites wherof were daily reaped in svndry of the faithfull servantes of God, (as well strangers vnto her, as of her own kindred

---

[385] In his will, Sir Thomas referred to 'the affectionate care which my said late wife did in her life-time take of his [John's] well doing and of his education in his youngest years'. NYCRO ZF 2/9–13.

Monument to Lady Margaret Hoby (1633), St Peter's Church, Hackness.

and Allies) whose wantes were largely svpplied by her christian charitie : and all svch as were eye witnesses of her Godly manner of lyfe and conversation, and of Gods great mercy shewed vnto her in her laste sicknes by givinge vnto her memory to pray vnto him, and in the manner of separatinge her sovle from her bodie with soe little bodily payne, had an assvred hope fixed in their heartes that her fvtvre resvrrection will be to inherit that Eternall habitation in Gods heavenly Kingdome which, whilst she lived with vs, herselfe often expressed (both by her worde and deeds) that she was assvred, only through the meer mercy and preciovs merites of her only Saviovr IESUS CHRIST, to enioy after her departvre ovte of this mortall lyfe, as the crowne of that faith which she professed and practized heer on earth.

> Non ero vobiscvm donec devs ipse vocabit:
> Tvnc cineres vestros consociabo meis.
> Thomas Posthvmvs Hoby.

Lady Hoby would have been touched by the sentiments expressed, and perhaps even more delighted with the little chapel of St Margaret in Harwood Dale erected in her memory a year later (see p. 227). It served the congregation of this part of the estate until such time as it became too small and was replaced by a new church built in the village.[386] She would not, however, have been as happy with the outcome of her estate. Sir Thomas knew that she had expressed a particular wish that certain of her property should be sold, with the amount raised to be distributed among her relatives. Sir Thomas failed to fulfil his wife's last wishes, and on his own death, in 1640, the bulk of her estate, along with his own, went to his cousin and heir, John Sydenham, to whom he also bequeathed 'the flaggon bracelet of gold with the picture of my late

---

[386] A black marble tablet in the existing church commemorates the old chapel: 'When Sr Thomas Posthvmvs Hoby knight and the lady Margarett his late wife were vnited together in this world they both resolved to have a Chappel erected for devine service for ye good of ye sovles and bodys of ye Inhabitantes dwellinge w^thin Harewood dale and w^thin very fewe monthes next after his said wives decease he did erect this Chappell in ye yeare 1634 And as they had both formerly resolved he hath by conveyance provided that his assigne (vnto whom he hath assvred the inheritance of Harewooddale in reversion after his owne death) and his heires and assignes shall for ever finde one svfficient preacher to preach GODS word, and to Catechyse herein on every Lords day comonly called Svnday'. This generous and very public gesture should refute a local legend that informs us Sir Thomas hastened his wife's death by kicking her downstairs.

Monument to Sir Thomas Posthumous Hoby (1682), St Peter's Church, Hackness.

most dear and only wife in which is fastened there unto and which I do purpose, if God shall permit, to wear about mine arm untill and at the time of my death'.[387] The Sydenhams, however, did not long retain the lands which became heavily mortgaged to the Earl of Leicester. They were put up for sale and purchased in February 1707/8 by John van den Bempde, a rich landowner of Dutch origin with substantial commercial interests, who was buying land all down the east coast.

A monument in Hackness church was erected in 1682 by the Sydenhams to the memory of their benefactor (see p. 225); but it is the combined presence of the two inside the altar rails, those of Lady Hoby and her father, which evoke the period in which this diary was written. To visit Hackness now, embellished as it is by luxuriant scenes, by wooded hills, by springs of water and green pastures, still manages to conjure up her life and times. Although the house is no longer the same, the place she lived in nevertheless makes our sense of her seem close. We can walk beside the beck through the village and enter the church where she worshipped. We can follow the lane to the dales, warmed by the sun on our backs as the wind from the moors rustles through the sheltering trees. We can climb out of the valley on to the high ground looking out over Harwood Dale and pick out the ruins of the old chapel in the distance. All around us are the sights and sounds of a country life rooted in the traditions of the past. It is in the diary itself, however, that we have the best memorial, for it is here that we can read and listen to a singular and secret voice, that of a very private Elizabethan lady recording her life in this glorious part of Yorkshire all those centuries ago.

---

[387]   Sir Thomas Hoby's will. NYCRO ZF 2/9–13.

St Margaret's Chapel, Harwood Dale, erected in memory of Lady Margaret Hoby by her husband (1634).

Appendix 1

CORRESPONDENCE: HOBY COURTSHIP

Extracts from the Hoby courtship correspondence (1591, 1595–6), to be found in the Preface to *The Fortescue Papers, New series, Vol. 1., consisting chiefly of Letters relating to State affairs, collected by John Packer, secretary to George Villiers, Duke of Buckingham, MSS in the possession of the Hon. G. M. Fortescue*, ed. Samuel Rawson Gardiner (London, The Camden Society, 1871), i–xxv. (Gardiner notes that the letters were then at Dropmore, but they were subsequently sent to Hackness, where they were destroyed in a fire.)

1591

Letter i from William Cecil, Lord Burghley, to the Earl of Huntingdon, 21 September 1591, promoting his nephew's interests.

My very good Lord: The harty love and dutyfull goodwyll that I knowe to be borne your Lp. by my good La. and syster in lawe the La. Russell, maketh me bowlde to joyne with her, as a mother for hir sonne, and my self for my honest servante and nephewe, to commend to your Lps. favore his intentione to seeke, by your Lps. both meanes and advyce, to be a suter to a late yonge wyddowe that was wyfe to Mr. Walter Devereux. And yf your Lp. shall please to geve my La. comforte therin, I wyll joyne with hyr in prosecutione therof both to the wyddow, and any other her freynds she may be advysed by. And I doubt not but the yonge gentlemane, thogh he be Posthumus by his father's death, beyng borne after, yet my La. hath such respect to hym, and he soe well doth and wyll deserve yt, as he shall be made able to be a father of lyvelode. And I can assure your Lp. by the proofe that I have had at his good nature and conditions, he wyll prove a good and corteous husbande, and a keeper and noe spender. And soe wyshynge to heer of your Lps. good recovery of your broose, from Elvetham the xxi^th of 7^ber 1591.

Your Lps. moste assuredly at com.

Letter ii from Lord Burghley to Arthur Dakins, 29 October 1591, supporting his nephew but apologising for doing so soon after the death of W. Devereux.

After my very harty commendations. Thogh yt may be that some have already moved you to understande your dyspositione for your assent to have suyte made to your daughter Mrs. Devereux, wyddowe of Mr. Walter Devereux deceased ; yet, I beynge in mynde, for a speciall particuler freynde of myne, to have, within some tyme after the death of the sayde Mr. Devereux, to have sought to have knowne your mynde, and to have alsoe obtayned your assent to my desyre; yett for some respect of the reputacione of your daughter, whome I accompted woolde rather myslyke of any that shoulde make suyte unto her soe suddeynly after her husbands death, and therefore have dyfferred my purpose untyll nowe that I ame informed that some have be wyll shortly attempt to make some request both to you and the yonge gentlewomane your daughter, and not knowynge what success they may have, I beynge very loath to be prevented by any delay, have presently fownde yt very necessary for me to delay noe farther tyme, and therfore, havynge a great desyre to preferr a yonge gentlemane of good byrth, honesty and understandynge, beynge allyed unto me, and of neer kyndred to dyvers my chyldren, I doe lett you knowe, the party is the sonne of Sir Tho. Hoby deceased and the La. Russell nowe lyvinge, syster to my late wyfe, and his name is Thomas Hoby with an addition of Posthumus, because he was borne after his father's buryall, whoe dyed in Fraunce, wher he was Embassador for hys Ma^ty to the then French Kynge, havynge but one brother lyvinge named Sir Edw. Hoby, knyght, whoe hath noe children, soe as this gentlemane is lykely to inherytt all his lyvelode. And besyds that, my La. Russell, his mother, hath provyded a good portione of lyvelod to be left to hym, yf he shall content her in his marryadge, and wyll deal very honorably and kyndly with hym, to enhable hym to make to his wyfe a convenient joynture, in case she shall lyke of his choyse. And accordyngly, her La. and I have of late conferred heerupon, and wee both woolde be glade to procure a maryadge for hym with your daughter, and to that purpose I doe by thes present lettres sygnify to you both hys and my request, prayinge you to accept the same as proceedinge from our harty goodwylls, and of the allowance of your daughter's vertues and conditiones soe reported to us very credybly. And heerunto we both requyre your answer of your inclynatione heerto, soe as the party may have comforte to repayre thyther, to see and acquaynte hymselfe with your daughter, and to make his suyte to herself, to obtayn heyr love ; and I shall moste kyndly accept your speedy answer. 29 Octob. 1591.

Letter iii from Arthur Dakins to Lord Burghley, 10 November 1591, regretting that his daughter has already gone to London and is now in the care of her former guardians.

May it please your Lo. to understande that your lettres, dated at Westmynster the 29th of Octob. laste, wer delyvered unto me heer at Hackenes, neigh Scarborough, by a gentlemane one Mr. Peerse Stanly, this present day the xth of Novemb. the which to answer as I woolde I noe ways can, which breedeth some greefe in me for that my daughter toke her jorney towards London the 2. of this instant November laste with my lettres to the Right Honorable therle of Huntyngdon, and the Countess his wyfe, her owlde mistress ; yeeldynge therby my consente to theyr honors for the disposynge of my daughter in her maryadge, which God knoweth is meane, and farr unworthy the proferr your Ho. doth make by your sayde lettres. Yf I wer able to gratify your honour by any meanes, I stande moste bownd soe to doe for your former goodness towards me, the which as your Ho. doth not remember, soe shall I never forget them, but shall dayly yeelde my harty thanks to Almighty God, whome yt hath pleased to prepare you a stronge pyller for this owre common weal. The L. preserve you, and sende you longe contynuance amongst us. Thus I moste humbly take my leave; from Hackeneys aforesayde; the sayde xth of Novemb. 1591.

Your Lo. honour's moste humble
at com. with his service,
ARTHURE DAKYNS.

Letter iv from Lady Dorothy Perrot (sister-in-law to Margaret) to Thomas Posthumous Hoby, about her attempt to discover the whereabouts of Margaret in London. Lady Perrot hopes to be in good favour with the influential Lady Russell.

Mr. Hoby; I sent a man of myne who long served her to see my Lady of Huntingdon from me, who as of hime selfe did inquier of the gentill woman you knowe of; but coulde learne nothing of her coming up. If you will have me send to know as from my selfe, I will, or what else I may to do your liking; I pray you remember me humbly to my Lady, and so I leave you to all good happs, this first of November.

Your frend that wisheth you well,
D. PERROT.

Letter v from Lady Elizabeth Russell to her son, Thomas Posthumous Hoby, telling him to hurry along his suit, but she also suggests that Margaret is already lost to Thomas Sidney 'in affection'.

Posthumus. I have sent you what I have rec[eived]. Shew Mr. Stanley's letter to me unto my Lord your master. Now, chyld, it standeth yow aper for your owne creditt's sake to trye your frends. My La. Perrott the wisest, surest, and fittest to your good, who, after she hath fownd her disposityon tooching Sidney, may, on some tyme of the gentlewoman's comming to visitt my La. Dorothie, let you understand of the tyme when yowrself may mete her there. Yf this prove a matche, I will be bownd to leave to yow that which shall be worth v c li. by yere, wherof iii c li. of it joynter to her after my death, and a howse presently furnished to bring her to. Yf in affection she be gon to Sidney, it is one thing: if by reason she be willing to be ledd to her owne good, yow will be fownd the better mache of bothe.

I have promised your brother to defray the charges of assurances for the entayle of Bisham, which I consent to for feare of sayle. He sayth it will cost me 40 li. I pray God it be worth so much to yourself.

Your most loving mother,
ELIZABETH RUSSELL.

I woold you coold so use the matter that the widdow be here this Christmas. I have appoynted your brother's musityons : have hard them and given the master v s. earnest.

Let Anthony Cooke help to steale her away. She hath her father's consent to match where she list.

1595

Letter vi from the Earl of Huntingdon to Sir Edward Stanhope, 12 September 1595, inviting him to meet up with Hoby and assist him in his suit.

Mr. Stanhope. This gentleman, Sir Thomas Hobby, taketh a longe jorney into the North for a good cause, as himself will shewe you. My Lady his mother did first write unto me to give him my best freindly meanes in the matter. And since my Lo. Trea. hath also required the same of me, both by his letters and speaches to me, which I am willinge to performe; but, as I have said to the Knight himself, I take it to be **verry** sone for me to deale therein, yet; and, to speake the trewthe, though I be verry willinge to do any good office towards him that may lye in me, yet so bad hath bin my successe that yf I might be spared I woulde never deale that way agayne for any such matter. And for this tyme I am spared to write, but he requireth that I would assigne some man to accompany him to the place that he may the redilyar have a sight of the gentlewoman. And because you are his kinseman, I hope shortely to see you in Yorkesheire, and for this tyme, with my harty commendacions, I do comitt you to our Lord.

Your loving freind,
H. HUNTINGDON.

At Highgate the xiith of Septemb., 1595.

Appendix 1

Letter vii from Sir Edward Stanhope to the Earl of Huntingdon, 27 September 1595, informing him of the visit to Hull.

My humble duetie to your good Lp. premysed. It may please you to be advertised that of Saterday last the xx[th] of this moneth, I receyved your Lps, lettres by my cosen Sir Thomas Hobby, and understandinge that night at Yorke that the gentlewoman was newely removed to Hull, wee spent the Sabbath at Yorke. The next daye, good Mr. Cotrell's funerall beinge to be solemnized, in respecte he put me in trust as a supervisor, wee staid ther till that afternoone, and then went towarde Hull, accompanyed also with Mr. Peres Stanley, whither we came upon Tuesday by one of the clocke, and went to the manor, where my cosen Sydney after a while admitted mee to her chamber. I founde her layde complayninge of payne in her eyes and heade, which I founde to proceede of greate lamentacion for the losse of the worthy gentleman her late husbande, for she coulde not then speake of him without teares.

After some speches of curtesey and entertaynment, I recomended your Lps. favor un to her, apperenge by your lettres which I shewed her, whereby finding the occasion of my cominge, she shedd teares againe, sayinge that thoughe she helde her selfe bounde to your Lp. to whom she was wholly devoted, yet the tender love she bare to him that was dead, made yt grevous to her to hear of any newe; and much more to be thought of the gentleman that she were to be delt with in any suche matter soe soone, which I excused, as I had receyved from himselfe before, that he had that reverend regard of her, as that in his owne opinione he might be thought to blame; but that two respects ledd him.

One, in desier his eyes to witnes that which publicke reporte had delivered him, that the guyftes of nature had in some sorte equalled her vertues.

Thother, havinge bene longe drawne to affect her for thes guyftes, he was desirous to be made knowne to her, as the first that shoulde seeke her, though he after forebore for some tyme to entertayne or prosecute his suyte.

In thend, unwillingly, but in duetifull regard of your Lps. recomendacion, and to avoyd to offer that discurtesey, not to be sene to a gentleman of his worth that came soe farr for that purpose, in very modest sort she yelded that after some tyme of my withdrawinge from her, she woulde admytt him to doe your Lps. comendacions her.

In which meane while my cosen Alred's wief cominge thither, after some half hower, my self was required to bringe Sir Thomas and Mr. Peres Stanley into her chamber, where curteousley and modestly intertayning him with fewe speeches, she retired to the gentlewomen, and, after smal tyme spent in the chamber, wee left her, I sayinge to her that if your Lps. cominge downe were not very shortely, this gentleman woulde be boulde in his cominge up, to knowe if she woulde comaunde him any thinge to your Lp. and my good Lady.

That eveninge I acquainted my cosen Aldred and his wief both with your Lps. faver to recomende the gent. to this match, and with the licklyhoode how well, by the naturall affeccion borne him of his honorable mother, his owne industry, his educacion in soe good a schoole of experience as my L. Threasorer's chamber, and his alyence and kindered, he might prove a very good match to the gentlewoeman.

They both cheifely respectinge that it was mocioned with your Lps. speciall liking, which they doubted not but woulde be seconded by my Lady, when tyme had overworne the great grefe she takes for the losse of a kinsman of soe greate good parts and expectacion, did not onely yeelde to geve there best furderance to the match, as occasione might be offered them, but my cosen Alred entred into consultacion with us, what course might be helde in prosecuting of yt, best beseminge the reputacions of them boeth.

Whereupon, although Sir Thomas at the first was desirous to have procured some place in or nere the towne of Hull, to the which, within a weeke or thereabouts, he might have repaired the better to take oportunitye to intertayne the gentlewoman ; yet, upon better advisement, be yeelded to this counsell, that he woulde retyre himselfe for v or vi dayes, and if in that tyme he harde not of your Lps. presente cominge into the cuntry, he woulde take his journey by Hull to your Lp. and there salutinge the gentlewoeman, woulde let her knowe that he was so fully satisfied by sight of her, that all things was answerable to the goode reporte he had receyved of her before, as he ment to settle himselfe upon her favor. Nevertheles, tenderly regardinge her reputacion, he woulde for a tyme retyre himselfe into the southe, and there eyther awayte your Lps. cominge downe, or if it were not soe soone as he wished, hoped to receyve your Lps. recomendacion to her as well of himselfe, as by his freendes, for his state and haviour.

And this course he meaninge to observe, and apperinge to as desirous to be onely behouldinge to your Lp. and my Lady for this matche, which, chefelie in regard of the gentlewoeman's vertues, whereof he heareth by all that speake of her, he will accompt a greate preferment to him, we came of Wedensday from Hull soe farr together towardes Doncaster as I comytted him to Mr. Stanley nere his house at Womersley, and I repaired to Doncaster, where I was in respect of my place ther to attende the next day the eleccion of the [mayor], where by foresight and good meanes, without contradiction or shewe of faccion (not usuall heretofore), William Hansley, one in duetie and service towards your Lp. was chosen there maior.

I humbly cease to trouble your Lp. 27 7br 1595.

Your Lps. humbly to command,

E.S.

Letter viii from Sir Thomas Hoby to the Earl of Huntingdon, 20 November 1595, concerning his ill success.

R[ight] H[onorable]. Beynge very loath to neglect the fytt opertunity of this bearer, I have presumed by hym to troble your Lp. aswell to manyfest my dutyfull desyres to become thankfull for your honorable favoure shewed in your furtherynge of myn endevours, as to lett your Ho. understande howe I have proceeded, synce your Lps. departure. And because I can not my self render unto your honour due thankes for your honorable coorses helde in the cause, I wyll referr that unto thos honorable persons that fyrst recomended myself and cause to your favoure, and wyll be bould to relate unto them at large withowte any omyssyone the honorable care you have pleased to have of my suyte. Now, concernynge the state wherein I nowe stande, yt ys soe weake that I fynde noe reasons as yet to hope for better, neyther wyll my affectione be drawne altogether to despayre ; for the favourable access which your Lp. obtayned for me ys soe unwyllyngly performed as, had I not learned a former lessonseof *audaces fortuna juvat,* wherby I ame ledd contynually to exceed good manners in beynge more ruled by my love then reasone, it woold have been longe synce absolutely denyed me. But as I came not soe farr to be dyscouradged with some fewe repulses, soe wyll I not departe untyll I have performed the uttermoste of my strengthe in seekynge her, styll referrynge the sequell to God's good pleasure and her own self and to that ende, God wyllynge, I wyll remayne heer untyll your Lps. retourne from the North parts, and then I wyll my selfe wayte upon you ; and soe for this tyme I wyll humbly leave to troble your Lp. any farther. This xx[th] of Novemb. 1595.
Your Lps. moste humbly to commaunde.

Letter ix from the Earl of Huntingdon to Margaret, 9 December 1595, regretting her refusal of Hoby's suit.

Mrs. Margarett. Beare with me whatsoever I wryte, for I was not in a greater payne synce my laste jorney then I even nowe ame in. I did acquaynte hym with the contents of your lettre, and at the laste I dyd geve hym the lettre to peruse, but yt moved him not to that purpose you desyred. And soe he toulde me he woolde tell your self, yet withowte my lettre he woolde not returne. He doth not beleeve that you wyll geve such a denyall as your lettre mentioneth. For God's cawse have care of all our credyts, and soe handle the matter as his commynge agayne may be neyther offensyve to you nor dyspleasynge to hymself. And so with wysh of all good and happynes to you, for this tyme I ende and commytt you to the L. Jesus. At Yorke this 9th Decemb.
Your lovynge freynde,
H. HUNTYNGDON.

Correspondence

Letter x from Sir Edward Stanhope to Margaret, 1596, advising her to accept Hoby and thereby make use of his powerful contacts in the lawsuit over the Hackness estate.

Now, my good cosen, what course for you to take in the meane while to make yt [ie. the chancery suit] sure, I cannot so well advise you, as if I were voyd of suspicion that my advise tended not to serve some other's turne, which I protest I am free from intencion, and therfore will let you simply know what I thinke for your good ; which is that having thes great folks to stand against you, (and you having none greater, that you may make account as sure to you, that may sway with my L. Keeper to cast the ballance being indifferent of your syde,) if you would so farr use your faithfull servant Sir Thomas as dyrect him by your appointment to trye his credytt with my L. Threr. for you, I know his Lp. may sway the matter wholly, and I am assured he so much affecteth his kinsman, as if he fynde that the mocion proceedeth from your self, and that Sir Thomas shall have kynde thanks of you for yt, he will stryke it sure for you.

Herein use your owne discrecion, for if I were not assured that the speciall favour I wish you to afford Sir Thomas for his long service and entyer affeccion should not fall out as much to your good and comfort hereafter, as his, and that I know his estate shall be so well supplyed by his honorable mother as that he shall be able (without that which you bring) to maintaine you according to his degree, I protest to you, by the faith of an honest man, I would not use thes speeches unto you, or seeke any way to draw you to your hinderance, and knowing the trust you repose in me, which I will never deceyve and therfore what I have ingaged my creditt unto you for, I doubt not but be able always to maintaine, and even so referring you to your owne good wisdome and honorable government, which hitherto you have carved of yourself to your great creditt, I leave the report of the rest of the buysines to Mr. Mease, and so betake you to God.

Letter xi from Sir Thomas Hoby to the Dowager Countess of Huntingdon, 26 June 1596, thanking her of his now anticipated success in the courtship of Margaret.

R[ight] H[onourable]. Fyndynge by sundry reports howe greatly I ame bownde unto your Ho. For your favorable coorse helde in my present sute unto my M^{rs}, wherin your La^p hath pleased neyther to advyz her unto me, nor to geve her counsell agaynst me, but, with some favourable speaches not a lyttle tendynge to my good, your Ho. hath suffyciently publyshed the same to be a matter by you helde very indyfferent, and soe have her to her owne free choyce, I have at this tyme presumed to troble your Ho. with thes rude lynes, that in them I myght both yeeld unto your Ho. moste humble thankes for your soe greate and by me altogether undeserved favoure, and alsoe that I myght the better manyfest my dutyfull desyres to become moste servyceable for the same. And althogh I have hitherto been but a meer stranger, and soe have wanted meanes to merrytt your Ho. favourable conceyte, and much less to deserve the leaste furtheraunce in my present proceedinges; yet shall your Ho. heerafter fynde me moste ready in all dutyfull endeavours to doe you all dutifull servyce. And when I shall prove soe happy as to possess the happynes I doe nowe seeke for (wherof my self-unworthynes myght make me dyspayre) I wyll be fownde as dutyfully servyceable, as if I wer a naturall branch of the stocke yt self, whereto I shall then be but grafted. But I wyll leave at this tyme to be further troblesome unto your Ho. and wyll humbly submytt my servyce to your Ho. comma^nt. This 26th of June, 1596.

Appendix 2

CORRESPONDENCE AND EVIDENCE: HOBY V. EURE LAWSUIT

[I] Extracts from correspondence and evidence relating to the Hoby v. Eure lawsuit (1600–02), found in *The Cecil Papers. Calendar of the MS of the most Honourable the Marquis of Salisbury.* Hist. MSS Com., 1883–1923.

Vol. X, 302–4.

SIR T. POSTHUMUS HOBY TO SIR ROBERT CECIL

1600, Sept 5.–Impute my presumption to my urgent cause, which for justice' sake I cannot swallow. There has been some dryness in the Lord Ewre (whose tenants are my next neighbours) almost ever since I was employed as a commissioner in these parts; which, if it has been for my partiality, or injustice, I desire on proof thereof to be punished; if it be for want of partiality (as I shall rather prove) I hope my wrongs will appear in time which I have sustained. On 26 August last, his son and brother came to my house at Hackness, whose visit I have related in the enclosed complaint to the Council, which I beseech you to read and to have delivered to the Council. I assure you it is not otherwise for me to remain in these parts, nor for any other but their own followers, that will fashion justice to their greatness. If the matter may come to judicial hearing, I shall prove all my complaint, and shall lay open the partial customs of these frozen parts. I crave your pardon for appealing from the Council here, which I did in respect of my Lord President's absence, to whom I have sent a copy of the misdemeanour; and in respect that our Vice-President (the Lord Ewre) is father, brother, and cousin to the offenders, and who has showed natural affection already in the cause.– My house at Lynton, 5 Sept, 1600. (**251.**74).

THE SAME TO THE PRIVY COUNCIL

1600, Sept. 5.– I beg leave to inform you of a great misdemeanour offered me in mine own house at Hacknes by Mr. William Ewre, son of the L. Ewre, Sir William, his brother, and others, whose names and facts are expressed in this enclosed. My suit is that the parties be bound before the Council at York to appear before your

Correspondence and Evidence

Lordships to answer my complaint, for it is not for me to serve any process upon them in these parts, in respect of my L. Ewre's greatness, who is our Vice-President, and hath summoned me to appear at York, to exhibit my complaint, though he is father, brother and cousin to the offenders. If you shall please to send commission to the Bishop of Lymryke, Mr Heskett and Dr. Bennett to examine my witnesses, your Lordships shall find somewhat more than I can deliver at this instant. I shall easily derive this outrage against me conceived from envy and malice for want of partiality in me in the executing of my place and calling.– From my house at Lynton in the East Riding of Yorkshire, 5 Sept, 1600. (**88.19.**)

The Enclosure:–
The manner of the riotous assault on Sir Thomas Posthumus Hoby, knight, at his house at Hackness in the N. Riding of Yorkshire by William Ewre, Sir William Ewre, Richard Cholmey, William Dawny, William Hylliarde the younger, Stephen Hutchenson and ——Smyth, yeoman falkner to the L. Ewre.

i. On Tuesday the 26ᵗʰ Aug. Sir Thomas Hoby was standing in his hall at Hackness, when there came in Sir. W. Ewre's footboy and said that his master and sundry other gentlemen would come that night. Sir Thomas answered that he was sorry, his wife was ill and he not so well provided for them as he wished, and desiring the footboy to tell his master as much, he answered that his master was hunting in the forest of Pyckering Lyth, so as he knew not where to find him. About two hours after, the above-named, Mr. Dawny excepted, came to Hackness with sundry other servants and boys, and Sir Thomas hearing they were come into his dining-room went to them and told them they were welcome. Presently after this Sir William Ewre's footboy took forth cards and laid them on the table, wherewith some of the gentlemen were exercised until supper. In the beginning of supper, Mr. Ewre pretending he had come to hunt, Sir Thomas sent for his servant that had charge of his deer, who dwelt three miles from him, to come the next morning, and so continued with them all the time at supper, which was spent by the gentlemen partly in discoursing of horses and dogs, sports whereunto Sir Thomas never applied himself, partly with lascivious talk where every sentence was begun or ended with a great oath, and partly in inordinate drinking unto healths, abuses never practised by Sir Thomas. In supper time came in a footboy whom they had sent for Mr. Dawny, and brought word he would come in the morning. After supper Sir Thomas willed to have their chambers made ready, and came himself to bring them to their lodgings, but they being at dice told him they would play awhile, so he did leave them and went down and set his household to prayers as they were accustomed. When Sir Thomas and his family had begun to sing a psalm, the company above made an extraordinary noise with their feet, and some of them stood upon the stairs at a window opening into the hall, and laughed all the time of prayers. The next morning they went to breakfast in the dining-room, and Sir

Thomas hearing them call for more wine, sent for the key of the cellar and told them they should come by no more wine from him. Presently Sir Thomas sent to Mr. Ewre to know how he would bestow that day, and told him if he would leave disquieting him with carding, dicing and excessive drinking, and fall to other sports, they should be very welcome. After this message Mr. Ewre sent to Sir Thomas's wife that he would see her and begone, whereunto she answered she was in bed and when she was ready she would send him word. At his coming she prayed him to depart the house in quietness, and going to the rest of the company, he called a servant of Sir Thomas, and said "Tell thy master he hath sent me scurvy messages, and the next time I meet him I will tell him so, if he be upon the bench, and will pull him by the beard." Coming to the uttermost court, Mr.Ewre said he would go to the top of the hill and fling down mill-stones and would play young Devereux, at the same time throwing stones at the windows and breaking four quarrels of glass.

    ii. A list of reasons to prove that this was done to disgrace Sir Thomas Hoby, and force him to a quarrel to save his reputation. (**88**. 17.)

SIR T. POSTHUMUS HOBY TO SIR ROBERT CECIL.

1600. Sept. 26.– Details of proceedings taken before Lord Ewre, the Vice-President, Sir William Mallory (whose eldest son married Lord Ewre's sister), Mr. Heskett, Mr. Stanhope, Mr. Bevercoats, Mr. D. Bennett, and Mr. Fearne. Hoby was charged with wronging certain gentlemen, unnamed, by charging them to the Council with bearing murderous minds, with committing atheistical contempts, and to have exceeded in drink. A pacification was arrived at, which resulted in the gentlemen protesting their innocence of the matters imputed, and that they never meant anything in disgrace of Hoby's wife.

    The following passage occurs: "The Lord Ewre told me a long tale of Duello, and that your Honour, whom he knew to be my most honourable friend, would but make the matter a jest to sport at: for that you made sport with his son Will Ewre about the last unkindness between us, that fell forth the last year, about his son's bringing cards into my house: in which matter he told me before all the Council that your Honour did make his son imitate my preacher, by using such gestures as my preacher did use in his evening exercises, and that your Honour did laugh very heartily at it."–York, 26 September, 1600. (**251**.39.)

Vol. XI, 11–12.

RALPH. LORD EURE TO SIR ROBERT CECIL.

[1600–1,] Jan 16,.– You know how Sir Thomas Hobbye is renewing before the Star Chamber, the complaint which he made before the Council at York, against my son and other gentlemen, for having misconducted themselves in his house. Be pleased to read the truth, which my son, the bearer, did affirm before this Council.–

Inglebye, this16ᵗʰ January. (**180. 4.**)

The Enclosure:–

Statement by William Eure of such things as passed in Sir Thomas Hobie's house in August last, whereupon myself and divers other gentlemen then in my company are drawn in question in the Star Chamber.

Being myself accompanied with six other gentlemen hunting at that time near to Sir Thomas Hobie's house in Yorkshire, and purposing to lodge with him in kindness, I sent beforehand my footman to signify so much unto him, and some three hours after we followed. Finding none of his servants ready to receive us, we sent our horses into the town, and went into the house ourselves. First, into the hall where we found nobody. Then into the great chamber, where we stayed some quarter of an hour or more before Sir Thomas came to us, which seemed to us strange and not answerable to our northern entertainments. Coming at last, he bade us coldly welcome, and accompanied us till after supper, when he retired to his chamber. We fell to cards to beguile the time and continued the play the longer for that none of his servants came to show us any lodgings. At last, being sleepy, and understanding that his servants had been at prayer in the hall under the great chamber, where we were, and were gone to bed, we were forced to seek out lodgings, which we found prepared, and so we rested that night. The next day we rose early to hunt, and word was brought by one of his servants that breakfast was ready. Whereupon I willed one of his men to entreat Sir Thomas' company, who returning answered that Sir Thomas was not yet stirring; so to breakfast we went. Which being done, we fell again to play, expecting Sir Thomas' coming forth. Shortly after one of his servants came and told me peremptorily our play was offensive to his lady, and therefore willed us to depart the house. I told him our stay was only to take leave, and he repeating the former words, I said the message was a scurvy message, and willed the servant to tell Sir Thomas I would gladly speak with him before I went. I wished to understand whether the message had proceeded from him, or that the fellow of himself had abused us. Whereupon the servant departed and presently returning told me my lady was willing to speak with me, and guided us into a inner room next adjoining to her chamber. I going into my Lady, the others withdrew themselves into the great chamber again. Sir Thomas Hobie had shut himself into the study, being unwilling to be spoken with, but watching there, as now I may conjecture, to take advantage if I should use any unseemly speeches. I expostulated a little with my Lady about the message and entertainment, whereupon she, with some show of dislike of her husband's strange fashions, entreated me with patience to depart. Which accordingly we did, and going out of the court in some discontent, I took up a little stone and cast it towards the house, not touching any windows, and so I took horse. His suggesting of tearing any commission is merely untrue, neither was any man's heels tript up, as he incerteth. (**180**. 3.)

See also *Cecil Papers, Vols. X,* 325, 391; *XI,* 456, 546; *XII,* 32, 105.

[II] PRO STAC 5/H22/21 [STAR CHAMBER 5, Proceedings 43. Eliz., Bdle. 22, no 21: the evidence of Robert Nettleton].

Robert Nettleton told the Court that he had nine fellow men-servants at Hackness, William Jarden, John Wasse, Henry Brathwhaite, Peter Campleman, Thomas Wraie, and four others, while the women servants consisted, at this time, of Mistress Everell Aske and three widows, to whom Hoby, of his charity, gave shelter and board. This witness described the coming of a hunting party of young men to Hackness. A footman was sent before them, two or three hours earlier, to beg the hospitality of Sir Thomas and his lady, but, when they finally arrived, Sir Thomas received them alone as Lady Hoby was sick. Immediately after their coming, declared the witness, they fell to cards in the great chamber, and these they must have brought with them, for, Nettleton declared, he knew there used to be none in his master's house. At supper time, his master keeping them company, Mr. Stephen Hutchinson drank a health unto his master, and Sir William Eure did drink a health unto his master and to my lady's health: to whom his master replied that, if drinking would make my lady well, he could find it in his heart to drink himself drunk but otherwise, since it would do her no good and himself hurt, he desired them to pardon him, for he would drink but his ordinary. After supper his master went first to my lady, and afterwards to see each of their lodgings prepared; then came to them again, and, finding them still at play, told them that, if they would repair to their chambers, they were fit, and he would bring them to their lodging. They, however, desired him to bear with them, for they would play awhile. Then he told them that he would bid them goodnight, for he would go keep my lady company as she was sick. Sir Thomas then gave order to his servants to go to prayers in the hall, which were usually, declared Nettleton, said in the great chamber morning and evening. His master also gave commandment to his chamberlain to show every gentleman's man his master's lodging, which he did. Then, continued this witness, when they were singing of the psalms, three of the guests' servants came and stood in the hall, laughing and making of a noise during the whole time of prayers. In the chamber over them the guests also made a noise, and some, coming out to the stairs that led down into the hall, made a noise with singing of strange tunes which, he was sure, were not psalms. The next morning breakfast was prepared, and he and others were in attendance. Some drank healths one to another, beer and wine in plenty being provided for them, and Mr. Richard Cholmley filled his glass so full as it ran over into the rushes, one of his company telling him it was a sin to spill drink. Mr. William Hilliard, somewhat before breakfast was done, rose from the table and swore he would drink no more healths. After breakfast the guests made a great noise in the great chamber with hallowing and shouting, and, my lady's chamber being very near, Sir Thomas sent them word that, if they would use some other quieter exercise they should be welcome, for that they did disease my Lady. Thereupon it was answered they would but see my lady and go their ways. Soon after Sir William Eure's man came to Nettleton and required him to tell my lady that Mr. William Eure was desirous to see her before he went, and that then they would be gone. Whereupon Nettleton brought my lady's answer which was, that she was not ready, but as soon as she were she would send him word. After, she sent for Nettleton and willed him to tell Mr. Eure that she would be willing to see him but not the rest of the company, because she was sickly and kept her chamber. To this Mr. Eure answered, By god thy master sends me such scurvy messages as I care not for them. I came not for his meat and his drink but to see my lady and therefore let him send me word what it lies him in and I will pay for it, and will set up horns at his gate and be gone. Whereupon Nettleton asked his fellow servant Jarden whether he were best to deliver the message in those terms, or make it better if he could. Jarden told him he were best to deliver it as it was for truth would never shame itself, which he thereupon did in my lady's chamber and in her presence. Whereto Sir Thomas willed him to answer Mr. Eure that he wished him and his company to depart his house and ground quietly, and, when he was off his ground, if he sent him either that message or any other, he would take it. After this being delivered to Mr. Eure, he being in a little chamber betwixt the dining chamber and my lady's, he said he came to see my lady and would see her ere he went, for they were strong enough to keep that chamber if there came twenty or forty against them. And Sir William Eure, looking out of a window, seeing country-men come towards the house, said the country was raised. Whereunto Jarden answered him that they were country people that came to the town about a commission that was appointed to be sitten on that day. Sir William replied that he and his company were strong enough to keep that little chamber against all the country, and Mr. William Eure said he cared not for the commission; he would tear it. After this my lady was willing to see Mr. William Eure, who wished the rest of the guests to go forth of that room into the dining chamber, and Jarden ordered Nettleton to bolt the door after them because my lady would speak only with Mr. Eure. When Nettleton tried to do this, the guests thrust the door open upon him, and took hold of him, and threw him against the table end in the great chamber, being two fathoms in length. And so they went into that little chamber again, and would not afterward suffer him to bolt the door. Whereupon he, Nettleton, going down into the hall, saw all the defendants come through the hall, and there George Smith, one of them, seeing a pair of stag's horns nailed on the screen, swore, by god's heart, I would the stag's horns were as hard-nailed or as hard fastened upon Sir Thomas his head as they were there. And thereupon the said George Smith went forth and fetched his horse, and, having pulled up two stiles, passed through a newly levelled courtyard, and trampled it across to and fro, galloping up and down. Nettleton told him it was not well done, for the ground cost money before it came to that pass. Smith answered that he did it in despite. Nettleton also testified to seeing four "quarries" of glass broken in one window in his master's dining chamber, which was said to be done with throwing of stones by one of the defendants or some of their company.

Select Bibliography

MANUSCRIPT SOURCES

British Library, London: MS Egerton 2614: The Diary of Lady Margaret Hoby, 1599–1605

North Yorkshire County Records Office (NYCRO): ZF 2/1–3, ZF 2/9–13, wills, settlements, mortgages; ZF 1/12/11 & 12, title deeds; MIC 951, survey, 1608; ZF4/3/10, survey, 1696

Public Records Office (PRO): STAC 5/H22/21 (Star Chamber 5, Proceedings 43. Eliz., Bdle., 22,21)

York Minster Library: Catalogue Hackness Church Library (1701)

PRINTED SOURCES

Amherst, Alicia. *A History of Gardening in England*, 2nd edn, London, Bernard Quaritch, 1896

Aylmer, G.E. and Cant, Reginald. *A History of York Minster*, Oxford, Clarendon Press, 1977

Bacon, Francis, Sir. *The Works of Francis Bacon, Vol.X*, J. Spedding, R.L. Ellis and D.D. Heath (eds), London, Longman, et al., 1857–74

Barley, William. *A New Booke of Tabliture*, London, 1596

Bilson, Thomas. *The effect of certaine Sermons Tovching the full redemption of mankind by the death and bloud of CHRIST JESUS*, London, 1599

Blodgett, Harriett. *Centuries of Female Days: English Women's Private Diaries*, London, Alan Sutton, 1989

——. *Capacious Hold-all. An Anthology of English-Women's Diary Writings*, Charlotteville, University Press of Virginia, 1991

Bowen, Catherine Drinker. *The Lion and the Throne: the Life and Times of Sir Edward Coke (1552–1634)*, London, Hamish Hamilton, 1957

Bradford, Gamaliel, *Elizabethan Women*, Harold Ogden White (ed.), Freeport, New York, Books for Libraries Press, 1969

Bright, Timothy. *A treatise of melancholie*, London, 1586

Select Bibliography

Broughton, Hugh. *An Epistle to the Learned Nobilitie of England*, Middeleurgh, 1597

Bulmer, T. *History, Topography, and Directory of North Yorkshire*, Preston, T. Bulmer, 1890

Camden, Carroll. *The Elizabethan Woman*, London, Cleaver-Hume Press, 1952

Cecil Papers. Calendar of the MS of the most Honourable the Marquis of Salisbury. Hist. MSS Com. 1883–1923

Clifford, Lady Anne. *The Diaries of Lady Anne Clifford*, D. J. H. Clifford (ed.) Stroud, Alan Sutton, 1992, 1994, 1996

Collier, John Payne, (ed.). *A Book of Roxburgh Ballads*, London, Longman, Brown, Green and Longmans, 1847

Devereux,Walter Bouchier. *Lives and Letters of the Devereux, Earls of Essex, 2 vols.* London, John Murray, 1853

Duncan-Jones, Katherine. *Sir Philip Sidney, Courtier Poet*, London, Hamish Hamilton, 1991

Ezell, Margaret J. M. *The Patriarch's Wife. Literary Evidence and the History of the Family,* Chapel Hill and London, University of North Carolina Press, 1987

Fortescue Papers. New Series, Vol 1, MSS in possession of Honourable G. M. Fortescue, Samuel Rawson Gardiner, (ed.) London, The Camden Society, 1871

Fothergill, Robert A. *Private Chronicles. A Study of English Diaries*, London, Oxford University Press, 1974

Fox, Evelyn. 'The Diary of an Elizabethan Gentlewoman', in Trans of the Royal Hist. Soc. 3rd Series, Vol II, 1908, 153–74

Foxe, John. *Actes and Monuments (The Book of Martyrs)*, London, 1596

Fraser, Antonia. *The Weaker Vessel. Woman's Lot in Seventeenth Century England*, London, Weidenfeld and Nicolson, 1984

Gerard, John. *The Herball Or Generall Historie of Plantes*, London, 1597

Gifford, George. *Foure Sermons*, London, 1582

Graham, Elspeth, et. al. *Her Own Life. Autobiographical writings by seventeenth century Englishwomen*, London, Routledge, 1989

Green, Ian. *The Christian's ABC, Catechisms and Catechizing in England c. 1530–1740.* Oxford, Clarendon Press, 1996

Hammond, Reginald J.W. *Complete Yorkshire*, London, Ward Lock, 1973

Hannay, Margaret P. *Silent But for the Word. Tudor Women as patrons, translators, and writers of Religious Works*, Kent, Ohio, Kent State University Press, 1985

——. *Philip's Phoenix: Mary Sidney, Countess of Pembroke.* Oxford, Oxford University Press, 1990

Hoby, Lady Margaret. *Diary of Lady Margaret Hoby 1599–1605*, Dorothy M. Meads, (ed.) London, George Routledge, 1930

Hogreve, Pearl. *Tudor Women: Commoners and Queens*, Ames, Iowa State University Press, 1975

Select Bibliography

Hole, Christina. *English Home Life, 1500–1800*, London, Batsford, 1947, 1949

Johnson, Samuel. *A Dictionary of the English Language*, London, 1755

Keeble, N.H. *The Cultural Identity of Seventeenth-Century Woman*, London and New York, Routledge, 1994

Kellett, Arnold. *The Yorkshire Dictionary of Dialect, Tradition and Folklore*, Settle, Smith, 1994

Latimer, Hugh. *Fruitfull Sermons*, London, 1596

Lemmon, Kenneth. *The Gardens of Britain, Vol. 5: Yorkshire and Humberside*, London, Batsford, 1978

Lewalski, Barbara Kiefer. *Writing Women in Jacobean England*, Cambridge, Mass., Harvard University Press, 1993

MacCaffrey, Wallace. *Elizabeth I*, London, Edward Arnold, 1993

MacDonald, Michael. *Mystical Bedlam*, Cambridge, Cambridge University Press, 1981

Mildmay, Lady Grace. *With Faith and Physic. The Life of a Tudor Gentlewoman, 1552–1620*, Linda Pollack (ed.), London, Collins and Brown, 1993

Mornai, Philip of. *Fowre Bookes of the Institution, Use and Doctrine of the Holy Sacrament of the Evcharist in the Old Chvrch*, London, 1600

——. *A Treatise of the Church, wherein are handled the principall Questions Mooued in our time concerning that matter*, translated by John Molle at request of King James, London, 1606

Moss, Ann. *Printed Commonplace-Books and the Structuring of Renaissance Thought*, Oxford, Clarendon Press, 1996

Page, William, (ed.). *The Victorian History of the County of York, North Riding, Vol.2*, London, St Catherine Press, 1923

Perkins, William. *An exposition of the creede in the Foundation of Christian Religion: Gathered into six principles*, London, 1597

Perry, Sir Thomas Erskine. *The Van den Bempde Papers. The Bibliographical and Historical Miscellanies of the Philobiblon Soc.*, Vol. 12 (1868/69)

Planche, James Robinson. *A Cyclopaedia of Costume or Dictionary of Dress, 2 vols.* London, Chatto and Windus, 1879

Pontefract, Ella and Hartley, Marie. *The Charm of Yorkshire Churches*, Leeds, The Yorkshire Weekly Post, 1936

Sadie, Stanley, (ed.). *The New Grove Dictionary of Music and Musicians Vol. 13.* London, Macmillan, 1980

Schleiner, Louise. *Tudor and Stuart Women Writers*, Bloomington and Indianapolis, Indiana University Press, 1994

Stephen, Sir Leslie and Lee, Sir Sidney, (eds). *Dictionary of National Biography*, London, Oxford University Press, 1917–

Stone, Lawrence. *The Crisis of the Aristocracy 1558–1641*, Oxford, Clarendon Press, 1965

Select Bibliography

Strong, Sir Roy Colin. *The Renaissance Garden in England*, London, Thames and Hudson, 1979

Thornbury, Walter. *Old and New London: A narrative of its History, its People and its Places, Vol.1*. London, Cassell, 1887

Tipping, H. Avrey. *English Homes of the Early Renaissance*, London, Country Life, 1912

Travitsky, Betty. *The Paradise of Women. Writings by Englishwomen of the Renaissance*, New York, Columbia University Press, 1989

Tusser, Thomas. *A hundreth good pointes of husbandrie*, London, R. Tottell, 1557

———. *Five hundred pointes of good Husbandrie*, London, Denham, 1580

Udall, John. *A Commentarie Upon The Lamentations of Ieremy*, London, 1593

University of York. *The Kings Manor*, York, University of York, n.d

Vives, Juan Luis. *The Instruction of a Christian Woman*, Richard Hyrde (tr.), London, 1540

Walker, Kim. *Women Writers of the English Renaissance*, New York, Twayne Publishers, 1996

Wear, Andrew. 'Puritan perceptions of illness in seventeenth century England', in Roy Porter (ed.), *Patients and Practitioners Lay Perceptions of Medicine in pre-industrial Society*, Cambridge, Cambridge University Press, 1985

Wilson, Violet A. *Society Women of Shakespeare's Time*, London, John Lane, The Bodley Head,1924

Winterbotham, J.J. *Hackness in the Middle Ages*, London, Hackness Press, 1985

Wright, Louis B. *Middle Class Culture in Elizabethan England*, Chapel Hill, University of North Carolina Press, 1935

(Numbers in *italics* refer to illustrations.

Index

(Numbers in *italics* refer to illustrations)

Index